QUESTIONS & ANSWERS

A LEVEL LAW

Questions and Answers Series

Series Editors   Margaret Wilkie and Rosalind Malcolm

Titles in the Series

Other titles in preparation

BLACKSTONE'S
LAW Q&A
QUESTIONS & ANSWERS

A LEVEL
LAW

TIMOTHY BLAKEMORE
LLB, LLM, Cert. Ed
Solicitor

BRENDAN GREENE
LLB, MA

BLACKSTONE PRESS LIMITED

First published in Great Britain 1998 by Blackstone Press Limited, Aldine Place, London W12 8AA. Telephone: 0181-740 2277

© T. Blakemore, B. Greene, 1998

ISBN: 1 85431 534 X

British Library Cataloguing in Publication Data
A CIP catalogue record for this book is available from the British Library

Typeset by Montage Studios Limited, Tonbridge, Kent
Printed by Bell & Bain Limited, Glasgow

Contents

Preface

Our aim in writing this book has been to produce material that is useful to students in a variety of ways. It can be used almost as a textbook, in that certain topics can be revised by scanning the appropriate 'Suggested Answer'. Certainly the legal content covered is wide-ranging — all aspects of the English legal system; criminal law (including public order offences); criminal procedure (including sentencing); contract and consumer law; tort; family law and employment law. We feel that this is a very limited use for the book, however, as a text of this nature cannot hope to cover more than a small part of one A level syllabus, let alone the range of subjects included in the syllabuses of all the different examination boards in England and Wales. We have therefore tried to produce a book that can be used as a tool for learning throughout any A level course, and a revision aid at the end of the course. Because of this approach, although the legal content has been prescribed by the coverage of the different English and Welsh A level syllabuses, the book could also be used by students on other courses such as the Institute of Legal Executives or even for first year undergraduates, as the skills involved are transferable to any law examination.

We have tried to provide a clear explanation and framework for each question and answer. In this way, we hope that the manner in which the material is structured will encourage students to plan their answers, and learn by comparing their plans to those given in the book, before considering the full Suggested Answer. Furthermore, by deliberately duplicating a small amount of material in the context of different styles of question, we have also sought to encourage students to be adaptable in the way in which they use their knowledge. By using the book in these ways the student should develop important examination skills and be able to cope with any type of question, as well as revising the actual law and procedure covered in the answers.

Each question has been given a notional number of marks (either 25 or 50). This is on the basis that the question is being answered in an examination which will last three hours and be marked out of 100, and so appropriate adjustments may have to be made. Because many questions are sub-divided, however, there is a wide range of questions of differing length and complexity, in both essay and situation-based style. Bearing this in mind, the only style of question which could be encountered in an A level examination and which is not included here is the 'data' style question now set in the Oxford board's Paper 2. The necessary material to deal with this is covered throughout the text, however, and we feel that the techniques needed for that type of question are best learned in the classroom. Otherwise the questions are all in the basic essay or situation-based format used in any type of law examination, at any level.

We know that some students use books like this in the hope that they can learn the 'model answers' and reproduce them from memory when required. The book has not been designed for that purpose — each answer is specific to the question given, and it is highly unlikely that exactly the same question would turn up in an examination. Furthermore, we do not pretend that our Suggested Answers are perfect; they merely represent one way of dealing with the question, and could easily be altered both in style and content without detracting from their coverage of the issues. Students should seek to adapt them to their own style, therefore, using our answers merely as a guide, and they will be much more successful if they do so.

Finally, we would like to thank our colleagues at Nene College, Northampton, who have helped us out in various specialist areas. In particular, Ian Hardcastle gave us invaluable assistance with the European law questions in chapter 2, and we think that students will benefit from his considerable expertise in that area. A mention must also go to the staff at Blackstone Press, whose patience has been sorely tested as a rich variety of problems has prevented us from meeting their deadlines. They are probably used to such expressions of gratitude and apology from various authors, but will not have received any more heartfelt than these!

The answers contained in this book should not be affected by any changes in the law before 31 January 1998.

Tim Blakemore and Brendan Greene
January 1998

Table of Cases

Table of Statutes

1 How to Use This Book

This book has been written to help students studying for A level law examinations. We have designed the contents so that they cover the syllabuses and examination styles of the three major examination boards — AEB, Oxford, and JMB/NEAB. Students studying for the examinations of other boards (EDEXCEL Foundation and Welsh, for example) will find that the major part of the syllabus that they are following is covered in the main chapters, but each of those boards includes one subject in its syllabus which is not touched on in any other board's syllabus. We have therefore included one chapter which deals with four of these 'unusual' subjects, namely consumer law, employment law, civil liberties and family law. In this way we feel that all students will have adequate coverage of their boards' syllabuses.

The three major syllabuses cover the same material (with some minor exceptions), but certain topics are organised differently. The sentencing of people convicted of a criminal offence may be dealt with under the General Paper, or under a Criminal Law option, for example. We have therefore organised this book into separate chapters for distinct topics, so that, no matter which syllabus you are following, you can easily look up the topic in which you are interested.

Each chapter has a short introduction explaining the types of questions which you will come across in that area of the law, and how you should approach them. There is then a selection of questions based on past examination questions from each of the three major boards. These have been designed so that every question will be useful, no matter which board's syllabus you are following. Each question has a short commentary, explaining the background to the question and the general approach you should adopt in structuring your answer. At the end of this commentary, we have included an outline of the key points which you should cover in your answer. Lastly, a full suggested answer is set out. These suggested answers have been deliberately designed so that they are realistic in the context of the typical examination, i.e., an A level student with outstanding knowledge of the area, and excellent examination skills, could produce it in the time given.

You will note that occasionally the same topic crops up in more than one question. This happens rarely, as we want to cover as much of the syllabus as possible. It is, however, impossible to cover the whole of the syllabus in any event, and we felt that it was important to illustrate how the same material can be adapted to answer different types of question. An area of law may be raised in a situation-based question, for example, but that answer will require a completely different technique to an essay question on the same topic. Similarly the same topic can occur as part of a long question, or as a short, discrete question in its own right. When that happens, note how the same material must be integrated into the text of the long answer, with appropriate links and references; and adapted for the short answer in such a way as to fit the number of marks allocated. By working through this book you will develop important examination skills at the same time as you are testing your knowledge on specific areas of law.

To get the best use out of this book, you should discipline yourself to try to answer the questions *before* looking at the commentary or suggested answer. The best way may be to follow a two-stage strategy. First, draft an outline answer yourself, and then compare it with the commentary. Once you have understood the reasons for any differences in approach between your outline and that suggested in the commentary, go on to write an answer in full, setting yourself a realistic time limit (and bearing in mind that you would have already spent time in the examination in writing your plan!). When comparing your outline and answer with those given here, please do not forget that you would not need to reproduce our suggestions in order to pass, or even to get a high grade. Matters of style are not necessarily important, and our answers are (we hope!) the best that could be devised.

Lastly, a few words about examination technique. Much general advice applies to A level law exams as to any other examination, and we would not wish to bore you by repeating it here. In any event, different people have different strategies for coping with the peculiar pressures which a pending exam imposes. In the examination itself, there are two key points which cannot be repeated too often, however:

- Ensure that you follow the instructions on the paper (some papers are in two sections, requiring at least one or two questions to be answered in each).

- Answer four questions (or however many the paper requires). An additional page to an already excellent answer may get you another 5 marks out of a hundred. The first page to a new question may get you 20 marks. Which would you prefer?

When answering individual questions, the following points are particularly important in the context of a law examination:

- Distinguish between 'problem' (or 'situation-based') and 'essay' type questions, and follow a different technique for each.

- State the law (when you have to) clearly and simply. This is not always easy to do, as it may involve explaining conflicting cases.

- If there are conflicting cases, do not be afraid to say that the law is uncertain. Give your opinion on which case should be preferred, however.

- For every statement of law, cite a case or a statute as authority. Even saying 'a decided case', or 'in an Act of Parliament' will get you marks.

Problem type questions require a special technique which you will be taught on your A level course. Again, however, the following points bear repetition:

- Follow a logical pattern for every point in the problem. What is the issue? What is the relevant law? How does the law relate to the facts given?

- Be prepared to set out arguments both ways ('... on the one hand ... on the other hand ...') before reaching a conclusion. A good lawyer always considers all sides of an issue.

- Deal with each issue in full, then move on to the next one. Do not confuse issues.

- Restrict yourself to the *relevant* law (you are not writing an essay!) and the law 'as it is' (avoid references to law reform, or general comments on the social, political or economic context!).

- Do not waste time with 'street-wise' advice ('he is in serious trouble and he should throw himself on the mercy of the court ...'). The examiner is concerned only that you know the law, not that you would make a good Citizens Advice Bureau adviser.

Lastly, law essay questions have some pitfalls as well. The typical question will ask you to criticise a particular area of law. This calls for a special approach:

- Think of the essay in three distinct sections. What is the law? What is wrong with it? What could be done to put it right?

- When stating the law, be careful to be succinct. You will get only limited marks for writing everything you know, as all the boards require you to show critical awareness.

- Examples of typical situations are needed for illustrating defects in the law — it is not enough merely to say what is wrong, without explaining why.

- When looking at possible reforms, cite Law Commission papers, Parliamentary reports, academic criticism etc. to show what options are available. But give your own opinion in the end.

2 English Legal System

INTRODUCTION

This chapter includes questions on general matters relating to the English legal system. You should carefully check the syllabus of the board whose exams you will be sitting, as the content of each (and therefore the precise nature of the material it covers) can differ considerably. We have tried to devise questions which are typical of all syllabuses, but the areas covered by some of the more philosophical questions (e.g., Questions 1 and 2) may not be included in their syllabuses by certain boards. Furthermore, much of the material covered in Chapter 3 'Sentencing and Criminal Procedure' is also relevant to the general papers of all the boards, and we have kept any overlap between that chapter and this to a minimum, so that as wide a range of topics is covered as possible.

You will encounter a mix of essay and situation-based questions, although the emphasis tends to be on fairly traditional essay-style questions, even where a short scenario is given to 'set the scene' (see, for example, Questions 3 and 6). We have put each question in the style in which it most often occurs, but you should also note that some of the questions can crop up in the optional papers of some boards, and in the AEB paper 2 on 'Liability in English Law'. Short questions on legal aid or the jury in a 'Criminal Law' paper (or the criminal liability section of AEB paper 2) are good examples of this practice.

QUESTION 1

Evaluate the extent to which morality and the criminal law overlap.

Commentary

This is a typical essay-style question which calls for some knowledge of both the relevant law and legal writers on the topic. The answer given here is by no means prescriptive, as there are many other examples which could be given and writers who could be cited. Rather, it is intended to show how you can structure an answer and weave critical comment into the text. It also illustrates how you can give weight to such an essay by citing case law and statutes as illustrations, and bolster your arguments by quoting from (or, perhaps more realistically, citing and paraphrasing) key writers in the field. Too often with this type of essay the answer will be too general, with little discussion of any real weight. The structure therefore should cover the following areas, finishing, of course, with a conclusion dealing specifically with the question posed:

- define 'criminal law' and 'morality'

- natural law and positivism

- international Conventions

- morality in English law: Wolfenden Report, statute and common law

- enforcing morals: Hart and Devlin, Dworkin

- contemporary legal/moral issues.

Suggested Answer

The starting point for this essay is to define what is meant by the terms 'criminal law' and 'morality'. The criminal law is that body of law which prohibits certain activity on the basis that it is a wrong against the community as a whole, rather than a wrong against an individual. Its aim is to punish, whereas the civil law seeks to compensate. Unfortunately that simple distinction is blurred, because criminal courts can award compensation, and the civil courts can award 'punitive' damages. Kenny has therefore defined crimes as 'wrongs whose sanction is punitive and is in no way remissible by any private person, but is remissible by the Crown alone, if remissible at all'. Even this, though, is not very helpful. First, it is a circular argument. If the question is 'What is a crime?', the answer would be 'Something which the Crown alone can pardon'. But, 'What type of activity can the Crown alone pardon?' — 'Something which is a crime'! Therefore it is difficult to define the type of activity which is criminal. Austin attempted to do it by stating his 'positivist' theory that it is activity which is forbidden by a sovereign power on pain of punishment. Hart distinguished between primary rules which are concerned with basic matters such as violence and theft; and secondary rules which are more regulatory in nature. All that these theories serve to illustrate, however, is that there is a wide range of activity which is covered by the criminal law, from murder to parking on double-yellow lines.

Morality is likewise difficult to define. In a general sense it can be said to consist of those rules which society uses to regulate the conduct of members of the community. The starting point here is to acknowledge that such rules are more in the nature of principles, which change from time to time and place to place, rather than clearly defined regulations. Even then, there will not necessarily be perfect agreement as to every rule, so that instead there must be reliance upon a broad consensus at any one time and place.

These difficult issues of definition are tied up in the central topic of this question, the extent to which law and morality overlap. In legal terms this is usually seen as the conflict between natural law and positivism. Positivism is that school of thought which holds that the only proper study is of the law as it is, not as it should be. As already noted above, Austin attempted to define law purely in those terms. Natural law is much older, going back to the ancient Greek philosophers, and being developed by early and medieval Christian thinkers. It is based on the idea that there are rules which are higher than human law, and that therefore any law which conflicts with those rules is not valid and need not be obeyed. This argument clearly has inherent dangers, as many people disagree with certain laws and would like to have an excuse to disobey them! The debate had a very practical arena in the twentieth century, however, when Nazi war criminals were prosecuted at the end of the Second World War at the Nuremberg trials. Several defendants could point to laws in force under the National Socialist government which authorised terrible 'crimes', such as involvement in the mass extermination of Jews. Nevertheless they were convicted, and — perhaps as a result of that debate — the United Nations and the European Community (as well as many other international bodies) have promulgated bodies of rules seeking to protect fundamental human rights. It is not uncommon for European governments to be required to change their laws by a ruling of the European Court of Human Rights. Although such rulings are strictly unenforceable, they are almost always complied with.

In English law the modern approach has been to distance law from morality, in the sense that purely personal morality should not be punished by the law. Thus the Wolfenden Committee *Report on Homosexual Offences and Prostitution* (1957) said that 'it is not the function of the law to intervene in the private lives of citizens, or to seek to enforce any particular pattern of behaviour'. The function of the law was only to 'preserve public order and decency, to protect the citizen from what is offensive or injurious, and to provide sufficient safeguards against exploitation or corruption of others'. Certainly in many areas there is a clear overlap between law and morality. Murder and violence, for example, are both immoral and unlawful. But there are many matters of immoral conduct which are not unlawful (adultery, for example); and several 'crimes' are not regarded as immoral (parking on double-yellow lines, for example). There is even a statutory offence involving immorality, namely 'for a man persistently to solicit or importune in a public place for immoral purposes' under the Sexual Offences Act 1956, s. 32. This offence will be committed even where the 'immoral purpose' would be lawful, as an homosexual act in private would be (*R v Goddard* (1991) 92 Cr App R 185). The English courts have developed their own system of 'enforceable morality' even further than this, by utilising the common law. In *Shaw v DPP* [1962] AC 220, the defendant had been prosecuted for publishing a *Ladies' Directory*. This was a list of advertisements by prostitutes detailing their specialities. The argument was that prostitution itself was not illegal, as long as it was not carried out in public. The House of Lords, however, stated that there was a common law offence of 'conspiracy to corrupt public morals'. Their reasoning was that 'there remains in the courts ... a residual power to enforce the supreme and fundamental purpose of the law, to conserve not only the safety and order, but also the moral welfare of the state'. This decision was followed in *Knuller v DPP* [1973] AC 435, this time involving advertisements by homosexuals for partners. As the Sexual Offences Act 1967 had legalised homosexual acts in private, it was again argued that nothing unlawful was being planned or encouraged. Once again, however, the House of Lords upheld the conviction for 'conspiracy to corrupt public morals'. The matter has also been considered by the courts in the context of sexual activity involving violence. In *R v Brown* [1992] Crim LR 586, CA several sado-masochists had been prosecuted for assaults upon one another, despite the fact that they had all gathered together in a private house for that very purpose. The assaults had never been life-threatening and had only been for their own pleasure, but certain minor injuries had been caused. The House of Lords ruled that consent to an assault could be a defence only in certain limited categories, such as regulated boxing matches, tattooing and body-piercing etc. There was a strong element of morality present in the judgments of the majority, which enabled them to state that public policy could not allow such behaviour to be practised lawfully. Even the two dissenting judges were morally neutral at best, stating that if Parliament wished to prohibit such behaviour, it should pass specific laws against it.

There are certainly, therefore, several examples in English criminal law of the boundary between law and morality being blurred. The conflicting arguments as to the extent to which law should incorporate moral attitudes were debated in the 1960s in books by Lord Devlin ('The Enforcement of Morals') and Professor Hart ('Law Liberty and Morality'). Hart recognised that law and morality are related (as most criminal activity is also deemed immoral), but was concerned with the question as to how moral rules could be determined with certainty, and therefore applied fairly. He did, however, concede that in certain situations (such as the Nazi government's legislation) law could be so evil as to allow — if not demand — disobedience to it. Lord Devlin argued much more strongly that morality is embedded in the law, and was an essential element which could be determined by representatives of the community — namely, the jury. Commenting on the judgments in *DPP* v *Shaw*, he said: 'morality in England means what twelve men and women think it means — in other words it is to be acertained as a question of fact'.

There was certainly some overlap in Hart's and Devlin's views, and the modern approach has been to emphasise this overlap. Professor Dworkin's writings have focussed on the part played in legal decision-making by 'policy', determined by principles derived from moral or even political considerations. It is in difficult cases that these 'non-rule standards' come into play. The latter half of the twentieth century seems to have been particularly afflicted by complex legal and moral issues. Despite the benchmarks laid down by the Wolfenden Committee, issues such as abortion, use of human embryos, sterilisation of mentally-handicapped women and euthanasia have all proved difficult to resolve. Some issues have been dealt with by statute, as with the Abortion Act 1967 and the Human Fertilisation and Embryology Act 1990. Other issues have had to be dealt with by the courts. In *Re F (Mental patient: sterilisation)* [1990] 2 AC 1, the court set out guidelines for the sterilisation of a mentally handicapped woman who was sexually active but clearly incapable of coping with pregnancy. In *Airedale NHS Trust* v *Bland* [1993] AC 789 the House of Lords devised a procedure whereby a person in a 'persistent vegetative state' could be 'allowed to die' by having all artificial nutrition and medication removed. It is notable, however, that the House of Lords affirmed that positive actions resulting in a patient's death (such as injecting the patient with a fatal drug) would still amount to murder. This case, perhaps more than any other, showed how the courts adopt a pragmatic, if illogical, approach to difficult moral situations. There is no legal distinction between killing by omission and killing by positive act — the phrase 'allowing to die' is merely a euphemism in this context. Furthermore, the House of Lords were being asked to give a declaration that the doctors' actions would not amount to unlawful killing, and they responded by setting out guidelines, including the requirement that leave of the court be sought before such actions take place. But if actions are 'criminal', the House of Lords cannot 'make' them lawful by a declaration (and *vice versa*).

To conclude, therefore, it seems that there must be a place for moral principles in the law, and therefore to a certain extent law and morality must — and do — overlap. The dangers of following this course too far, however, are perhaps illustrated by the *R v Brown* case. It cannot be said that there is one moral code in English society which is followed by everyone, especially in a society with such a strong multi-ethnic and multicultural element. The three judges forming the majority in *Brown* could be said to be imposing their own moral values in circumstances where the criminal law should tread warily. Certainly two judges were prepared to disagree, and the case was taken to the European Court of Human Rights by the defendants (where it was dismissed). This perhaps indicates that it is only bodies such as the European Court of Human Rights, or Parliament itself, which should take such decisions except in the most extreme cases.

QUESTION 2

Examine the need for 'fault' to be proved before liability can be established in English law. (25 marks)

Commentary

This question calls for a consideration of the fundamental principle of 'fault' in both civil and criminal law, with careful distinction being drawn between the two areas. Rather than merely writing two essays, however, you should look to compare and contrast approaches taken by the civil and criminal courts, commenting in particular upon areas where there appears to be an overlap (the law on 'gross negligence' manslaughter, for example). Inevitably your discussion will touch on those civil and criminal offences where no fault, or minimal fault, is required; but, while mentioning these briefly, you should be careful not to turn the essay into an examination of the reasons or justification for strict liability. Follow this pattern and cover the following points:

- Aims of the law and the purpose of 'fault'.

- Fault in the criminal law — *mens rea*.

- Strict liability crimes.

- Fault for civil liability — contract, tort, strict liability.

Suggested Answer

A system of law is meant to ensure that the conduct of every person in that society conforms to certain specified standards, so that the society can function properly. Civil liability is imposed so that losses suffered are compensated, thereby reducing the extent to which the person wronged is put at a disadvantage. Criminal law seeks to punish for the breach of certain standards of behaviour, on the basis that some types of behaviour are so harmful to the community as a whole (as opposed to just an individual) that they need to be prevented. A system of punitive sanctions aims to prevent 'criminal' behaviour by deterrence, simple physical incapacitation (e.g., imprisonment) or possibly rehabilitation. The modern approach, however, is 'just deserts', which seeks to prevent crime by establishing a coherent system based on proportionate punishment. These basic aims of the civil and criminal law overlap, however. The civil law includes the concept of 'exemplary damages', when people in established positions of authority (such as the police) wantonly exceed their powers and therefore must be discouraged from such behaviour in the future. Similarly, criminal procedure allows the court to award compensation to the victim of a crime, and for this to be collected and enforced by the criminal process. Indeed, under the Powers of Criminal Courts Act 1973 (as amended) the court must give reasons why it is *not* awarding compensation in certain cases. The requirement for fault is also a common feature of both civil and criminal law. This is on the basis that behaviour cannot be discouraged unless the perpetrator has a choice about whether to behave in that way or not. 'Fault' therefore implies that the offender chose to behave improperly. The issue is much more complex than that, however, as the law includes situations of so-called 'strict liability', where no fault is required, as well as many other types of behaviour where the element of choice on the part of the defendant may be very difficult to detect. It is those situations which this essay will focus upon.

Fault in the criminal law is prescribed by the principle *actus non facit reum nisi mens sit rea.* This means that the prohibited act (the '*actus reus*') is not criminal unless the defendant also had a 'guilty mind' (*'mens rea'*). The *mens rea* for every crime differs, usually being specified by a statute, but sometimes described by the courts for common law offences such as murder. *Mens rea* should not be confused with 'motive'. Thus 'mercy killing' is still murder, as the *mens rea* for murder is 'intention to kill', regardless of the purpose for killing unless it falls within certain categories (such as killing an enemy in action in time of war).

There are three recognised forms of *mens rea* — intention, recklessness and negligence. 'Intention' has a wider meaning than in the everyday sense. It includes not only 'purpose' (direct intention) but also 'oblique intention'. Thus if a person foresees that a result is 'virtually certain', that is evidence that she 'intended' the result, and the inference of intention 'may be irresistible' (*R* v *Nedrick* [1986] 1 WLR 1025). The test in both situations covered by the *mens rea* of intention is subjective, in that the the prosecution must prove that the defendant either wished the result, or knew that it would occur. The need for 'fault' is thus clear. Some crimes only require recklessness as the *mens rea*. The position here as regards fault is a little less clear. Recklessness concerns unjustified risk-taking, and the difficulty lies in determining whether the prosecution have to prove that the defendant knew of the risk (subjective recklessness), or merely that the defendant should have known of it (objective recklessness). Subjective recklessness is required for any offence where the word 'malice' is used to describe the *mens rea* (*R* v *Cunningham* [1957] 2 QB 396); for offences involving assault (*R* v *Parmenter* [1991] 4 All ER 698); and for rape (*R* v *Satnam and Kewal* (1983) 78 Cr App R 149). The need for fault is apparent, because the defendant took a risk despite knowing the possible results. Objective recklessness, however, requires only that the defendant be judged by the standards of a reasonable person. This applies to all offences where the word 'reckless' is actually used in the statutory definition (with the exception of rape), as decided by the House of Lords in *R* v *Caldwell*. The element of fault could be argued to apply on the basis that the defendant was not paying sufficient attention to the consequences of her actions. However, the Court of Appeal in *R* v *Coles* [1994] Crim LR 820 decided that a person would be guilty of an offence requiring objective recklessness even if she was incapable of appreciating the risk herself, as long as the risk was obvious to a 'reasonable person'. This approach is very difficult to justify, and there are *dicta* in the House of Lords decision in *R* v *Reid* (1992) to suggest that allowance should be made for the defendant's incapacity to appreciate risks. Certainly the courts are not consistent in their decisons regarding the *mens rea* of recklessness, and it is also difficult to distinguish between objective reckless-ness in the strict *Coles* sense, and negligence. Negligence is sometimes required for fairly minor offences, such as 'careless driving', and again requires that the defendant be judged by the standards of ordinary people. The argument for regarding this as 'fault' is similar to that for objective recklessness, but perhaps less controversial because it usually applies only to minor offences. It has been confirmed by the House of Lords that the crime of manslaughter can be committed by 'gross negligence' (*R* v *Adomako* [1995] 1 AC 171), but this formulation requires the jury to assess that the negligence is so great as to amount to a serious criminal offence, bearing in mind the risk of death involved in the defendant's actions.

Lastly, some crimes do not require *mens rea* at all. Generally there is a presumption that the prosecution must prove *mens rea* (*Sweet* v *Parsley* [1970] AC 182), but the courts have ruled that many quite serious offences (e.g., criminal libel, blasphemy and public nuisance) involve at least an element of strict liability. Many 'regulatory' offences (e.g., consumer protection and public health legislation and minor road traffic offences) are strict liability also, although sometimes a specific provision in a statute will allow the defendant to escape liability by proving that all reasonable steps had been taken to avoid the problem, or that somebody else was to blame. The arguments here often revolve around the idea of social protection, in that the risk of harm to society is so great, especially where the activity itself is clearly potentially harmful, that imposing strict liability is necessary to encourage careful assessment and avoidance of all risk (*Gammon (UK) Ltd* v *Attorney-General for Hong Kong* [1985] AC 1).

The principle of fault does not play such an important role in civil law, but nonetheless the law is often based on the moral principle that you are liable only if you are to blame, i.e., at fault. Strict liability, which is liablity without fault, underpins the law of contract and surfaces in a number of torts.

In the law of contract, as a general rule, a party does not have to be at fault to be made liable for a breach of contract. For example, if a shop sells goods to a customer and the goods are not of satisfactory quality, this is a breach of contract even though the shop is not at fault. In *Rogers* v *Parish* [1987] QB 933, the defendant garage was liable for selling a new car, which was defective, to the plaintiff. But in some circumstances contract law imposes liability only if one of the parties is at fault, for example, in relation to the doctrines of frustration and common mistake. The doctrine of frustration provides that if something happens which makes performance of the contract impossible, illegal or radically different from what was agreed, without the fault of either party, then the contract is frustrated. The legal effect is that neither party is liable. In *Taylor* v *Caldwell* (1863) 3 B & S 826, the defendants were not liable for breach of contract when the hall they hired out was burned down. If one party is at fault and caused the frustrating event, he or she cannot rely on the doctrine of frustration (as in *Maritime National Fish* v *Ocean Trawlers* [1935] AC 524) and he or she would be in breach of contract. Similarly, if the parties make a contract but unknown to both of them something happened before the contract was made which makes performance impossible, this is treated as a common mistake and the contract is void. An example of this is *Couturier* v *Hastie* (1856) 5 HL Cas 673 where at the time of the contract the subject-matter, the corn, had already been sold and did not, effectively exist. However, if one party has taken the risk that the subject-matter exists, and it doesn't, they cannot claim that the contract is void. Statements made before a contract may be terms of the contract, in which case liability is strict. But if they are classed as representations then the person making them will usually be held liable only if he or she is at fault in some way. The law imposes liability for both fraudulent and negligent statements in the law of tort. A fraudulent statement is one made knowing it is wrong or recklessly, i.e., without caring, and in such circumstances liability would also arise in criminal law. A negligent statement is made by someone who had no reasonable grounds for believing it to be true. In *Hedley Byrne* v *Heller* [1964] AC 465, the court said that in principle the defendant bank was liable for negligently providing a reference, which it knew the plaintiff would see. Under the Misrepresentation Act 1967, a party to a contract is given the right to sue for a negligent misrepresentation made by the other party to the contract. Damages can be claimed for all direct losses for fraudulent misrepresentation and under the Misrepresentation Act.

The rule of strict liability does not apply in contract in the case of provision of services. Under the Supply of Goods and Services Act 1982, s. 13, if a service is provided in the course of a business there is an implied term it will be carried out with reasonable care. This does not make the provider strictly liable, but only liable if they are at fault and fall below the standard of 'reasonable care'. This distinction between goods and services is necessary because of the nature of services, particularly professional services — a guarantee of the outcome cannot be given, for example, by a doctor carrying out an operation.

The whole concept of a tort as a 'wrong' shows that it is based on the principle of fault. To establish liability in the tort of negligence the plaintiff must show that the defendant has broken a duty of care or, in other words, was at fault. In deciding if the defendant has broken this duty the courts use the idea of the 'reasonable man', which is an objective standard, rather than looking at the particular individual. If someone does not meet this standard he or she is liable, so in *Donoghue* v *Stevenson* [1932] AC 562, the manufacturer was liable for the injury caused by a snail in a bottle of ginger beer. However, the objective test may mean that a defendant is held liable even though they have done their best and are not morally 'at fault'. Sometimes tort imposes strict liability; for example, in *Rylands* v *Fletcher* (1868) LR 3 HL 330, the defendant was held liable for bringing something dangerous on to his land (water) which escaped and caused damage to the plaintiff's land. In the tort of private nuisance a defendant will be held strictly liable for activities on his land which interfere with other land owners.

Fault remains an indispensable element in a legal system which requires the culpable to 'pay' for their misdeeds.

QUESTION 3

Susan has just been convicted in Walford Magistrates' Court of stealing goods to the value of £14 from an off-licence. She was arrested outside the off-licence two months ago, charged and detained in the police station over night. The next day she was brought before the local magistrates' court, when the case was adjourned and bail granted. Her trial took place four weeks after that.

(a) Explain critically the arrangements for legal advice and assistance which would be available to Susan at different stages of the criminal proceedings if she could not afford to pay for it herself. (15 marks)

(b) Susan was tried and convicted in the local magistrates' court. Evaluate the role played by lay magistrates in the criminal justice system. (10 marks)

(c) Explain briefly the other functions of lay magistrates in the English legal system. (5 marks)

(d) Susan could have asked to be tried at the Crown Court before a jury. How satisfactory is trial by jury? (20 marks)

Commentary

This question is in the style of an AEB paper 2 question covering issues of 'Liability in English law', and any of the short questions could crop up in the section on liability in criminal law, as additional elements to the questions concerning the substantive criminal law (see Chapter 4, Question 1). When combined with the similar style question in Chapter 3 (see Question 3 and 4), this gives you a wide range of questions which could crop up in this way. These shorter questions could also occur in almost any combination as parts of a question on the general papers of any of the boards, however. Allow yourself 90 minutes to complete the whole question, or a proportionate amount of time for any individual part. The particular points which should be included in your answer are as follows:

Question 3(a)

- duty solicitor scheme

- 'Green Form' legal aid and ABWOR

- problems with these schemes — availability, remuneration, quality of advice

- legal aid for the trial

- inconsistencies in awarding certificates, remuneration, quality of representation.

Question 3(b)

- outline of functions — summary trial, committal to Crown Court

- appointment — the system and criticisms

- training — the system and criticisms

- advantages of lay magistracy — cost, involvement of community

- disadvantages — prosecution bias, inconsistency, do not represent community.

Question 3(c)

- family proceedings court

- licensing

- civil debts (council tax).

Question 3(d)

- 'random' selection

- finders of fact and the judge's role

- intellectual ability

- representatives of community against professionals

- perverse decisions.

Suggested Answer

(a)   There are various arrangements for people to receive legal advice and assistance in criminal proceedings even though they cannot afford to pay for the services of a lawyer. These schemes are governed by the Legal Aid Act 1988 and associated regulations, and fall into two categories — advice and assistance short of representation in court; and 'full' legal aid, which will cover everything including court hearings. The first point at which Susan would have needed legal advice and assistance would have been when she arrived at the police station after she had been arrested. Under the Police and Criminal Evidence Act (PACE) 1984 and the associated Code of Practice, she is entitled to free legal advice and to be informed of that entitlement. She could use her own solicitor, or if this was not possible she could make use of the duty solicitor scheme. These schemes are run by local law societies and provide a rota of solicitors willing to be called out at any time (day or night) to advise people who have been arrested and detained, or even those merely being questioned by the police. The solicitor's charges will be covered by the special Green Form scheme, with no assessment of the suspect's means being necessary. This means that the solicitor will have to fill in a claim form and submit it to the Legal Aid Board, for payment at a fixed rate. If Susan did not make use of the 24-hour duty solicitor scheme, she could have asked to see, and be represented by, a solicitor on her first day at court. There are also local duty solicitor schemes with a rota of solicitors attending court every day; or the magistrates could ask any solicitor who was available in court to see Susan. The legal aid scheme in such a situation also covers representation on that day only, and is known as 'Assistance by Way of Representation' (ABWOR). Again, no means test is necessary, and the solicitor must complete a slightly different form for submission to the Legal Aid Board for payment, again at fixed rates of remuneration. Both of these schemes rely upon local solicitors to organise and staff a rota system, and some areas may not have a suitable scheme in operation. The rates of pay offered by the Legal Aid Board (which are fixed by Regulations made by the Lord Chancellor) are not regarded as adequate by the legal profession, especially in view of the fact that a solicitor on the rota may have to turn out in the early hours of the morning, and be ready to do so even if there is no call for the duty solicitor that night. As a result, the rota tends to be staffed by less experienced solicitors, and there is therefore a suspicion that the advice and assistance given to suspects will not be of the highest quality. There is also obviously a temptation for a solicitor to give advice over the telephone to the suspect, rather than go all of the way out to the police station in the middle of the night.

After her initial consultation with a solicitor, Susan will have needed to apply for full legal aid to cover preparation for, and representation at, her trial. This is done by completing forms showing the nature of the charge and giving a detailed breakdown of her income and outgoings. These forms are sent to the local magistrates' court, and legal aid will be granted only subject to certain criteria. First, the case itself must justify legal aid 'in the interests of justice', by reference to guidelines. These include factors such as: that the defendant is likely to be sent to prison if convicted; that complicated issues of law are involved; that the defendant has an inadequate knowledge of English; or that conviction might affect the defendant's livelihood. If the application passes that test (the 'merits' test) then the defendant's income (after deductions and certain allowances) and capital must come within certain specified limits (the 'means' test). These limits are updated regularly, but anyone in receipt of income support will always fall within the scheme. Those whose net income or capital is too high will be liable to pay a contribution towards the costs of their defence. As with the legal advice and assistance schemes, the concern is that the rate of remuneration paid to solicitors is too low to make it worthwhile taking on cases such as Susan's. The Lord Chancellor, as a member of the Government, has consistently kept increases in legal aid rates at below the rate of inflation for many years, and Regulations brought in in 1993 tightened up the system even more. This is because the legal aid bill has risen dramatically over the past few years and shows sign of spiralling out of control as more and more demands are made on it. The result of the increased limits on remuneration, however, has been that many firms of solicitors will no longer undertake criminal legal aid work, let alone take part in duty solicitor schemes. Those firms that do still take on such work have to reduce to a minimum the time spent on cases by senior staff, and ensure that they have a constant flow of cases to justify a team of lawyers specialising in such matters. Preparation for trial must typically be undertaken by unqualified staff, so that the qualified solicitors (who are obviously paid more) only have to deal with the court hearing itself, when the legal aid rates of pay are higher. The fear is that legally aided defendants will get a poorer quality service than wealthy defendants who can pay their solicitors properly themselves. The conflict is therefore between the need to ensure that justice is freely available to everybody, regardless of means; and the need to keep public expenditure under control. Traditionally, solicitors themselves have been allowed to monitor both the merits of cases which receive legal aid and also the amount of time which needs to spent on each case, with only partial supervision by the legal aid authorities. There is now a growing tendency for the authorities to take much stricter control of expenditure, and it therefore seems likely that people such as Susan will in the future find themselves with a much more limited choice of legal adviser and possibly a lower quality of representation.

(b) A lay magistrate is one who is not paid but receives expenses only to cover loss of earnings, travel etc. Lay magistrates play a key role in the criminal justice system. Magistrates' courts deal with all criminal cases in one way or another, and hear 95% of them in full, yet out of nearly 30,000 magistrates, only a handful (about 75) are qualified, professional (or 'stipendiary') magistrates.

The lay magistrate will usually sit as one of a bench of three magistrates to hear criminal cases, assisted by a legally qualified clerk. They deal with cases which can be tried summarily, as opposed to cases which must be transferred to the Crown Court. If a case is 'triable either way', the magistrates must first decide on 'mode of trial'. This involves hearing a brief outline of the facts of the case, and then deciding if it is a suitable case for summary trial. A charge of theft, for example, may involve a tin of baked beans, or a million pounds of gold bullion. The latter case would clearly need to be dealt with by a Crown Court judge. Even if the case is suitable for summary trial, the defendant can nevertheless then elect to be tried by a judge and jury. Under the Criminal Procedure and Investigations Act 1996, the magistrates must now also ask the defendant to give an indication of his or her plea before deciding where the case will be tried. If the defendant wishes to plead guilty, the magistrates must proceed to deal with the case and only commit the case to the Crown Court for sentence once they have heard all the facts and the defence mitigation. If the defendant indicates a plea of not guilty, mode of trial will be decided in the usual way, with the defendant still able to elect for trial at the Crown Court if necessary. The aim of this provision is to keep as many cases as possible in the magistrates' court, so if the defendant then pleads guilty in the Crown Court, he or she will lose a certain amount of the usual discount for a guilty plea and may also have to pay towards the prosecution costs.

If a case is tried summarily, the magistrates will hear the evidence from witnesses and decide if the defendant is guilty or innocent. Once a defendant has been convicted of, or pleaded guilty to, an offence, the magistrates have certain powers of punishment limited to a fine of £5,000 and/or imprisonment for up to six months for one offence, or 12 months for two or more offences. If they feel that their powers are insufficient, they can commit the defendant to the Crown Court for sentence. The new procedure under the Criminal Procedure and Investigations Act 1996, as outlined above, will mean that the magistrates will have an increased responsibility in dealing with serious cases which previously they would have committed to the Crown Court immediately. In particular, it will present them with many more difficult sentencing decisions, as they will frequently have to decide whether their sentencing powers are adequate in borderline cases.

If the offence is only triable on indictment, or is a case which is triable either way but which has to be sent to the Crown Court, the magistrates must hold a 'committal hearing'. At this hearing, the prosecution will produce statements by all their witnesses, shown in advance to the defence. If the defence so require, the magistrates must consider whether the prosecution case is strong enough to justify a Crown Court trial. If not, they must dismiss the charge. If they decide that the prosecution case is strong enough, they will transfer ('commit') the case to a suitable Crown Court, where the trial will take place some weeks afterwards.

There are various advantages and disadvantages of using lay magistrates to such an extent in the criminal justice system. There are clear benefits in involving the local community in the legal process, especially as this enables the magistrates to utilise their knowledge of special problems in the locality of the court. It also helps to prevent the community feeling alienated from the process of justice. Generally, the use of lay people also prevents the process becoming dominated by the natural tendency of professionals to run matters 'their way', with an emphasis more on set rules and accepted formalities rather than on the justice of the case. There is also an enormous cost benefit to using lay magistrates. As already explained, over 99% of magistrates are unpaid, apart from expenses, and they deal with over 95% of all criminal cases. The rota system, whereby magistrates sit only once every few weeks, also helps to prevent their becoming 'case-hardened', so that they consider each case on its merits without recourse to standardised sentences for stereotypical offenders such as drunks and young offenders.

The disadvantages are mainly concerned with the manner in which lay magistrates deal with the cases before them. There is at least a perception that they are prosecution biased and accept police evidence too readily. There is also much concern about inconsistency in sentencing practice, with the same offence in similar circumstances likely to receive a much harsher punisment depending upon whereabouts in the country the case is tried. The Magistrates Association has gone some way to addressing this problem by developing guidelines for sentencing purposes, but there is still a lot of discretion within those guidelines. Perhaps the main objection to lay magistrates, however, is the fact that they are not representative of the community, but only of small sections of it. The stereotypical magistrate is white and middle-class, either self-employed, retired or (if a married female) not seeking employment. These problems could be seen as stemming from the system for appointing magistrates, which used to rely upon a secret selection process apparently relying upon the appointment of traditional figures of standing in the community. Steps have been taken to broaden the base of the magistracy by bringing in people from all walks of life, but the traditional image of magistrates is proving difficult to overcome, and is probably discouraging many potential applicants from ethnic minorities, for example. Once appointed, magistrates then receive some basic training in how to conduct themselves and run trials, but not in the law. There is also criticism that this process should be more strictly controlled and more carefully thought out, as it could help to correct some of the perceived problems mentioned above.

To conclude, therefore, there is no doubt that the English criminal justice system depends a lot on the lay magistrate, and the system is so well established that drastic changes are unlikely. The importance of the role of magistrates suggests that problems should be addressed with more urgency, however, to ensure that public confidence in the system is not diminished.

(c)   Lay magistrates deal with criminal matters in both the adult court and the youth court, where people under 18 years of age are tried. They must be specially trained for this function and their sentencing powers are different. They also have an important function in civil family matters. In these proceedings they are called the family proceedings court, and magistrates who sit in this court also require special training. The family proceedings court deals with a wide range of matters connected to married life and children (whether of a married or unmarried couple). Under the Domestic Proceedings (Magistrates' Court) Act 1978, magistrates can award financial provision between married couples who are separated rather than getting divorced. This provision can consist of maintenance (i.e., payment of a regular sum) and/or a lump sum, limited to £1,000, but the magistrates cannot deal with disputes involving property. Under the Family Law Act 1996, they also have powers to issue orders to protect people from violence at the hands of an 'associated person', typically a spouse or cohabitant, but extending to certain relatives or friends who have shared a house with the victim. They can even exclude one party from a house or the area of a house in some circumstances. Lastly, the family proceedings court has a major role to play in child law. Under the Children Act 1989, the court must deal with a wide range of matters concerning children, such as residence and contact orders, and maintenance where the dispute is between the parents of the child. The magistrates might also be involved in dealing with applications by local authorities for children to be taken into care or protected in some other way, or for adoptions to be formalised.

Apart from their criminal and family jurisdictions, the magistrates also have various administrative roles. They will deal with applications for gambling or alcohol licences, for example, and with disputes concerning non-payment of civil debts such as the council tax (the 'poll tax' or community charge, as was).

(d)   The jury comprises 12 people, supposedly selected at random to hear a criminal trial in the Crown Court. Their role is to decide matters of fact, and ultimately the guilt or innocence of the accused. Although Crown Court trials account for only about 1% of all criminal cases, the right to trial by jury has been described by Lord Devlin as 'the lamp that shows that freedom lives'. There are, however, serious misgivings about trial by jury, both in general and in specific types of case.

The process starts by the local Crown Court office selecting a number of people at random from the electoral register, without knowing whether they are eligible or not (they may be ineligible, for example, because they are connected with the administration of justice, or have serious convictions for a criminal offence). The 'randomness' of this process is, however, difficult to verify, as there is no set procedure. Without strict controls, for example, it would be possible for the Crown Court official to have unwittingly chosen 'at random' only from certain areas of the city. These areas might be predominantly white, middle-class, or contain a disproportionately high number of households from a particular ethnic minority.

Everyone selected will be sent a summons through the post requiring their attendance at court on a specified day and at a given time. The period of attendance could be for up to two weeks, but some complex cases may take several months. As jury service is an onerous duty, certain people can claim exemption as of right. These include those who have served within the last two years, or who have been excused further service for life because of involvement in a lengthy trial before. Other categories are those who are over 65, MPs, doctors, and people whose religious beliefs are incompatible with jury service. Others may be excused by the Crown Court office (e.g., students who are about to sit exams), but this obviously again could affect the true randomness of the selection. Although great care is certainly taken only to allow unusual situations to excuse service, it is possible for different Crown Courts to have differing interpretations of what amount to 'unusual situations'. Job-related difficulties, for example, should never be a suitable excuse, as otherwise everyone in employment could be excused and the selection process would thereby be far from random, but it is possible that some situations might 'slip through the net', depending on the rigour with which a particular Crown Court approaches its task.

At the trial there will be a number of potential jurors from which the jury for a particular trial will be selected. Any individual juror may be challenged by the prosecution or defence advocate. The challenging party must satisfy the judge on the balance of probabilities that there is good reason for the challenge. The difficulty here is that the defence will have little idea in advance of the list of potential jurors, nor any realistic way of making quick investigations as to their backgrounds. The prosecution, on the other hand, can quickly access the police national computer, or possibly check in advance of the day of the hearing. No questioning of the jurors is allowed, except in exceptional circumstances in which there may be a special reason why certain people would be prejudiced (for example, by having seen a biased account of one of the parties in a certain television programme). The prosecution, however, also have the right to vet the jurors in advance in cases involving terrorism or national security; and have the right to 'stand by' a juror. This right is governed by the Attorney-General's Guidelines 1989, and must be exercised with caution, especially in view of the abolition of the defence right to 'peremptory challenge' in 1988 (i.e., the right to challenge up to three jurors without giving a reason). There is, nevertheless, a danger now that the make-up of the jury may be unfairly influenced by the prosecution without the defence being able to prevent it. There is also the continuing problem of producing a 'suitable' jury for certain trials. Where the defendant is black, for example, a random selection could result in an all-white jury, especially if the Crown Court has unwittingly tended to select only from certain areas of the city. There is no mechanism for avoiding this situation at present.

During the trial itself the jury are supposed to act as the finders of fact, with direction from the judge as to points of law. The rules of evidence allow the judge to exclude certain facts from the jury's consideration, however, if it is felt that they would be unduly prejudiced by them. The defendant's previous convictions are almost always excluded therefore, as is 'hearsay' evidence. Under PACE 1984, even the defendant's confession will be excluded unless the prosecution can satisfy the judge that it was obtained fairly. Possibly the most controversial area, however, is the judge's summing up of the evidence, which occurs right at the end of the trial. This enables the judge to influence the jury's attitude towards the evidence of certain witnesses, sometimes subtly, but sometimes quite blatantly. Thus in the first trial of the 'Birmingham 6' (*R* v *McIlkenny* (1991) 93 Cr App R 287) the judge openly stated that a key defence witness was a perjurer (i.e., telling deliberate lies) 'of the worst kind'; whereas in the libel trial involving Jeffrey Archer, the judge referred to Mrs Archer (who gave evidence in support of her husband's case) as 'fragrant'. There is therefore serious doubt as to the true independence of the jury as fact-finders.

Lastly, there remains the question whether a jury will have the intellectual capacity to follow certain complicated trials, particularly trials involving complex frauds in the context of the activities of a large company. Such trials can last for months and involve a vast volume of documents, including detailed scrutiny of company accounts. In 1986 the Roskill Committee on Fraud Trials recommended that expert 'lay assessors' should be used in such cases instead of a jury, possibly with two such assessors sitting with and assisting the judge. This recommendation has been debated on and off ever since, and was raised as a possibility once again by the Royal Commission on Criminal Justice in 1995. The opposing arguments, however, are that the use of a jury forces the prosecution to keep their case as simple as possible; and that the key issue of 'dishonesty' is uniquely suitable for ordinary people to decide upon, no matter the context in which the defendant's behaviour took place. There is also a deep-rooted suspicion of professionals taking over the criminal process, as their culture can easily slide from an impartial search for truth and justice into formalism, i.e., the trial process can become 'part of the job' and thus the rules of procedure can become the be-all and end-all. Juries are, after all, the representatives of the community, on whose behalf the prosecution is being brought. They have shown an ability to ignore the strict law in the past, in preference for a just verdict. Thus, in *R* v *Ponting* [1985] Crim LR 318, the jury acquitted Clive Ponting despite the judge's ruling that he had no defence recognised by the law. He had released details about the sinking of the Argentinian ship *General Belgrano* during the Falklands conflict, which showed that the Government was giving misleading information to the public. This was clearly a breach of the Official Secrets Act, but the jury acquitted Ponting anyway. This is an example of a 'perverse decision', and is sometimes used by critics of the jury system as an argument against the use of unqualified jurors. Other cases are sometimes cited where a jury have acquitted a defendant who was 'clearly guilty', and judges have been known to make the jury listen to the prosecution reading out an acquitted defendant's previous convictions where, unknown to them, the defendant had been found guilty of a similar charge already. These arguments must be viewed with scepticism, as it may be that the prosecution simply did not put up a strong enough case. The jury cannot be blamed in such a situation; but it is of course possible that some perverse acquittals occur which cannot be overturned, whereas perverse convictions can be subject to an appeal. The issue, therefore, is the extent to which perverse decisions occur, such as to invalidate the whole system, and there does not seem to be convincing evidence one way or another.

To conclude, therefore, there are strong arguments that trial by jury is an important part of the criminal process, but that there are flaws in the present system which need to be addressed to ensure that the system is fair to all parties. Ascertaining and correcting the flaws is made difficult by the prohibition on any research which involves questioning specific jurors, and so a determined approach to the issue by Government is needed before the full facts can be brought to light by properly conducted research, rather than reliance upon hearsay and anecdote.

QUESTION 4

Answer *both* parts:

(a) Describe and explain the appeal system in criminal cases up to the Court of Appeal. (10 marks)

(b) Evaluate the effect of the Criminal Appeals Act 1995 in reforming this system. (15 marks)

Commentary

As a whole, this question requires a good knowledge of the basic criminal appeals system (including the new Criminal Cases Review Commission), together with an understanding of the recent history of miscarriages of justice. Only if you are confident of your knowledge in those areas will you be able to describe the system and give some critical comment on the changes brought about by the 1995 Act. The short question on appeals could be encountered by itself, or as part of a longer question (e.g., on the AEB paper 2). The second part would perhaps be more likely to appear with different wording, in the context of a question concerning miscarriages of justice. The same material would be called for, however. The following points should be covered in your answer :

Question 4(a)

- appeal to the Crown Court

- appeal by case stated

- judicial review

- appeal to the Court of Appeal.

Question 4(b)

- background — the Royal Commission 1995

- make-up of the Criminal Cases Review Commission

- the Commission's powers

- role of the Court of Appeal

- criticisms — resources, political independence, criteria for investigation, scope of investigatory powers, criteria for referral, reliance on Court of Appeal

- new grounds of appeal compared to former

- criticisms — pre-Act case law, effect of Act.

Suggested Answer

(a) The first situation in which a defendant may wish to appeal is after conviction in the magistrates' court. Such appeals are covered by the Magistrates' Courts Act 1980, and there are two basic possibilities. The defendant could appeal to the Queen's Bench Division of the High Court on a point of law, or to the Crown Court as of right. An appeal to the Queen's Bench Division can, in fact, be made by either the prosecution or the defence and involves requesting the magistrates who presided to 'state a case' within 21 days of the conclusion of the proceedings. This means that the magistrates must draw up a document which sets out the arguments by the parties on questions of law, the facts on which the magistrates based their decision, and the decision itself. The hearing in the High Court will be before at least two judges of the Queen's Bench and will consist purely of argument on the relevant points of law (i.e., no evidence will be heard). The court can quash a conviction or substitute a conviction (and sentence) for an acquittal, but it is more usual (in the latter case) for the case to be remitted to the magistrates with a direction to convict or to retry the case. An appeal to the Crown Court is available as of right to any person convicted by the magistrates, but not to the prosecution. Notice of appeal must be given to the the prosecutor and the magistrates' court which dealt with the case, within 21 days of the conclusion of the case. The appeal will be heard by a judge sitting with two magistrates and will consist of a complete re-hearing of the case, with all witnesses having to give evidence all over again. The judge can confirm, reverse or vary all or any part of the decision being appealed against, including increasing the sentence or remitting the case for the magistrates to re-hear. Lastly, there is a third possibility for appeal, namely by way of judicial review. The High Court has a general supervisory function in that it can oversee all lower courts and tribunals, including any magistrates' court. Both the prosecution and defence can therefore ask the High Court to review any decision — whether on law or procedure — of the magistrates, but the High Court is likely to refuse any application which could have been made in the usual appeal process. This method of appeal is therefore used only in unusual circumstances, such as a refusal by the magistrates to issue a witness summons.

A defendant convicted after a trial on indictment in the Crown Court can appeal to the Court of Appeal (Criminal Division), under the terms of the Criminal Appeal Act 1968, as amended by the Criminal Appeal Act 1995. The grounds of appeal were amended and simplified by the 1995 Act so that the Court of Appeal 'shall allow an appeal against conviction if they think that the conviction is unsafe; and shall dismiss such an appeal in any other case'.

It is possible, although rare, for the trial judge to grant a certificate that the case is fit for appeal. This would usually happen only where there is a clear element of doubt about a point of law, and the ground of appeal must be identified in the certificate. More typically the defendant will have to apply for leave to appeal to the Court of Appeal itself. This will entail setting out the grounds of appeal in a formal document and submitting it within 28 days of the conviction. The application will be heard in the first instance by a single judge, and if leave is refused the defendant may 'renew' the appeal by notice within 14 days. This means that the full court will then consider the appeal in open court, but there is a danger that they will agree with the single judge and order that the time that the defendant has spent in custody awaiting their decision will not count towards the sentence of imprisonment imposed at the original trial. A defendant is treated as an unconvicted prisoner while awaiting the outcome of the appeal process, and can therefore receive certain benefits in prison which are not available to a convicted prisoner. The rules are therefore an attempt to ensure that the court will only have to hear realistic applications, by discouraging defendants spinning out the appeal process for as long as possible

At the appeal (if leave is granted) the defendant (now known as 'the appellant') is entitled to be present unless the appeal is purely on a point of law, when specific leave is necessary. Three judges (Lords Justices of Appeal) will hear argument from counsel for the appellant and the prosecution, but only rarely will oral evidence be given. This will usually happen only when a new witness is available who could not give evidence at the trial for some reason. The Court of Appeal may quash the conviction, order a re-trial, substitute a conviction for an alternative charge, or dismiss the appeal altogether.

(b) The Royal Commission on Criminal Justice was set up in 1991 in the wake of a series of successful appeals by people who had spent many years in prison for crimes they did not commit. The Royal Commission reported in 1993 and included a recommendation that a new body be set up which could investigate and redress miscarriages of justice. The Government eventually published a White Paper, resulting in the Criminal Appeal Act 1995. This Act set up a new body along the lines of that recommended by the Royal Commission, namely the Criminal Cases Review Commission (CCRC). The CCRC is to replace the former procedure whereby the Home Secretary could refer cases back to the Court of Appeal where, for example, new evidence gave rise to doubts about a person's conviction for an indictable offence. In fact, the Royal Commission had criticised the approach adopted by the Home Office under successive Home Secretaries whereby it restricted itself in practice to cases where fresh evidence had been brought to its attention. Because of this policy, it failed to investigate other cases where there was unease about the conviction and where there was a need for a more critical scrutiny of the prosecution case at the trial and a more positive search for additional evidence which could be relevant. The Royal Commission felt that the Home Office had been constrained by its position as a Government department, and that therefore a new body was needed which would be independent of Government.

The CCRC consists of at least 11 people, all of whom should have knowledge or experience of the criminal justice system, and at least a third of whom will be legally qualified. It has the power to investigate cases and to refer a case to the Court of Appeal for either a conviction or a sentence to be considered. The Act stipulates certain preconditions, namely that the CCRC must consider that there is a 'real possibility' that the referral will be successful; that the reason that it so considers is that there is evidence or argument which was not raised in the original proceedings or appeals; and lastly, that the usual route of appeal through the courts has been exhausted. There is, however, a further provision which enables the CCRC to make a referral in respect of a conviction (rather than a matter only of sentence), despite the last two restrictions, if there are 'exceptional circumstances'. The Court of Appeal is also specifically empowered to call upon the CCRC to investigate a case on its behalf, and to submit a report.

There are various criticisms of the new system. First, it is not truly independent of Government, in that the members are appointed by the Queen on the recommendation of the Prime Minister. Whether this will affect the attitudes of the members towards their duties is a matter for speculation, but at the least it enables the Prime Minister of the day to attempt to influence the CCRC's approach by appointing members who are likely to comply with Government policy. Secondly, its powers of investigation limit it to instructing the police to re-investigate their own original investigation, although it can require the investigating officer to be appointed from a different area. There is some possibility under the Act that the Commission can make its own arrangements for inquiries, but it remains to be seen how often and to what extent it will make use of this power. An additional limiting factor will be the resources available to it, especially in the light of the number of cases it will be called on to investigate. There are also no criteria in the Act which specify how it should select cases for investigation, and this is perhaps at the root of the third concern. Many recent miscarriages of justice have been overturned only after many years of dogged investigation. The Birmingham 6, for example, succeeded in having their convictions quashed only after several appeals to the Court of Appeal over a period of over 15 years (*R* v *McIlkenny* [1992] 2 All ER 417). There is not even any provision in the Act for legal aid for representations to the Commission, despite a recommendation to that effect by the Royal Commission. Any or all of these different factors could dramatically affect the value of the work done by the CCRC in uncovering miscarriages of justice. Lastly, the criteria for referrals to the Court of Appeal are actually more restrictive than those under which the Home Secretary used to operate (which merely allowed the Home Secretary to refer cases as he thought fit). The Court of Appeal must also treat a referral as it would any other appeal, and so the prospects of success are linked to the powers of the Court of Appeal and the way in which it chooses to exercise those powers.

This brings us to the second aspect of the 1995 Act which needs to be considered. The Act also revised the grounds for an appeal against conviction to the Court of Appeal, and as noted in the answer to (a) above, the grounds of appeal have thereby been simplified. Previously the Court of Appeal had to allow an appeal in three situations:

(a)   if the decision was 'unsafe or unsatisfactory';

(b)   if there had been a wrong decision on a point of law; or

(c)   if there had been a 'material irregularity' in the trial.

The 1995 Act replaced all three with one ground, so that now the Court of Appeal 'shall allow an appeal against conviction if they think that the conviction is unsafe; and shall dismiss such an appeal in any other case'. There is no other guidance as to the circumstances in which a conviction might be deemed 'unsafe', and the pre-1995 Act case law presumably still applies. In cases such as *R* v *Cooper* [1969] 1 QB 267, the Court of Appeal explained its approach by referring to the need for 'some lurking doubt in our minds' as to the validity of the conviction. It went on to state that the Court's decision may not be based on the evidence but 'can be produced by the general feel of the case as the court experiences it'. During the Bill's progress through Parliament, it was stated several times that the 'new' test merely restated the existing practice of the Court of Appeal. It seems clear, therefore, that this intuitive approach will still form the basis of most successful appeals, and that there are no grounds as such for believing that the Court of Appeal will be more or less likely to correct a miscarriage of justice than before. It may be, however, that the Court will be more sympathetic in practice to cases presented by the CCRC than by the Home Secretary under the former procedure, and that this spirit of cooperation is the best source of hope for the victim of a wrongful conviction.

QUESTION 5

Critically examine the role of lay persons in trying cases in the English legal process. (25 marks)

Commentary

This is a fairly standard essay-style question requiring a consideration of the full range of lay people involved in the legal process. Note the key words 'critically examine' however. You must not be tempted merely to write everything you know, but should try to adopt a theme which can be used to start and finish the essay; and also to weave critical comment into your answer throughout. This should be done at the expense of much detailed description, as the topic is potentially so wide that you could easily spend the whole of the exam writing on it! Remember instead that after you have written for a certain length of time, you will not gain any extra marks for carrying on regurgitating basic information. Careful planning is therefore essential, and the areas you should cover are:

- the meaning of 'lay people' and their basic role

- criminal cases — magistrates: cost, appointment, effectiveness

- criminal cases — juries: 'randomness', vetting, effectiveness

- magistrates' other functions — domestic, licensing, civil debts

- juries in civil cases and coroners' courts

- tribunals

- conclusions — community representatives, criticisms of particular classes.

Suggested Answer

A 'lay person' in this context is a person who has no formal legal qualifications, as opposed to a legally-qualified judge. There are several situations where such lay people are involved in trying cases in the English legal process. Criminal cases are dealt with by lay magistrates in the magistrates' court, or by a jury in the Crown Court. Lay magistrates also deal with some family disputes in the family proceedings court, and with licensing applications and certain civil debts. Industrial tribunals hear cases with two lay people sitting with a legally qualified chairperson, as do several other types of tribunal. Lastly, there is a right to a jury in certain civil trials, and certain coroners' courts involve a jury.

There is thus a strong tradition of lay involvement throughout the English legal process, but undoubtedly the most important areas are those criminal cases which are dealt with by lay magistrates or a jury. Lay magistrates deal with probably 95% of all criminal cases, and are therefore a vital part of the criminal justice system numerically. Trial by jury, on the other hand, although accounting for only a small number of cases, has been described by Lord Devlin as 'the lamp that shows that freedom lives'. It therefore has a strong symbolic function, and is seen as the fundamental right of defendants for all but the least serious criminal charges. This essay will therefore concentrate on these two types of lay involvement, before moving on to look more briefly at other instances.

A lay magistrate is one who is not paid but receives expenses only to cover loss of earnings, travel etc. Lay magistrates play a key role in the criminal justice system, as magistrates' courts deal with all criminal cases in one way or another. Out of nearly 30,000 magistrates, only a handful (about 75) are qualified, professional (or 'stipendiary') magistrates. The lay magistrate will usually sit as one of a bench of three magistrates to hear criminal cases, assisted by a legally qualified clerk. Magistrates deal with cases which can be tried summarily, hearing the evidence, deciding on guilt and passing sentence. Other cases involving more serious charges (or cases 'triable either way' where the defendant has elected for jury trial) must be transferred to the Crown court as a matter of course. In these cases, if requested by the defence, the magistrates must consider whether the prosecution case is strong enough to justify a Crown Court trial. If they decide that the prosecution case is strong enough, they will transfer the case to a suitable Crown Court, where the trial will take place some weeks afterwards. If not, they must dismiss the charge and discharge the defendant. If a defendant pleads guilty or is found guilty by the magistrates, their powers of punishment are limited to a fine of £5,000 and/or imprisonment for up to six months for one offence, or 12 months for two or more offences. If they feel that their powers are insufficient, they can commit the defendant to the Crown Court for sentence.

There are various advantages and disadvantages of using lay magistrates to such an extent in the criminal justice system. There are clear benefits in involving the local community in the legal process, especially as this enables the magistrates to utilise their knowledge of special problems in the locality of the court. It also helps to prevent the community feeling alienated from the process of justice. There is also an enormous cost benefit to using lay magistrates. As already explained, over 99% of magistrates are unpaid, apart from expenses, and they deal with over 95% of all criminal cases. The rota system, whereby magistrates sit only once every few weeks, also helps to prevent their becoming 'case-hardened', so that they consider each case on its merits without recourse to standardised sentences for stereotypical offenders such as drunks and young offenders.

The disadvantages are mainly concerned with the manner in which lay magistrates deal with the cases before them. There is at least a perception that they are prosecution biased and accept police evidence too readily. There is also much concern about inconsistency in sentencing practice, with the same offence in similar circumstances likely to receive a much harsher punisment depending upon whereabouts in the country the case is tried. The Magistrates Association has gone some way to addressing this problem by developing guidelines for sentencing purposes, but there is still a lot of discretion within those guidelines. Perhaps the main objection to lay magistrates, however, is the fact that they are not representative of the community, but only of small sections of it. The stereotypical magistrate is white and middle-class, either self-employed, retired or (if a married female) not seeking employment. Steps have been taken to broaden the base of the magistracy by bringing in people from all walks of life, but the traditional image of magistrates is proving difficult to overcome, and is probably discouraging many potential applicants from ethnic minorities, for example.

As already explained, a small proportion of criminal cases will be dealt with in the Crown Court by a judge and jury. The jury consists of 12 people whose role is to decide matters of fact, and ultimately the guilt or innocence of the accused, in much the same way as the magistrates. Like the magistrates, they are supposed to represent the community, but there are also misgivings as to the extent to which this is true in reality. First, it is not so certain that selection is a totally random process. The process starts by the local Crown Court office selecting a number of people from the electoral register, but the 'randomness' of this process is difficult to verify, as there is no set procedure. Furthermore, as jury service is an onerous duty, certain people may be excused by the Crown Court office for personal reasons, but again this could easily affect the true randomness of the selection if excuses are too readily accepted. Randomness of the eventual make-up of the jury can also be affected by events at the trial. At court on the day of the trial there will be a number of potential jurors from which the jury for a particular trial will be selected. Any individual juror may be challenged by the prosecution or defence advocate. The challenging party must satisfy the judge on the balance of probabilities that there is good reason for the challenge. The difficulty here is that the defence will have little idea in advance of the list of potential jurors, nor any realistic way of making quick investigations as to their background. The prosecution, on the other hand, can quickly access the police national computer, or possibly check in advance of the day of the hearing. The prosecution also have the right to vet the jurors in advance in cases involving terrorism or national security; and have the right to 'stand by' a juror. This right is governed by the Attorney-General's Guidelines

1989, but there is, nevertheless, a danger now that the make-up of the jury can be unfairly influenced by the prosecution without the defence being able to prevent it. There is also the continuing problem of producing a 'suitable' jury for certain trials. Where the defendant is black, for example, a random selection could result in an all-white jury, especially if the Crown Court has unwittingly tended to select only from certain areas of the city. There is no mechanism for avoiding this situation at present.

During the trial itself the jury are supposed to act as the finders of fact, with direction from the judge as to points of law, just as magistrates are guided by their clerk. The jury are much more susceptible to the influence of the judge, however. First, rules of evidence allow the judge to exclude certain facts from the jury's consideration if it is felt that they would be unduly prejudiced by them. Secondly, the judge's summing up of the evidence, which occurs right at the end of the trial, enables the judge to influence the jury's attitude towards the evidence of certain witnesses, sometimes subtly, but sometimes quite blatantly. There is therefore serious doubt as to the true independence of the jury as fact-finders. Lastly, there is the question whether a jury will have the intellectual capacity to follow certain complicated trials, particularly trials involving complex frauds in the context of the activities of a large company. Such trials can last for months and involve a vast volume of documents, many of a technical nature. In 1986 the Roskill Committee on Fraud Trials recommended that expert 'lay assessors' should be used in such cases instead of a jury, possibly with two such assessors sitting with and assisting the judge. This recommendation has been debated on and off ever since, and was raised as a possibility once again by the report of the Royal Commission on Criminal Justice in 1995. The opposing arguments, however, are that the use of a jury forces the prosecution to keep their case as simple as possible; and that the key issue of 'dishonesty' is uniquely suitable for ordinary people to decide upon, no matter the context in which the defendant's behaviour took place. There is also a deep-rooted suspicion of professionals taking over the criminal process, as their culture can easily slide from an impartial search for truth and justice into formalism, i.e., the trial process can become 'part of the job' and thus the rules of procedure can become the be-all and end-all.

Like magistrates, juries are seen as the representatives of the community, on whose behalf the prosecution is being brought. They have shown an ability to ignore the strict law in the past, in preference for a just verdict, as in the *Ponting* case (1985). This is an example of a 'perverse decision', and is sometimes used by critics of the jury system as an argument against the use of unqualified jurors. Other cases are sometimes cited where a jury have acquitted a defendant who was 'clearly guilty'. These arguments must be viewed with scepticism, as it may be that the prosecution simply did not put up a strong enough case. The jury cannot be blamed in such a situation, but it is of course possible that some perverse acquittals occur which cannot be overturned, whereas perverse convictions can be subject to an appeal. The issue, therefore, is whether the extent to which perverse decisions occur is such as to invalidate the whole system, and there does not seem to be convincing evidence one way or another.

Other situations where lay people are involved must now be considered briefly. Lay magistrates deal with criminal matters in both the adult court and the youth court, where people under 18 years of age are tried. They must be specially trained for this function, and their sentencing powers are different. They also have an important function in civil family matters. The family proceedings court also requires special training, and sees the magistrate dealing with financial provision between married couples who are separated (as opposed to getting divorced). Magistrates must also deal with a wide range of matters concerning children, under the Children Act 1989, such as residence and contact orders and maintenance. Lastly, under the Family Law Act 1996, they have powers to issue orders to protect people from violence at the hands of 'associated persons' such as their spouse or cohabitant, even to the extent of excluding one party from the matrimonial home in some circumstances. Apart from their criminal and family jurisdictions, the magistrates also have various administrative roles. They will deal with applications for gambling or alcohol licences, for example, and with disputes concerning non-payment of civil debts such as the council tax (the 'poll tax' or community charge, as was).

The growing use of tribunals is an important area for consideration, as there are several types dealing not only with employment matters such as unfair dismissal, but also with welfare benefits, fair rent, and a variety of other social welfare and financial matters of considerable importance to ordinary people. It is customary in these instances for the case to be dealt with by a qualified chairperson assisted by two lay people. The lay people will often be experienced in the relevant area, so that (for example) in industrial tribunals one will be a trade union representative, and the other will be from an employers' organisation.

Lastly, a jury is used in some proceedings other than criminal cases. There is a right to a jury trial in civil cases where the claim is based on defamation, false imprisonment, fraud or malicious prosecution. The judge has a discretion to refuse trial by jury in complex cases, however. Coroners hearings might also require a jury. Where it is suspected that the death has occurred as a result of murder, manslaughter or a road traffic accident, for example, a jury must be empanelled. Coroners may also inquire into the ownership of property which has been found but where the actual owner is not apparent.

To conclude, therefore, there is no doubt that the English legal system depends a lot on lay persons, but that there are several important questions which should be addressed as to the effectiveness of their involvement in particular cases. Where they bring certain knowledge and expertise there seems to be little controversy, as in the case of tribunals. Lay magistrates and juries are a different matter. In the case of lay magistrates, at least in criminal cases, the system is so well established that drastic changes are unlikely. The importance of their role suggests that problems should be addressed with more urgency, however, to ensure that public confidence in the system is not diminished. Similarly, there are strong arguments that trial by jury is a vital part of the criminal process, but that there are flaws in the present system which need to be removed before it can be said with confidence that the system is fair to all parties. In civil cases the role of the jury has already been watered down by the increasing tendency of the Court of Appeal to substitute its own assessment of damages in defamation cases for that of the jury. Generally, however, the use of lay people can be seen as a necessary restriction on the domination of justice by professionals, and of symbolic as well as of practical importance in retaining a link between the community and the legal process.

QUESTION 6

Tajjinder claims that Robert owes him money from a business transaction last year. Robert denies this, and so Tajjinder wants to start court proceedings.

(a) Explain which courts might deal with Tajjinder's claim, outlining the criteria which would be used to decide which would be the most appropriate and describing briefly the procedure for appeal should he lose his case. (10 marks)

(b) Describe and critically examine the provisions which would allow Tajjinder to have access to legal advice and representation for his case, if he could not otherwise afford it. (15 marks)

Commentary

This two-part question deals with some aspects of civil procedure in the context of a simple situation-based problem. Part (a) calls for a concise overview of a typical civil action for debt, while part (b) requires a more detailed examination of the civil legal aid system. This second part could sometimes crop up as part of a question asking for explanation and criticism of the general scope of provision for legal advice and assistance to people who cannot usually afford it, i.e., covering criminal legal aid as well as civil legal aid. See Question 3(a) for the extra material which you would be expected to include in your answer to such a question. The marks for such a question would typically amount to 25 in total, thus giving you about 40 minutes to complete your answer. If you combine the material for this question and Question 3(a), you should be able to work out how you could cut out duplicated material and thus in effect answer both questions together in much less time than it would take to answer both questions separately. The points you should cover in this question are as follows:

Question 6(a)

● Courts and Legal Services Act 1990

● county court jurisdiction, small claims court, default procedure

● High Court jurisdiction, transfers from county court

● appeals.

Question 6(b)

● Legal Aid Board procedures

● 'Green Form' scheme

● merits and means tests

● Statutory charge

● Government restrictions — rates of pay, eligibility thresholds, franchising

● criticisms — reduced eligibility, choice of representation.

Suggested Answer

(a) Tajjinder's claim appears to involve a contract. This is an important point, as under the Courts and Legal Services Act 1990 there are different rules for the allocation of civil claims, depending upon the nature of the action. The usual court in which to bring civil claims would be the county court. There are 300 or so of these courts around the country, and so there should be one in Tajjinder's town or a nearby town. Proceedings are started by taking the relevant documentation to the court's administrative office and paying the appropriate court fee. The administrative staff will then open a file on the case, give Tajjinder a reference number and send a copy of his claim to Robert. Robert then has the opportunity to file a defence or admission with a request for time to pay. If he fails to do so within 14 days, Tajjinder can obtain judgment against him by default, merely by attending the court office again and filling in the appropriate form. If Robert denies the claim and a full trial is needed, this will take place in due course before a judge in open court. If Tajjinder's claim is below £3,000, however, he may be able to use the 'small claims court'. This is, in fact, a special procedure rather than a different court. It allows the claim to be dealt with informally, with few procedural rules, and the final hearing would usually be held in private, in an office in the administration building before a district judge. In order to discourage the use of lawyers, no costs are usually awarded against the unsuccessful party, except expenses such as travelling costs or the loss of wages for time off work on the day of the hearing. If Tajjinder wins he would also be able to recoup the court fee from Robert. This procedure is only suitable for cases which involve simple issues of fact which can be presented by ordinary people with no legal training, although the district judge (typically a local solicitor appointed to this post) will help both parties to outline their cases. If it transpires that a point of law is involved, or if the case is otherwise too complex for the small claims court procedure, the district judge will transfer it to the full county court for hearing, and the usual rules of evidence and procedure will apply.

If Tajjinder's claim is for a large sum of money, he may have to start proceedings in the High Court, or have the case transferred there from the county court. All claims in contract involving more than £50,000 should normally be started in the High Court, and claims of between £25,000 and £50,000 will be transferred there if they appear to be particularly complex. The procedure for starting a claim in the High Court is similar to the county court procedure, and there are similar rules allowing a default judgment if the defendant does not respond to the claim. In the High Court, however, the onus is on the plaintiff to draw up and serve the details of the claim (the 'writ'), so Tajjinder would almost certainly need to instruct a solicitor to undertake this work for him. The nearest administrative office should be used, although there are fewer of these and so Tajjinder may have to travel to the nearest big town to start his action. The High Court comprises three divisions, and the appropriate one for claims in contract is the Queen's Bench Division. If the case results in a full trial, it will be heard by a High Court judge of the Queen's Bench, although as there are only 80 or so such judges, it is common for less important cases to be dealt with by a county court judge given temporary promotion!

If Tajjinder were to lose his case, he could consider an appeal. Regardless of whether the case had been dealt with in the county court or High Court, such an appeal would lie directly to the Court of Appeal (Civil Division). This court sits in London, and the case would be heard by at least two, and possibly three, Lords Justices of Appeal. The appeal could be based on issues of law or fact, but it is rare for the Court of Appeal to overturn a trial judge's findings of fact. Tajjinder would therefore have a realistic chance of a successful appeal only if there was a point of law at stake. In simple cases of debt this is unlikely to be the case.

(b) If Tajjinder cannot afford to pay for a lawyer to represent him, he will have to rely upon the legal aid scheme. Legal aid for civil matters is administered by the Legal Aid Board, under the Legal Aid Act 1988, and over £1,000 million is spent annually on the Green Form and civil legal aid scheme. The high cost of the scheme is at the root of most controversies and criticisms, as there is a continual conflict between the needs of justice and the desire of the Government to restrict public spending. In recent years the costs of the scheme have increased dramatically, with corresponding attempts to limit its coverage.

The first stage that Tajjinder would have to go through would be to see a solicitor and ask for the costs of the initial interview to be covered by the 'Green Form' scheme. This enables the solicitor to assess Tajjinder's means in accordance with a simple set of allowances for dependants. If his 'disposable income' (i.e., his net income after deductions and allowances) and his 'disposable capital' (again, his net capital after certain allowances) are below stipulated figures, the solicitor will be able to claim up to two hours' worth of work for advice and assistance. It is possible for the solicitor to obtain an extension, by applying for authorisation from the Board to exceed the limit by a specified additional amount, but the assistance given can never cover taking court proceedings. For that purpose Tajjinder must apply for full legal aid, and the Board will also insist that this be done after only a limited amount of work has been completed under the Green Form scheme. This will involve completing a lengthy form covering his financial situation in more detail (the 'means test'). In addition he will have to outline the basis of his claim against Robert, so that the Legal Aid Board can judge whether Tajjinder has a realistic prospect of winning his case (the 'merits test').

The means test will usually be conducted by an assessor scrutinising a detailed form completed by the applicant, supported by documentary evidence of income and outgoings. If necessary a full assessment can be undertaken. This used to be done by the Department of Social Security (the Benefits Agency, Legal Aid Assessment Office), but is now the responsibility of the Legal Aid Board pursuant to new regulations approved by Parliament in March 1997. The means assessment process will now be undertaken by staff at the Legal Aid Board's area offices. The test will involve an assessment of disposable income and capital, and although more circumstances can be taken into account than with the Green Form scheme, otherwise the system is similar. There are therefore set deductions from net income and capital for dependants, with a cut-off figure for both over which the applicant will be deemed ineligible, and provisions for paying a contribution if income or capital falls inbetween the figures giving unrestricted legal aid and rendering the applicant completely ineligible. Over 80% of those people in receipt of legal aid pay no contribution.

The merits test involves a two-stage assessment of the applicant's case. First, are there reasonable grounds for bringing the action (or defending it, where appropriate); secondly, is it reasonable in all the circumstances for legal aid to be granted? The first stage involves an assessment of the likelihood of the claim being successful. This can be a complex process and will oblige the applicant to provide full details of the evidence backing up the claim, including all the documentation appertaining to the legal basis of the claim and written statements by witnesses, if relevant. This assessment will be done by the Legal Aid Board, whose staff includes qualified lawyers, but as it often calls for opinion rather than a clearly objective evaluation of the evidence, it can give rise to controversy. The second stage also involves subjective opinion and value-judgements, as the test is usually interpreted as meaning whether a solicitor would advise a client in that situation to spend his or her own money on the case. The Board's assessors may take into account the applicant's motives in bringing the claim; the balance between the amount involved and the costs of court proceedings; and the availability of other help. Most small claims will therefore be excluded, as a solicitor would usually advise a client not to waste money on a case where the costs would exceed the amount at stake. This is especially so as the small claims court procedure (as explained in (a) above) is set up to allow individuals to bring their own claims without the need for legal assistance. Other issues may be at stake, however, such as reputation and integrity, and the assessor will have to determine whether these factors outweigh the financial implications of the case. As these additional issues are almost certain to be personal to the applicant, the assessor's own prejudices could have an important bearing on the decision.

If there is some doubt about the validity of the claim, the Board can issue a certificate limited to (for example) obtaining an expert's opinion. Only if that opinion supports the claim will the certificate then be extended to cover the full costs of the action. There is, however, provision for appeals against the decision of the Board, which entitle the applicant to an oral hearing before the Area Committee.

Of particular concern to Tajjinder must be the rules regarding the statutory charge. This provides that the Board must have first call on any money or property recovered or preserved by the applicant as a result of the action, in order to meet the costs claimed by the applicant's lawyer. Tajjinder must therefore hope to recover his lawyer's costs from Robert in addition to the money he is claiming. Normally there will be an order for costs in his favour, should he win his case. But these costs have to be recovered from Robert after the exact amount has been fixed by the court (a process called 'taxation'). Furthermore, the amount recoverable from Robert may be slightly less than Tajjinder's lawyer's total bill, and the short-fall will have to be met from the damages recovered. This provision can be particularly onerous on an applicant where the action concerns property or goods rather than money. If land is involved, the Board can place a charge on it which will have to be paid off when the property is sold. There are special provisions restricting the operation of this charging process where the property involved is the matrimonial home and the proceedings were family proceedings (for example, after a divorce and concerned with dividing up the marital assets).

The growing costs of the legal aid scheme have led to various attempts to limit the amounts spent on it by Government. First, the rates paid to solicitors have been pegged so that they have been reduced in real terms. This means that solicitors claiming payment under a legal aid certificate will not be able to claim the same amount as they would from clients who are paying their own bills. The short-fall has reached the point where many firms of solicitors will no longer take on legal aid cases. The Government's response has been to develop franchising as a method of keeping down costs even more. This allows certain firms of solicitors to specialise in legal aid cases, with reduced paperwork and regular monthly payments 'on account'. The idea is that, eventually, legal aid will be available only through such firms, although the restrictions on client choice that this would involve have met with much opposition from the Law Society. Advice agencies such as the Citizens Advice Bureaux are also now able to apply for a franchise. The concern here is that a two-tier system of justice is being created, whereby those in receipt of legal aid are much more limited in their choice of representation than those who can pay for themselves.

Secondly, the limits on eligibility for legal aid have also been raised so that progressively fewer people can now benefit from a certificate in any event. It has been estimated that eligibility fell from 75% of the adult population in 1979 to 50% in 1996.

In July 1996 the Government published a White Paper, *Striking the Balance: the future of legal aid in England and Wales*. It was preceded by a Minister from the Lord Chancellor's Department calling the legally-aided 'state-funded Rottweilers' in an interview. Its proposals included making everybody pay a standard, fixed amount towards the costs of their case, regardless of means. The Lord Chancellor appointed by the new Labour government has indicated that he, also, will strive to limit the amount spent on legal aid. The principle that the English civil justice system should be open to all, rich and poor alike, and on an equal basis, is clearly under severe pressure.

QUESTION 7

Critically examine the current system of law reform.

Commentary

All the boards cover law reform on paper 1. The question requires a knowledge of all the agencies involved in reforming the law and an understanding of the process of how the law is changed. The key points which should be dealt with include:

- outline groups involved in law reform — committees, Government departments, Parliament, Royal Commissions, pressure groups and the courts

- outline the work of these groups and give examples

- comment on the successes and failures of the present system.

Suggested Answer

That the law should need reform may seem obvious today, but it was not until the early twentieth century that the need to reform the law was recognised and that bodies were set up to carry out reform. There is now a wide range of groups or organisations who make a contribution to reforming the law, including various committees, Government departments, Parliament, Royal Commissions, pressure groups and the courts.

The first formal committee to deal with reform was the Law Revision Committee which was set up in 1934 and became the Law Reform Committee in 1952. This was a part-time body made up of lawyers and academics. It produced a number of reports and some of these led to legislation, such as the Occupiers' Liability Act 1957. The Criminal Law Revision Committee was established in 1959 and also consisted of both lawyers and academics. It has produced reports on a range of matters which have led to legislation, such as the Theft Act 1968. The Committee has not met since 1985 and the Law Commission has taken over much of its work. Both of these committees suffered from being part-time and having inadequate resources, and although their work has produced some legislation it has not had a great impact on reform.

In 1965 the Law Commission was established as a full-time body. There are five Law Commissioners and they have a staff of approximately 20 lawyers and other research assistants. The aims of the Commission are to simplify the law, codify the law and repeal obsolete statutes. The areas of law the Commission mainly deals with are criminal, family, property, common law and statute. The Commission carries out its work in a number of ways, one of which is to publish a *consultation paper* on a particular topic, which is then sent to lawyers, academics and other interested parties. This is followed by a *report*, which is sent to the Lord Chancellor. If the report is accepted by the Government then legislation may follow. Two reports on family law, *Family Law: The Ground for Divorce* (1990) and *Family Law: Domestic Violence and Occupation of the Family Home* (1992) were largely implemented in the Family Law Act 1996. The Commission also publishes programmes of reform, which deal with particular areas of law, for example, the *sixth programme* (1995) deals with a range of 11 matters from contract law to involuntary manslaughter. One of the reports produced under this programme, *Privity of Contract: Contracts for the Benefit of Third Parties* (July 1996) recommends that the parties to a contract should be able to give a third party the right to sue on that contract where it is made for the benefit of the third party. The number of reports which have become law has varied during the lifetime of the Commission. Between 1966 and 1973, 28 out of 30 reports became law, but during the next two decades less than half of the reports were implemented. In the 1990s the success rate has improved and many important measures have become law, including the Trusts of Land and Appointment of Trustees Act 1996 which creates the new 'trust of land'. The Commission has also been successful in repealing hundreds of obsolete public statutes by passing a series of measures, for example, the Statute Law (Repeals) Act 1995. Local Acts of Parliament have also been repealed in large numbers. Another success for the Commission has been its work on consolidating the law, so where there are numerous statutes on a particular subject, the Commission aims to bring them all together. Examples of this are the Employment Rights Act 1996 and the Industrial Tribunals Act 1996.

Amongst the tasks of the Commission is the codification of the law, and in this there have been some notable failures (for example, it abandoned its attempts to codify the law of contract). The problems faced by the Commission include gaining support from the Government to pass legislation or from individual MPs under the Private Members Bills procedure, and having the resources to deal with the wide areas of law it examines. Many important measures have not become law, for example, the *Report on Offences Against the Person* (1993), which would simplify and bring up to date the Offences Against the Person Act 1861. Despite the fact that action is sometimes taken quickly — for example, the *Report on Offences of Dishonesty: Money Transfers*, which led to the passing of the Theft (Amendment) Act 1996, completed within six months — delay still frustrates the work of the Commission.

Both Parliament and the Government are involved in reforming the law. Many Parliamentary committees examine topics and recommend change. Government departments monitor the law in their particular field and make proposals for legislation. The Timeshare Act 1992, which gives consumers a right of cancellation of a timeshare agreement, was passed after a report by the Office of Fair Trading. But these methods of reform are often slow and usually deal with less important matters. Departments often cooperate with the Law Commission, particularly the Home Office and the Department of Trade and Industry, and this may be a way of bringing more proposals into law.

From time to time Royal Commissions are appointed to investigate particular areas of the law with a view to reform. Sometimes these lead to legislation, for example, the Royal Commission on Criminal Justice (1993) which led to the passing of the Criminal Appeal Act 1995. However, sometimes nothing happens after such an investigation, a notable example being the Royal Commission on Civil Liability and Compensation for Personal Injury (1978). The Woolf Report (1996) on the civil law has made numerous recommendations, but it remains to be seen how many of these will be implemented.

Pressure groups can also contribute to law reform, either by bringing particular issues to public attention or by putting forward proposals for legislation. The Legal Action Group campaigns to improve legal advice services for poorer groups in society.

The courts should not be overlooked as a possible route to reform of the law. By using the doctrine of precedent judges may change the law to reflect modern times. However, this is rather haphazard as it depends on particular issues reaching court, and then it may depend on an individual judge whether the opportunity is taken to change the law. The House of Lords in *R* v *R* [1991] 4 All ER 481, changed the common law rule that a man could not rape his wife. But in *C* v *DPP* [1995] 2 All ER 43, the House of Lords refused to change the presumption of *doli incapax*, i.e., that children between 10 and 14 years of age are presumed to be incapable of committing an offence; they said that it was not up to the courts to make such a radical move, but that it was the job of Parliament. Similarly, in *Alcock* v *Chief Constable of South Yorkshire Police* [1991] 3 WLR 1057 the claims of relatives who suffered nervous shock arising from the Hillsborough disaster were rejected and Lord Oliver called for legislation to change the law on nervous shock.

It may be questioned whether there is a 'system' of law reform in operation, as the work of law reform is shared by many groups and can hardly be described as systematic. Reform can generally be achieved only by passing legislation, and this seems to be a drawback as governments have little time in their legislative programme for law reform measures unless they relate to matters which have caused public concern. Using the Private Members Bills route is just as bad. The Law Commission has an important role in research and proposing reforms, but it may be that a Ministry of Justice is needed to ensure that the work of all the reform groups is given a higher priority. The law needs to be clear, up-to-date and understood, and this will be achieved only if the system for review is effective.

QUESTION 8

Critically discuss the effect that entry into the European Community has had on the sovereignty of Parliament.

Commentary

European law is covered in Paper 1 of all boards. The question requires a discussion of the doctrine of parliamentary sovereignty as it applies in the domestic constitution, and the modification of such doctrine in the light of the UK's entry into the European Community. The key points should include:

- introduction — outline exposition of doctrine of supremacy

- the effect of the European Communities Act 1972

- the attitude of the European Court of Justice to the issue of supremacy of EC law

- the initial reluctance of the UK courts

- the eventual acknowledgment of the primacy of EC law; its implications in practice

- conclusions — the erosion of sovereignty is set to continue, but it is always open to Parliament to call a halt.

Suggested Answer

It is one of the fundamental tenets of the British Constitution that Parliament is *the* sovereign law-making body. Statutes passed by Parliament are the supreme source of law, prevailing over all and any inconsistent rules of common law and equity. Once a statute has been passed, it remains in force until repealed by a later one; and any attempt to entrench a statute (Parliament's devising laws drafted in a way which attempts to bind its successors) is ineffective. No other body, particularly the courts, may question the validity of an Act of Parliament (*Cheney* v *Conn* [1968] 1 WLR 242): what Parliament has given, only Parliament can take away.

The UK's entry into what was then the European Economic Community (now the European Community, or 'EC') put rather a different complexion on the traditional Diceyan dogma, namely that Parliamentary Sovereignty is absolute and unqualified. The European Communities Act 1972 was passed to give expression to the UK's obligations under the Treaty of Rome 1957 (now the European Community Treaty) and came into force on 1 January 1973. Section 2(1) provides that EC measures are to be given legal effect 'without further enactment'. Debate over whether this tell-tale phrase amounts to the entrenchment of EC law in our legal system continues unabated, but whatever its effect, there can be little doubt that it has (perhaps irrevocably) modified orthodox thinking. The relationship between domestic law and EC law is dealt with more specifically by s. 2(4) which states that any Act of Parliament, present or future, 'shall be construed and have effect subject to' the provisions of s. 2. While this provision does not openly talk of EC law reigning supreme over UK law, that is the way it has been interpreted by the English courts.

The attitude of the European Court of Justice is clear enough; its decisions are binding on the domestic courts in all 15 member states of the EC, including those of the UK (see European Communities Act 1972, s. 3). Ever since *Van Gend en Loos* (case 26/62) [1963] ECR 1, [1963] CMLR 105, the judges in Luxembourg have been hailing the emergence of a 'new legal order in international law', for whose benefit states have limited their sovereign rights, albeit in restricted fields. The reception of Community law into the domestic legal system rules out any measure — even one subsequent to the EC Treaty — which gives priority to domestic law (*Costa* v *ENEL* (case 6/64) [1964] ECR 585, [1964] CMLR 425). The validity and effect of EC law must never be judged in the light of domestic law, no matter how superior its source or status; any other approach would, it is said, endanger the uniform application of Community law and undermine the very fabric of the system itself (*Internationale HandelsgesellschaftGmbH* (case 11/70) [1970] ECR 1125, [1972] CMLR 255). Most significant of all for British judges, Community law automatically renders invalid any domestic provision which is incompatible with it. The courts of member states have not merely the power, but the bounden duty to prefer and enforce Community law (*Simmenthal* (1978)), even before Parliament has got around to bringing municipal law into line. In adopting this radical viewpoint, the European Court is bolstered by Article 5 of the EC Treaty, which obliges member states and their organs of government to take all effective steps to ensure compliance with EC law. This provision has heralded a dramatic extension, in recent years, of the primacy of Community Law. As far as possible, the courts of member states are supposed to construe their own law in such a way as to give effect to the wording and purpose of EC measures (*Von Colson* v *Land Nordrhein-Westfalen* (case 14/83) [1984] ECR 1891; *Marleasing SA* v *La Comercial Internacional de Alimentación SA* (case C106/89) [1990] ECR I–4135). To the extent that domestic law contravenes EC law, it is 'inherent in the scheme of the Treaty', apparently, that member states are obliged to compensate any of their individual citizens who suffer loss in consequence of the breach (*Francovich* v *Italian State* (case C6 & 9/90) [1992] IRLR 84; *Brasserie de Pêcheur* (case C46/93 [1995] 1 CMLR 889)). The message is an unequivocal one: EC law supersedes the laws passed by Parliament in the event of any inconsistency between the two.

Does this mean, then, that Parliament has relinquished its sovereignty, at least partially? 'Not necessarily', commentators like Nigel Foster have reasoned. After all, Parliament was a voluntary signatory to the Treaties, and the process may always be reversed. We see distinct echoes of such thinking in the utterances of the British judiciary. At first, the signs were encouraging. In *Bulmer* v *Bollinger* [1974] 2 All ER 1226 (CA), Lord Denning openly embraced the superiority of EC law, describing it famously as an 'incoming tide' which 'cannot be held back'; but such optimism was to quickly give way to scepticism, when in *Felixstowe Dock & Railway Company* v *British Transport Docks Board* [1976] 2 CMLR 655, the same judge asserted that once a Bill has been made law 'that will dispose of all this discussion about the Treaty. The courts will then have to abide by the statute without regard to the Treaty at all'. In the context of s. 2(4) of the European Communities Act 1972 (referred to above), the House of Lords at first insisted on treating the provision as a rule of construction, requiring the court to construe English law in accordance with EC law only if this was plausible. Applying such an approach in *Garland* v *British Rail Engineering* [1982] 2 All ER 402 (HL), the House of Lords held that material provisions of the Equal Pay Act 1970 had to be reconciled with Article 119 of the EC Treaty (which provision embodies the principle of equal pay for equal work, regardless of sex), building on the overtly pro-European stance of the Court of Appeal in *Macarthy's Limited* v *Smith* [1979] 3 All ER 32 (CA). The hopes of those who hailed this new found judicial pragmatism were, however, dashed in *Duke* v *GEC Reliance* [1988] AC 618, where Lord Templeman resolutely maintained that s. 2(4) did not constrain an English court to go as far as distorting the meaning of a British statute simply to enable individuals to enforce EC laws which were never intended to be directly effective (i.e., to confer rights which are directly enforceable by individuals before their own national courts). It may be argued, in the light of cases like *Marleasing* (above), that EC law does indeed expect English courts to go as far as 'fitting square pegs into round holes', if that is what it takes to implement EC law. In fairness, the House of Lords have since gone some way towards recognising this fact in cases like *Litster* v *Forth Dry Dock & Engineering Co. Ltd* [1990] 1 AC 546, where it was decided that domestic law had to be construed in line with EC law, even if this amounted to a wide departure from the apparent meaning of the statute; or even if this entailed reading into domestic law words which had originally been absent. Euro-scepticism, however, returned to the fray in *Webb* v *EMO Air Cargo (UK) Ltd* [1992] 1 CMLR 793 (CA), and it took a contrary ruling from the European Court of Justice under Article 177 of the Treaty (which article enables the European Court to rule on questions submitted to it by national courts) to make the House of Lords see the error of its ways.

It may be argued that in cases where the courts have had to resort to rewriting statutes to ensure consistency with EC law, the constructionist approach to s. 2(4) is at best a fiction and at worst a distraction from the main issue, namely the obligation to protect individual rights conferred by Community law. After all, where an Act of Parliament is unambiguously different in meaning from a comparable EC measure, it will be futile to try to reconcile the two. In such instances, EC theory would have us afford priority to EC law; but has the theory translated into practice? The case of *Factortame Ltd* v *Secretary of State for Transport* [1990] 2 AC 85, suggests an affirmative response to that question — proof positive, to paraphrase James Hanlon, that 'Britannia no longer rules the waves'. The initial reluctance of the House of Lords to grant an interim injunction restraining enforcement of a statute which endangered individual rights granted by EC law was overcome by a robust ruling from the European Court, which proclaimed that domestic courts have no choice but to grant relief where that is necessary to protect vested Community rights. The constitutional heresy of a court being able to disapply an Act of Parliament, or to restrain its enforcement by injunction, poses a formidable threat to the doctrine of sovereignty of Parliament. The fears of the traditionalists were realised when their Lordships, in *R* v *Secretary of State for Employment, ex parte Equal Opportunities Commission* [1995] 1 AC 1, taking their cue from the 'precedent' set by *Factortame*, granted a declaration that provisions of the Employment Protection (Consolidation) Act 1978 (denying the majority of part-time workers protection from redundancy and unfair dismissal) were incompatible with both Article 119 of the Treaty and the Equal Treatment Directive 76/207. Steiner sees this as evidence that the House of Lords is taking on some of the functions of a constitutional court, although (unlike many of its European counterparts) the House is not yet able to annul legislation — something which remains the exclusive province of Parliament and which keeps its sovereignty alive.

Our conclusion may be, therefore, that the notion of Parliamentary sovereignty has been scotched but not killed. In truth, the early pronouncements of the European Court have proven prophetic, as member states have effectively surrendered their capacity to take independent decisions in large areas of law and policy under the Treaty of Maastricht. The 1997 general election once again breathed new life into the controversy, as James Goldsmith and the Referendum Party issued dire warnings that the advent of a single European currency and a European Central Bank would lead to the further erosion of nation statehood, with devastating consequences for the national interest. Lord Slynn prefers to call it the pooling or sharing of sovereignty, but whatever view is taken, the debate ought not to blind us to the reality, say authors like Jo Shaw. In the eyes of the courts — charged with the duty of applying laws according to the classic conception of the doctrine of separation of powers — Parliament remains the supreme law-making body. Lest we forget, Lord Denning in *Macarthys* observed that, if ever the time should come that Parliament deliberately passes an Act with the avowed intention of repudiating Community law, 'I should have thought it would be the duty of our courts to follow the statute of our Parliament'. More recently, in *R* v *Secretary of State for Foreign*

and Commonwealth Affairs, ex parte Rees-Mogg [1994] QB 552 Lloyd LJ
insisted that Title V of the Treaty of Maastricht 1992 had *not* signalled an
abandonment or assignment of prerogative powers in the realms of foreign and
security policy; it was in fact an exercise of those powers, and in the final
analysis 'it would be open to the Government to denounce the Treaty' or at least
to fail to fulfil its obligations under EC law. With what is often hailed as a
European-wide backlash against the integrationist ideals of the 1980s, the risk
that Parliament might take back what it originally saw fit to give away is one
which should not be taken lightly.

QUESTION 9

Some European Community laws are said to be 'directly effective'. Critically
assess what is meant by this.

Commentary

This question requires a treatment of the doctrine of direct effect: the notion
that some EC laws create rights enforceable by individuals before their national
courts. The following points should be addressed:

- introduction — definition and rationale of direct effect

- the application of the doctrine to primary and secondary EC laws;
  vertical and horizontal effect

- the direct effect of directives — problems and pitfalls; the prohibition
  on horizontal enforcement

- the same result via other means — widening of definition of 'the state'
  and 'emanations of the state'; the doctrine of indirect effect; the principle
  of state liability

- conclusions — if anything individual rights are more secure under these
  alternative doctrines than they ever were.

Suggested Answer

One of the things which marks out European Community (EC) law from other
sytems of international law is the doctrine of direct effect. Some EC laws are
capable of creating individual rights which a national court must recognise and

protect. In *Van Gend en Loos* (case 26/62) [1963] ECR 1, [1963] CMLR 105, the European Court of Justice invented the doctrine of direct effect, carving out for itself a pivotal role in the evolution of EC law by acknowledging that it has ramifications not merely for member states, but also for their subjects. The doctrine is said to be an essential tool in maintaining the supremacy of EC law over any national laws which threaten it. By asserting their rights, individuals police the Treaties just as effectively as the other EC institutions. *Van Gend en Loos* set in train the process which was eventually to lead to the establishment of a 'judicial liability system' (Snyder) under which:

(a)   member-states may be pursued by their own citizens in their own courts to the extent that they fail to carry out the obligations imposed on them by Community law; and

(b)   EC citizens are to be endowed with a range of rights which they are expected to protect.

At the same time, the European Court laid down the criteria (adapted and refined in later decisions) which have to be met by any directly effective EC measure. It must:

(a)   be clear and unambiguous;

(b)   be precise and unconditional;

(c)   take effect without the need for any further action on the part of state authorities or EC institutions.

These conditions have been used as a basis for making numerous articles of the Treaty judicially enforceable, making the doctrine one of the principal methods of enhancing the *effet utile* (the positive and binding nature) of EC law.

The European Court has often had occasion to decide that not only Treaty articles may be enforceable, but that the secondary sources of EC law specified in Article 189 of the EC Treaty — regulations (*Politi* v *Italian Minister of Finance* (case 43/71) [1971] ECR 1039), directives (*Van Duyn* v *Home Office* (case 41/74) [1974] ECR 1337), and decisions (*Grad* v *Finanzamt Traunstein* (case 9/70) [1970] ECR 825) — are all capable of creating rights which individuals may rely upon before their own national courts and tribunals. In English domestic law, s. 2(1) of the European Communities Act 1972 enshrines the principle of direct effect, stating that rights conferred by the Treaties should be 'recognized and made available in law'. Many such instances of direct effect have concerned the enforceability of EC law against the state and its agencies — so called 'vertical direct effect'; yet in *Defrenne* v *Sabena (No. 2)* (case 43/75) [1976] ECR 455, the European Court held that Article 119 was directly effective not merely as against public authorities but also by one private individual against another. The application of the doctrine to the relations between private persons (including companies) has come to be known as 'horizontal' direct effect. That Treaty articles and regulations are both vertically and horizontally effective has become a truism in EC law.

The position is somewhat different with regard to directives. By its nature, a directive is binding on those to whom it is addressed, but it leaves it to the member state to decide the 'choice of form and methods'. This broad discretion as to how best to transpose a directive into national law has led commentators like Gerard Bebr to argue that directives can never be of direct effect. Such misconceptions were dispelled in *Van Duyn* (above), the European Court stressing that simply because Article 189 reserves the phrase 'direct application' to regulations, that does not prevent other types of measure — most notably directives — from having direct effect as well. One of the main justifications for according direct effect to directives was said in *Pubblico Ministero* v *Ratti* (case 148/78) [1979] ECR 1629 to be the 'estoppel' argument — that states should not be able to rely on their own failure to implement Community law by way of defence to any enforcement proceedings brought by individuals against them. Until the time limit for implementing the directive has expired, however, states are to be given the benefit of the doubt (*Ratti*; *Vaneetveld* v *Le Foyer* (case C316/93) [1994] ECR I-763). If a directive *is* incorporated into English law by an Act of Parliament, it is the Act, not the directive, which must be enforced. Even then, however, the directive itself may be relied upon by individuals to the extent that domestic legislation wholly or partly fails faithfully to reproduce the intended effect of the directive (*Verbond van Nederlandse Ondernemingen* v *Inspecteur der Invoerrechten en Accijnzen* (case 51/76) [1977] ECR 113).

The biggest check on the expansion of the doctrine of direct effect was the reluctance of many member states to concede that directives could be, and should be, of direct effect. This reluctance eventually permeated through to the European Court of Justice, which in 1985 held, in *Marshall* v *Southampton and South West Hampshire Area Health Authority* (case 152/84) [1986] ECR 723, that directives could be invoked only against public authorities, i.e., the state and its organs, not against private individuals. Advocate General Slynn had warned that any other outcome would cause the distinction between regulations and directives effectively to disappear. The Court agreed. Directives, therefore, may produce vertical, but not horizontal, effects — a result which has been attacked on the grounds that it is arbitrary (an individual employed by a public body can enforce a directive; a person employed by a private company cannot — see, e.g., *Duke v GEC Reliance* [1988] 1 All ER 626); and that it endangers the uniform application of EC law. Despite such persuasive criticisms, the European Court has persisted in its refusal to make directives horizontally enforceable (see *Facchini Dori v Recreb Srl* (case C91/92) [1994] ECR I-3325) and *El Corte Inglés v Rivero* (case C-192/94) [1996] ECR I-1281).

Having definitively closed the door on the prospect of directives ever being horizontally effective, the European Court has switched its attentions to achieving the same result by other means. The definition of state agency — so-called 'emanations of the state' — has been drawn as widely as possible. It now includes any organisation, whatever its form, made responsible for providing a public service and which has for this purpose been given special powers (see *Foster v British Gas* (case C 188/89) [1990] ECR I-3313). The net has been cast wide enough to catch local authorities (*Fratelli Costanzo Spa v Commune di Milano* (case 103/88) [1989] ECR 1839); nationalised industries (*Foster* itself); and even, it seems, privatised utilities (*Griffin v South West Water* [1995] IRLR 15). Purely private companies, though, are ruled out, even if the government has a stake in them (*Doughty v Rolls Royce* [1992] ICR 538).

Another way of achieving direct effect by the 'back door', to quote Steiner, is via a process of interpretation. If member states are told that they must interpret their domestic law in a way which gives effect to EC measures, individuals may indirectly rely upon those measures. This is precisely what happened in *Von Colson v Land Nordrhein-Westfalen* (case 14/83) [1984] ECR 1891 and *Marleasing SA v La Comercial Internacional de Aimentación SA* (case C 106/89) [1990] ECR I-4135, [1992] 1 CMLR 305. Lastly, if a state cannot be trusted accurately and fully to implement a directive, it should be liable, the Court has said, to compensate individuals who suffer loss as a result (*Francovich v Italian State* (cases C 6 & 9/90) [1992] IRLR 84). The breach of EC law must be sufficiently serious (*Brasserie de Pêcheur v Germany* (1996); *British Telecom* [1996] 2 WLR 506), but it seems that failure to implement a directly effective EC norm is itself a sufficiently serious breach in this regard (*Hedley Lomas* (C-5/94) [1996] ECR I-2553). This general principle of state liability is proving to be one of the most important and dynamic areas of growth in EC rights and remedies in recent years.

Thus even if direct effect is, in some ways, a 'dog which has had its day', the development of European law, and the preservation of the rights which individuals acquire from it, has been continued and, if anything, stepped up.

3 Sentencing and Criminal Procedure

INTRODUCTION

Each of the three major boards requires some knowledge of criminal procedure, as well as sentencing law and theory. Such questions may appear in the general paper (Oxford and NEAB boards, for example), or in the criminal law option paper (AEB includes them in the general paper as well as in the criminal law question in the 'Liability in English Law' paper). In the area of criminal procedure there is a range of possible areas which could be examined, and you should ensure that you have a good overview of the whole criminal process. The process starts with the commencement of criminal proceedings by charge or summons; continues through various preliminaries, such as applications for legal aid and bail and committal for trial; covers trial procedures; and concludes with the law and practice of appeals. You might encounter essay questions on one part of this process, or be asked to explain a whole section, perhaps in the form of a 'what happens next' style of question. The question might be a straightforward essay title ('describe and explain'), or provide a brief scenario and ask you to advise the defendant. In either case you will be expected to show a good understanding of the way in which a defendant is taken through the process, with an awareness of the way in which the different parts of the process link together. A sound, concise description of the relevant procedure will usually be sufficient, but if you can also provide some critical comment about the defects in the system, you will easily achieve excellent marks.

We have selected some of the most common topics which have cropped up in the last few years. In the area of sentencing law and theory, the range of questions is smaller, focussing on sentencing options and aims, and this is reflected in the content of the questions and answers we have devised. It is perhaps more important, therefore, that you should have critical ideas about the sentencing process, and show an awareness of research and statistics, and a knowledge of the key White Papers and associated legislation. As with criminal procedure in general, on some boards' papers a question on sentencing may occasionally be posed in the context of a 'problem' or situation-based scenario, and therefore one example of this style of question has been included as well.

Lastly, we have included one 'multi-part' question. This style is typical of the AEB board paper 2, but a two- or three-part question may also often be encountered in other boards' papers.

QUESTION 1

Explain the different aims which may be pursued in the sentencing of criminal offenders, and discuss their validity.

Commentary

This question may be expressed in many different ways, but it always calls for a statement of the aims of sentencing (as they are traditionally identified); a simple explanation of each; and some discussion of their respective advantages and disadvantages. The topic may occur as a full question, or as part of a question, in which case you should limit your discussion to two of the aims, after identifying them all. In any event, ensure that you give theoretical explanations; practical examples (e.g., by referring explicitly to specific sentencing options, typical judicial statements, current events etc.); and as many references as possible to statistics about the criminal process (which should be accurate, but can be expressed in approximate terms). It is also good practice (and makes for a neat conclusion) to comment on recent developments in legislation, or proposals for legislation. The key points which should be covered are:

- introduction — criminal process, maximum penalties, sentencing options

- prevention — imprisonment, time limit on effectiveness, does rehabilitation 'prevent' better?

- deterrence — general and specific, does it work?

- rehabilitation — community orders, can prison rehabilitate, society's need to 'punish'

- retribution — denunciation and education, is revenge permissible?

- 'just deserts' — *Crime, Justice and Protecting the Public*, Criminal Justice Act 1991

- developments — Criminal Justice Acts 1993 and 1994, *Protecting the Public*, Crimes (Sentencing) Act 1997.

Suggested Answer

The aims of sentencing are linked to the aim of the criminal law generally, which can be simply expressed as the prevention of crime. Sentencing comes at the very end of the criminal process, and will obviously therefore occur only when a defendant has been found guilty of a specific crime. That crime will carry a maximum sentence, usually fixed by statute and expressed as the maximum length of time that the defendant can be imprisoned and/or as the maximum amount of money that can be imposed by way of a fine. The judge or magistrate who is passing sentence will usually have a wide range of possible sentences available, from immediate imprisonment down to an absolute discharge. Each of these will also often need to be fixed in further detail. For example, the maximum period of imprisonment, or the maximum fine, will often not be appropriate, and a lesser time or amount will have to be determined instead. Even community penalties need fixing in detail, as probation can be for one to three years, and community service can be imposed for up to 240 hours. The main aim will be to prevent crime, but there are several ways in which the sentencer may hope to achieve this. The sentencer will therefore be pursuing one or more aims when passing sentence, but all with that primary purpose in view. The most basic aim of a sentence may be that of prevention in a physical sense. Thus, the simplest way to stop a defendant committing crimes in the future is to send him or her to prison. Judges or magistrates can often be heard to use words to the effect that 'sending you to prison will give the community a rest from your criminal activities'. There are various problems with this approach. First, the community will benefit only for as long as the defendant is in prison, so that the effectiveness of the sentence is limited unless a very long sentence of imprisonment is imposed. This is done in situations where a serious, violent crime has been committed (e.g., rape) and where the judge determines that the defendant should not be released until he is deemed to be no longer a danger. A sentence of life imprisonment can then be passed, allowing the prison authorities and Home Secretary to decide when it is safe to release. The most extreme example of this theory is the system adopted in some states in the USA, whereby a defendant must be sentenced to life imprisonment on his conviction for a third serious offence. This approach was taken by the Home Secretary in the 1996 White Paper *Protecting the Public*, and was included in the Crimes (Sentencing) Act 1997. Automatic life sentences will now be imposed on defendants who have been convicted of a second serious violent or sexual offence. Defendants convicted of a third offence of drug dealing will receive a minimum sentence of seven years' imprisonment, and third time burglars will receive a sentence of three years' imprisonment. This system could have serious repercussions, however. The prison population would soar, at considerable expense in both building new prisons and keeping that many prisoners locked up. It could also seem offensive, and contrary to other principles such as 'just deserts' (see below), to sentence a person to life imprisonment for offences which are irritating to the community but not dangerous (as in the USA). Even the English legislation will result in a big increase in the prison population (estimates range from 12,000 to 30,000), and could give rise to anomalies. The severity of the provisions in the Crime (Sentencing) Bill was considerably reduced during its passage through Parliament, so that judges will now have much more discretion whether to apply the law or not as far as drug dealers and burglars are concerned. These amendments were described by the Home Secretary as 'driving a coach and horses through the Bill', but had to be accepted by him because of the lack of time before Parliament was to be dissolved for the forthcoming general election. The new Labour government has implemented all of the provisions except those relating to repeat burglars, despite continuing academic and judicial criticism.

Furthermore, there is evidence that imprisonment is not completely effective in preventing crime. Not only does crime continue within the prison itself, but the demand for illegal drugs can stimulate supply outside and encourage other people to obtain drugs so that they can be smuggled inside. There is also now evidence that prisoners sharing syringes to inject drugs has increased HIV infection, which can then be transmitted unknowingly on release. Prison walls are not as impermeable as may be thought. It could be argued that rehabilitative sentences such as community service orders are just as effective in preventing crime during the currency of the sentence, but without the disadvantages of cost. The majority of offenders (over 80%) complete their sentence without further convictions, but the cost of supervision is much less than the cost of keeping a person in prison (£1,000 per annum instead of £500 per week). The option of imposing a curfew order (i.e., restricting an offender to a certain place during specified hours) was introduced in the Criminal Justice Act 1991, together with the possibility of enforcing such an order by electronic monitoring ('tagging'). This would seem to have the aim of preventing offending by keeping the defendant at home during the most likely times for criminal activity (e.g., at night, if the relevant crime is burglary). Unfortunately, the pilot projects for electronic monitoring proved unsuccessful, and it was only in 1996 that new pilots were set up. Even if successful this time, such orders do not, of course, prevent offending during times not covered by the curfew.

Perhaps the most common aim of sentencing, as expressed by sentencers, is that of deterrence. This may be 'individual' deterrence ('Let this be a warning to you not to do this kind of thing again') or 'general' deterrence ('Let this be a warning to other people like you . . .'). It relies upon the idea that people make — or at least could make — a clear, rational choice when committing a crime by weighing up the advantages of the activity against its disadvantages (i.e., being caught and convicted). The problem is that, as was acknowledged in the 1990 White Paper *Crime Justice and Protecting the Public*, most crime is committed on the spur of the moment, with little thought, and by people who lead inadequate and shiftless lives. It is, in any event, unrealistic to expect people to be seriously concerned about the prospects of punishment, as it has been estimated that only 2% of crimes result in a conviction. The sentencing process is therefore far removed from the reality of criminal activity.

Thirdly, the possibility of rehabilitating offenders is often considered. This involves the sentencer selecting a sentencing option that would assist or encourage the offender to 'change his ways' (as it is often put). Community orders are perhaps most clearly focussed on this prospect. Probation orders started in the late nineteenth century when some courts allowed well-meaning and respected local volunteers ('police court missionaries') to promise to attend to the moral education of an offender (typically a juvenile) rather than see that offender merely sent to prison. The Probation of Offenders Act 1907 put this system into a formal framework, and eventually the probation order and the Probation Service developed into important parts of the criminal justice system. Community service orders were introduced by the Criminal Justice Act 1972, enabling the courts to order a defendant to be released but to perform a specified number of hours working in the community (up to 240 hours in 12 months). It was hoped that such work would give offenders a feeling of self-worth and encourage a sense of responsibility, and thus tend to reduce the prospects of their offending again. The combination order allows the court to impose community service with an element of personal supervision by a probation officer, and is seen as the toughest of the community orders.

It has certainly been recognised (*Crime, Justice and Protecting the Public*) that imprisonment is highly unlikely to rehabilitate, and may often make matters worse by reducing still further the offender's prospects of living off paid employment and instead encouraging involvement in the criminal community. Rehabilitation as an aim in itself, however, can be dangerous, by concentrating on the offender rather than on the crime committed. The result can be a tendency to impose a sentence disproportionate to the crime, as with Borstal training. This was an indefinite sentence of up to 18 months, with release depending upon the perception of Borstal officers that the young offender was ready for release. On the other hand, rehabilitative sentences can seem too 'soft' to the victim and the community in general, and this may reduce what little deterrent value the criminal process holds. Recent developments have seen an increasing emphasis on making community sentences 'tougher'. The National Standards issued by the Home Office have directed the Probation Service to ensure that work in the community is demanding, and that an offender who does not comply with the terms of the order is returned to the court for resentencing. The Criminal Justice Act 1991 allowed the courts to combine orders (for example by adding a fine), and also introduced the combination order. This new sentencing option allowed the court to order a period of probation combined with an element of work in the community, up to a maximum of 100 hours rather than the maximum of 240 hours for a full community service order. The consultation paper *Strengthening Punishment in the Community*, issued in 1995, made further proposals to give the courts more control over the form and content of community orders, at the expense of the Probation Service's discretion, but this has met with much opposition from judges and magistrates as well as from the Probation Service and academic commentators. It is felt that rehabilitation is such a personal process, peculiar to each offender, that the courts cannot possibily assess what is suitable at all, let alone for the whole term of the order. Any attempt to do so, and increases in the punitive side of the order, will merely reduce its rehabilitative value to next to nothing.

Lastly, undoubtedly one of the most central elements of any punishment is that of retribution. The community in general, and the victim in particular, feel instinctively that punishment must follow the commission of a crime. This can be rationalised as the need to educate the community that certain activities are wrong, and to indicate the extent to which some are worse than others. The difficulty is that such an approach can seem identical to revenge, which presumably is not something to be encouraged. The Criminal Justice Act 1991, building upon the 1990 White Paper *Crime Justice and Protecting the Public*, followed the aim of 'just deserts'. This idea seeks to impose fair punishment for every offence by focussing on the crime committed rather than on the offender. It recognises the weaknesses inherent in ideas of deterrence and rehabilitation, but also accepts that imprisonment usually serves little constructive purpose and therefore should be relegated to a last resort. The Act emphasised the need for a punishment proportionate to the crime, and imposed the need for a formal assessment of 'seriousness' before a community order could be imposed rather than a fine; and before imprisonment could be imposed rather than a community order. In this way the use of imprisonment was discouraged, and the effect was a drop in the prison population to about 40,000. This approach is still at the basis of the sentencing system, but it is not clear whether it will stand the test of time. The growing tendency to 'toughen up' rehabilitative sentences is perhaps a response to a new punitive atmosphere in criminal justice, signalled by the then Home Secretary Michael Howard in his speech to the Conservative Party Conference in 1992, and reinforced by the Criminal Justice Act 1993 and the overall approach of the Criminal Justice and Public Order Act 1994. The 1993 Act cancelled some key elements of the 1991 Act only a few months after they had come into force, e.g., by scrapping unit fines as a compulsory system. The 1994 Act introduced several new crimes, such as criminal trespass, and restricted the right to silence, amongst several other changes to criminal evidence and procedure. Further statements by the Home Secretary, both in public speeches and in the *Protecting the Public* White Paper, returned to and developed the idea that imprisonment was useful as a deterrent and to prevent crime, and as a result the prison population has risen steadily so that it is now over 60,000 in total, an increase of approximately 50% in six years.

It is clear, therefore, that no one of the traditional aims of sentencing can operate in isolation, and that individual sentencing options tend to have elements of two or three such aims. The theory of 'just deserts' seems fairly neutral, in that it merely tries to structure sentencing in a logical way, rather than leaving the process solely to judicial discretion. This at least has the advantage of discouraging drastic swings in sentencing practice as one of the traditional aims becomes temporarily more fashionable than another. The present developments in the criminal justice system show, however, how volatile the process is, and how easily its emphasis can be changed.

QUESTION 2

(a) Explain the different ways in which a judge's or magistrate's powers might be limited when passing sentence on a person convicted of a criminal offence. (13 marks)

(b) Describe the various community orders which a criminal court can impose on adult offenders. (12 marks)

Commentary

Either of these questions could crop up in the general paper for the Oxford and NEAB boards, and part (b) would be an appropriate question for AEB's paper 2 (Criminal Law option). They both require little more than a straightforward description of different aspects of the sentencing process, but it is as well to remember that additional critical comment will enable the examiner to award much higher marks. You should therefore try to show some awareness of any controversies about the topics, and of relevant research or statistical information. The important White Papers (*Crime, Justice and Protecting the Public* (1990) and *Protecting the Public* (1996)) should be referred to whenever possible, as they set out the aims of the legislation and perhaps explain the way in which the courts have reacted to it. Generally, if you show an awareness of trends in sentencing policy this will not only look impressive to the examiner, but it will also give you a structure for the essay. The following points should be covered:

Question 2(a)

- maximum penalties — general and magistrates' court

- guilty plea discount

- pre-sentence reports

- unit fines and previous convictions

- mandatory sentencing.

Question 2(b)

- the sentencing framework for community orders

- probation

- community service

- combination orders

- curfews and electronic monitoring.

Suggested Answer

(a)   The sentencer is constrained by various limits. In the magistrates' court there is a maximum fine of £5,000 and maximum term of imprisonment of 12 months, with only six months' imprisonment being possible for one offence. Otherwise there is a maximum penalty fixed by law for every crime, but no minimum except in special cases (for example, life imprisonment for murder under the Murder (Abolition of Death Penalty) Act 1965, or 12 months' disqualification for driving with excess alcohol under the Road Traffic Act 1972). It is unusual for these maximum penalties to be reached, however, and in practice the sentencer has a wide discretion as to the actual sentence which may be imposed. There are therefore various other statutory provisions which seek to structure that discretion.

The basic framework is set out in the Criminal Justice Act 1991. A defendant can be sent to prison only if either the offence was so serious that only a custodial sentence can be justified; or if only such a sentence would be adequate to protect the public from serious harm. A similar principle applies to the passing of a 'community sentence' (see below) instead of a fine, conditional or absolute discharge. This framework therefore imposes a clear relationship between the seriousness of the offence and the sentence, with an implied hierarchy ranging from imprisonment as the most serious sentence, community sentences as the next most serious, and fines and discharges as the basic forms of punishment. Under the 1991 Act the sentencer can pass a disproportionately long sentence if the offence was a violent or sexual offence and it is thought necessary to protect the public from serious harm. The statutory maximum for that offence still applies, however.

Within this framework there has been a shift in recent years, away from restrictions aimed at reducing the use of imprisonment, towards mandatory sentences of imprisonment. Perhaps the only 'neutral' requirement is that introduced in the Criminal Justice and Public Order Act 1994, s. 48. Under this provision the sentencer 'shall' take into account the stage in the proceedings at which the defendant indicated an intention to plead guilty. This puts into statutory form the customary practice of the courts whereby, if a defendant pleaded guilty, a 'discount' of up to one-third of the usual prison term would be given. The aim is to encourage guilty pleas, thus saving the costs of a full trial. The provision is so worded that a greater discount will be given the earlier the guilty plea is entered or indicated, as clearly more costs are saved in that way.

The Criminal Justice Act 1993 saw a change of approach in sentencing policy. This Act abolished restrictions introduced in 1991 whereby the sentencer could not take into account the previous convictions of a defendant except in limited circumstances, and also scrapped the requirement for a pre-sentence report where imprisonment was being considered. These reports are prepared by the Probation Service and give details about the background, home life and employment record of the defendant, as well as making suggestions and recommendations as to what sentence should be passed. The 1993 Act also made the unit fine system optional instead of mandatory. This method of setting the level of a fine is based upon the defendant's disposable income multiplied by a number of 'units' according to the seriousness of the offence. It should result in a close relationship between the amount of the fine and the ability of the defendant to pay, so that the same amount of punishment will be imposed regardless of the wealth of the offender. The court may use it, or depart from it if it feels that it is not producing a fair result.

The 1993 Act can be seen as the turning point in sentencing policy. The 1991 Act had implemented the ideas contained in the earlier White Paper *Crime, Justice and Protecting the Public* (1990) by trying to reduce the use of imprisonment by the courts. The Crime (Sentencing) Act 1997 has gone to the other extreme by imposing mandatory sentences of imprisonment in three situations:

(a)   On being convicted of a second serious violent or sexual offence (a list of such offences is included in the Act), a defendant must be sent to prison for life. The defendant will be released only when assessed as no longer dangerous to society. There is little or no guidance in the Act as to how this assessment will be made, and research shows that attempts at assessing dangerousness are notoriously inaccurate.

(b)   Offenders who are convicted of a third offence of drug dealing will receive a mandatory sentence of seven years' imprisonment.

(c)   Burglars of a dwelling-house will receive a mandatory sentence of three years' imprisonment on their third conviction.

The severity of the provisions for drug dealers and burglars in the original Bill was considerably reduced during its passage through Parliament, so that judges will now have much more discretion whether to apply the law or not. These amendments were described by the Home Secretary as 'driving a coach and horses through the Bill', but had to be accepted by him because of the lack of time before Parliament was to be dissolved for the forthcoming general election. The proposals in the White Paper (*Protecting the Public* (1996)) which preceded the Bill, stipulated that a judge could depart from the provisions only in genuinely exceptional circumstances (indeed, no one could think of a situation which would allow a departure, nor would the Home Office give an example). The judges were horrified at the limits thereby imposed on their discretion, seeing it as a constitutional issue as well as a potential cause of injustice. The new Labour government has already brought into force the provisions relating to violent offenders and drug dealers and shows no sign of heeding the judges' complaints.

The effect of these different statutory provisions is that the judges still have a wide discretion as to sentencing, as even the framework under the 1991 Act allows them to decide the sentence on vague concepts of 'seriousness'. At present only the maximum sentences fixed for each offence, and the limits on the magistrates, are truly restrictive, and in practice those are set so high as rarely to pose difficulties to the sentencer. The mood seems to be moving towards mandatory sentences, however, and future amendments to the 1997 Act might make those provisions much more restrictive.

(b) Within the constraints set out above (such as they are), the sentencer has various specific sentencing options, with a variety of community sentences available for consideration. In particular, Parliament has added different sentencing options over the last few years so that there is a middle course between punishments such as fines and discharges, and imprisonment. The Criminal Justice Act 1991 makes it clear that community sentences must be considered as more serious than fines by stipulating that the court may impose such a sentence only if the seriousness of the offence justifies it, or it is necessary to protect the public. On the other hand, the same restrictions apply to the imposition of a custodial sentence rather than a community sentence, so that a clear sentencing structure is apparent. The community orders are therefore an attempt to keep suitable offenders out of prison, which is seen as likely to corrupt rather than rehabilitate. Such community sentences are also much cheaper to run, costing as little as £1,000 per annum to supervise an offender, compared to £500 per week per prisoner. The difficulty is that these orders may be seen as 'soft' by the public, and therefore there has been a growing tension between the rehabilitative ideals of the Probation Service (which supervises offenders in the community) and a more punitive policy on the part of the Government.

The different options may be considered in approximate order of severity. Apart from fines, there are various other sentences which are not custodial; but although the offender will therefore remain in the community during the currency of the sentence, they are not really considered as community sentences as such, and are not covered by the restrictions on sentencing in the 1991 Act. An absolute discharge means that a conviction is recorded but no action taken against the defendant at all. Similarly, with a conditional discharge no action is taken, but this time on condition that the defendant stays out of trouble for a specified period (two or three years). Lastly, with a deferred sentence, sentence is adjourned for up to six months, to enable the defendant to show an intention to reform (e.g., by 'getting and keeping a job'). Objectives can be specified, and the implication is that, if achieved, a non-custodial sentence will be passed when the case comes back.

The following sentencing options are specifically described as community orders under the 1991 Act, and thus fall under the restrictions which prevent their use unless justified by the seriousness of the offence or the need to protect the public. Under a probation order the defendant agrees to be supervised by the Probation Service for a specified period of two or three years. This type of order dates its origin from informal arrangements in the late nineteenth century when some courts allowed well-meaning and respected local volunteers ('police court missionaries') to promise to attend to the moral education of an offender (typically a juvenile) rather than see that offender merely sent to prison. The Probation of Offenders Act 1907 put this system into a formal framework, and eventually the probation order and the Probation Service developed into important parts of the criminal justice system. Nowadays the order involves the defendant in regular reporting, residence at a fixed address and generally responding to advice and guidance by a specified probation officer. Under the 1991 Act, certain requirements can be attached by the sentencer, such as attendance at a centre; to take part in/refrain from specified activities; undergo medical treatment or attend courses to deal with drug or alcohol dependency.

The community service order was introduced in 1972. The defendant agrees to do a specified number of hours work in the community (up to 240 hours) within the next 12 months, the work being allocated and supervised by the Probation Service. It is hoped that such work will give offenders a feeling of self-worth and encourage a sense of responsibility, and thus tend to reduce the prospects of their offending again. National guidelines prescribed by the Government over the last few years have 'toughened up' this sentence to make it more obviously punitive, e.g., by requiring certain types of activity to be undertaken, stipulating that the activity must be physically or mentally demanding, and by limiting the Probation Service's discretion as to when the order has been breached. This last point is important, as breach of either a probation order or a community service order can lead to the offender being resentenced by the court for the original offence (as well as for a 'new' offence, if that was the substance of the breach). As the court will then take into account the fact that the offender has not responded to the opportunity offered by a community order, it is quite likely that a custodial sentence will be the result. There is some concern, therefore, that a more punitive approach to this type of community order could result in people being sent to prison for relatively minor offences.

Combined orders can also now be made under the 1991 Act. Not only can a fine be imposed as well as a probation order or community service order (previously such combinations were not allowed), but the Act specifically allows a combination order combining probation (plus any of the additional requirements possible) with community service of up to 100 hours. This is seen as the most demanding of the community orders.

Lastly, a curfew order is also possible, and is intended to be combined with electronic monitoring. The basic order requires the defendant, with his or her consent, to stay at a specified place (e.g., at home) during specified periods (e.g., between 9.00 pm and 8.00 am, up to a maximum of 12 hours per day). It can last for up to six months. The defendant will be supervised, and the possibility of 'electronic tagging' was introduced again by the 1994 Act. This requires the defendant to wear an electronic device which cannot be removed without setting off an alarm at a central point. This device enables the whereabouts of the offender to be checked at regular intervals, so that a breach of the conditions of the curfew order should be easily detected. Otherwise, curfew orders are practically impossible to enforce because of the manpower involved in keeping a check on those subject to them. Pilot projects on electronic monitoring in 1989 proved unsuccessful at a cost of over half a million pounds. New pilot projects are now underway, with perhaps more success as the technology has improved. There is still a reluctance on the part of magistrates to use tagging, however, and it seems unlikely that it will make much of an impact on the criminal process.

QUESTION 3

John has been arrested and charged with murder, and has been committed for trial at the Crown Court.

(a) John is worried about what is meant by 'trial by jury'. Identify for him the key points in the procedure for selecting a jury and how they will reach their decision, and explain the significance of these to John's case. (15 marks)

(b) At his trial John will wish to justify the killing on the grounds of self-defence. Explain to him the principles of burden and standard of proof and how they will be applied at his trial. (10 marks)

Commentary

As with Question 4 below, this style of question could occur in the AEB board paper 2, which covers the 'Liability in English Law' part of the syllabus. It would form part of a series of questions relating to a situation-based problem concerned with different aspects of criminal liability, with the rest of the questions on the substantive criminal law. Taken together with Question 1 in Chapter 4 and Question 3 in Chapter 2, the student for the AEB exam therefore has a wide range of questions which could form part of the question on criminal liability in paper 2. For the other boards, these questions would be found in the general paper, as the questions on their special criminal law papers tend to be restricted purely to criminal law.

The content of your answers can be basically descriptive, but again it is always useful to include critical comment as this is a good way to show your understanding of the topic and thus to encourage the examiner to award higher marks. You should make an effort to refer to John's situation whenever possible, and you should certainly use his situation to illustrate your answer to **(b)**. You should cover the following points:

Question 3(a)

- eligibility of jurors — those excluded and disqualified

- summoning jurors, and exempted persons

- empanelling

- challenges and 'standing by'

- discharge during the trial

- conduct while considering their verdict

- majority verdicts.

Question 3(b)

- evidence in a criminal trial

- legal burden of proof

- evidential burden for defences

- standard of proof in criminal cases

- how John's defence will be dealt with.

Suggested Answer

(a)   A jury for a Crown Court trial consists of 12 people, selected at random from the local community. Their role is to decide matters of fact, and to decide whether the defendant is guilty or innocent of the charges which are the subject of the trial. Everyone between the ages of 18 and 70 who is on the electoral register for the area is eligible for jury service, unless excluded or disqualified by specific provisions of the Juries Act 1974. These provisions exclude anyone concerned with the administration of justice, such as judges, magistrates, members of the legal profession, court staff, police, probation and prison officers. Even people who have been within one of those groups within the last 10 years are excluded. Those people who are disqualified consist of various categories of ex-offenders who have received serious sentences of imprisonment, or a lesser sentence (including a community service order) within the last 10 years, or a probation order within the last five years.

The local Crown Court office will select a number of people at random from the electoral register, without knowing whether they are eligible or not. The 'randomness' of this process is, however, difficult to verify, as there is no set procedure. Everyone selected will be sent a summons through the post requiring their attendance at court on a specified day and at a given time. The period of attendance could be for up to two weeks, but some complex cases may take several months. As jury service is an onerous duty, certain people can claim exemption as of right. These include those who have served within the last two years, or who have been excused further service for life because of involvement in a lengthy trial before. Other categories are those who are over 65, MPs, doctors, and people whose religious beliefs are incompatible with jury service. Others may be excused by the Crown Court office (e.g., students who are about to sit exams), but this obviously again could affect the true randomness of the selection, and so great care must be taken to allow only unusual situations to excuse service. Job-related difficulties, for example, are never a suitable excuse, as otherwise everyone in employment could be excused and the selection process would thereby be far from random.

On the day of the trial, 20 or more of the people summoned will be nominated as the 'jury in waiting'. They will be brought into the courtroom and the clerk of the court will chose 12 of them at random, typically by shuffling and selecting from cards with their names on. As each person's name is called, that person will step into the jury box and take the juror's oath, unless objected to by the prosecution or defence barrister. Once 12 people have been sworn in, the jury are formally empanelled and may hear the case for which they have been selected.

As mentioned, while the jurors are being sworn in, either the defence or prosecution may object to a particular person being on the jury. Since the Criminal Justice Act 1988, the prosecution or defence can only 'challenge for cause'. This means that there must be a specified reason, such as ineligibility, or a real danger that that specific person may be biased. If potential bias is alleged, there must be evidence that (for example) the person is related to (or perhaps employed by or employing) the defendant, the victim or a prosecution witness. The challenging party must satisfy the judge on the balance of probabilities that there is good reason for the challenge. The difficulty here is that the defence will have little idea in advance of the list of potential jurors, nor any realistic way of making quick investigations as to their background. The prosecution, on the other hand, can quickly access the police national computer, or possibly check in advance of the day of the hearing. No questioning of the jurors is allowed, except in exceptional circumstances in which there may be a special reason why certain people would be biased (for example, by having seen a biased account of the background of a party to the trial in a certain television programme). The prosecution, however, also have the right to vet the jurors in advance in cases involving terrorism or national security; and also the right to 'stand by' a juror. This right is governed by the Attorney-General's Guidelines 1989, and must be exercised with caution, especially in view of the abolition of the defence right to 'peremptory challenge' in 1988 (i.e., the right to challenge up to three jurors without giving a reason). There is, nevertheless, a danger now that the make-up of the jury may be unfairly influenced by the prosecution without the defence being able to prevent it. There is also the continuing problem of producing a 'suitable' jury for certain trials. Where the defendant is black, for example, a random selection could result in an all-white jury, especially if the Crown Court has unwittingly tended to select only from certain areas of the city. There is no mechanism for avoiding this situation at present.

When the jury have been empanelled and the case has started, the same people will have to hear the whole trial. Situations may arise, particularly during a long trial, where individual jurors have to be excused ('discharged'). This may be because of illness or family bereavement, for example, or even because the juror has been guilty of misconduct, such as talking to a witness. The judge can discharge up to three jurors before the point is reached where the trial has to be halted and re-started before a fresh jury. In a long trial, however, the judge may feel that the whole jury should be discharged if even two jurors have been lost at a relatively early stage of proceedings. The judge must discharge the whole jury if there is a danger of prejudice. This is most likley to occur when inadmissible evidence has been revealed to them, or in unusual circumstances, as in *R* v *Boyes* [1991] Crim LR 717 where the mother of a victim of an alleged rape shouted from the public gallery 'What about the other five girls he has attacked?' (or words to that effect).

When all the evidence has been given, and the prosecution and defence barristers have addressed them and the judge summed up the evidence for them, the jury retire to consider their verdict. This must be done in private, and without any outside interference or guidance. They may, however, ask the judge for guidance on particular points. This is done by sending a note through the jury bailiff, which is read out in open court and discussed with the prosecution and defence barristers. The jury will then be called into court and a direction given by the judge in open court. No further evidence can be called, however. During their deliberations, the jury are in the charge of the jury bailiff. This official should be ready outside the jury room, and must always accompany them if (for example) they have to leave the room for meals. If the jury cannot arrive at a unanimous verdict, under the Jury Act 1974 after a minimum of two hours the judge can allow a majority verdict. This can be 10 out of 11 or 12; or 9 out of 10 jurors. If the jury are unable to agree at all, the judge will eventually have to discharge them and order a new trial before a fresh jury. In that situation the prosecution must seriously consider whether it is right for the defendant to face another trial, but it happens regularly.

(b)   The trial of the charges against John will consist in the main of evidence given by witnesses, both for the prosecution and for the defence. This evidence will form the basis of the jury's decision to convict or acquit, in that the jury will have to decide certain facts by means of that evidence (for example, 'Was witness X correct in claiming that John was at the scene of the crime? If so, how far does that prove that John committed the crime?'). This assumes, however, that the evidence will always give the jury a simple 'either/or' decision to make, and that each decision will be clear-cut and easy. Unfortunately, in life decisions are rarely that straightforward, and indeed, if the matter were that clear-cut, there would probably be no need for a trial at all.

The rules on the standard and burden of proof are therefore designed to give the jury guidance as to how to deal with difficult decisions.

The expression 'burden of proof' is used to describe which party to the proceedings has to produce the evidence to prove the relevant facts. It applies to criminal cases in two ways, known as the legal and the evidential burdens of proof. First, the legal burden of proof is placed squarely on the shoulders of the prosecution in the sense that they have to overturn the presumption that the defendant is innocent, and thereby establish the specific allegations made against the defendant. The exceptions to this principle are rare. One example is the defence of insanity, which proceeds on the basis (under the so-called *M'Naghten* Rules dating from 1843) that every person is presumed sane. Apart from such exceptions, the legal burden never shifts to the defendant. This was clearly established by the House of Lords in *Woolmington* v *DPP* [1935] AC 462, where the defendant explained that he shot his estranged wife by accident, after producing a gun merely to frighten her. The House of Lords stated that the trial judge was wrong to say that the defendant had to 'prove' his explanation after the prosecution had established that he had fired the fatal shot. The principle of the presumption of innocence meant that the prosecution had to disprove his explanation. Similarly in John's case, as well as proving that he actually killed the victim in the first place, the prosecution will have to go on to disprove John's explanation that he killed in self-defence.

Secondly, the evidential burden of proof applies to both prosecution and the defendant, in the sense that both must supply enough evidence about specific facts to make them worthy of rebuttal by the other party. The evidential burden will move from party to party. At the end of the prosecution case the defence can ask for the case to be dismissed if the prosecution have not established a prima facie case (i.e., have not produced enough evidence by that stage to warrant the defendant even answering the allegations made). If the prosecution have made out a prima facie case, the defence must now at least raise enough evidence about facts which would establish the defendant's innocence to shift the burden back to the prosecution again. This evidential burden can be quite simple to discharge. It may, for example, merely entail the defendant giving evidence that there is an innocent explanation for certain facts. The prosecution would then have to try to disprove that explanation by (for example) cross-examining the defendant and showing that the explanation is unbelievable. John will therefore have to raise the issue of self-defence at some stage, either by cross-examining (through his barrister) a prosecution witness to that effect, or by giving evidence himself. Only then will the prosecution have the legal burden to disprove that possibility.

Even if the defendant cannot raise explanatory matters, the defence can still claim that the prosecution have not discharged their legal burden of proof to the requisite standard. This standard of proof is expressed as a requirement to prove the case against the defendant 'beyond reasonable doubt'. This is the standard of proof in criminal cases, except where the legal burden is placed on the defence (e.g., in cases of insanity) where the standard is the same as in civil cases, namely 'on the balance of probabilities'. The difference can be illustrated by explaining that, in a civil case, a fact can be proved by saying that it 'probably' happened as alleged; but that would not be enough to convict in a criminal case.

The combined effect of these rules as to the burden and standard of proof means that the benefit of any doubt must be given to the defendant. In John's case, if the prosecution produce enough evidence to show that he killed the victim, he will have to raise the issue of self-defence, perhaps by giving evidence himself, or by cross-examining a prosecution witness to that effect. The prosecution would then have to disprove his defence 'beyond reasonable doubt'.

QUESTION 4

Dwight has been charged with rape.

(a) Explain to Dwight the various stages in the criminal process which will now take place, up to and including his eventual trial. (15 marks)

(b) If Dwight were to be convicted and wished to appeal against his conviction, what courts or similar bodies might be involved, and how would the appeal progress? (10 marks)

Commentary

See the 'Commentary' to Question 3 above for an explanation of where you might expect to come across this style of question. Part (a) is fairly straightforward, but it requires a good knowledge of the criminal process, as it covers everything from bail and committal proceedings, to the new disclosure provisions and the trial itself. In some papers, if a question similar to (a) were included, it might carry only 10 marks, and you would therefore not be expected to include quite so much detail as in our 'Suggested Answer'. Once again, as with Question 3 above, the content of your answers can be basically descriptive, but again it is always useful and effective to include critical comment. You should make an effort to refer to Dwight's situation whenever possible, perhaps by using his case to illustrate your answer. You should cover the following points:

Question 4(a)

- Crown Prosecution Service

- preliminary hearing in magistrates' court — bail and time limits

- committal papers

- committal hearing

- preparation for trial

- primary and secondary disclosure of evidence and defence statement

- the trial — the jury, plea, opening, prosecution case, defence case, addressing the jury, judge's summing up, jury decision, sentence.

Question 4(b)

- grounds of appeal — statute and case law in outline

- Court of Appeal procedure (leave, renewal, loss of time, judges' titles)

- House of Lords procedure

- other possibilities (European Court of Justice, Review Commission).

Suggested Answer

(a) As soon as the police have charged Dwight, they will prepare a file containing all the details of the case, which will be sent to the Crown Prosecution Service. As the charge is so serious, Dwight is certain to be kept in custody, and therefore the first step will be a hearing before the local magistrates' court, where the issue of bail will be dealt with. The Bail Act 1976 says that bail 'shall' be granted unless the court find that there are substantial grounds for believing that the defendant will (*inter alia*) abscond or commit further offences while on bail. It goes on to specify that the court 'shall have regard' to certain matters, including 'the nature and seriousness of the offence'.

As rape is one of the most serious crimes which can be committed (it carries a discretionary sentence of life imprisonment), bail is almost certain to be refused. Indeed, under the Bail Act 1976, s. 9A, the court would have to give reasons for granting bail if the application was opposed by the prosecution in some circumstances. Furthermore, under the Criminal Justice and Public Order Act 1994, s. 25, if Dwight has a previous conviction for murder, attempted murder, manslaughter (if he received a prison sentence), rape or attempted rape he cannot be granted bail at all. If Dwight is remanded in custody, there will have to be regular short hearings before the magistrates for his position to be reconsidered. With successive remands in custody, it is usual for a hearing to take place every 28 days until the trial, but under the Prosecution of Offences (Custody Time Limits) Regulations 1987 committal to the Crown Court must take place after 70 days, and the full trial 112 days thereafter. Dwight may appeal to the Crown Court against the magistrates' refusal of bail, but it is unlikely to be successful.

Rape is an indictable offence and therefore can only be tried in the Crown Court. The magistrates will therefore have to transfer the case to the Crown Court for trial. This process has always been known as 'committing for trial', and the procedure commences when the prosecution serve upon the defence a schedule of the charge or charges and copies of the evidence upon which the prosecution will rely. This will usually consist of typewritten copies of the prosecution witness statements. The defence will consider these documents to ensure that they disclose sufficient evidence against the defendant to justify a full trial. If the prosecution evidence seems too weak, the defence can ask for a committal hearing where the magistrates must consider the prosecution evidence and hear submissions from the defence asking them to dismiss the charge(s). This can be done only by reading the witness statements, as the Criminal Procedure and Investigations Act 1996 abolished the rights of the defence to ask that those witnesses give oral evidence and/or to call their own witnesses. Contested committals are unusual because of the risk that they will merely reveal the defence's hand in advance of the trial. If there is a real chance of having the charge(s) dismissed, however, this would avoid much publicity, as committal proceedings cannot be fully reported by the press unless the defence agree. At present the vast majority of committal hearings involve no objections by the defence, and therefore the magistrates do not even have to read the prosecution witness statements. There have been proposals to scrap committal hearings altogether, but these have now been rejected. Although a shorter procedure would save the cost of the occasional lengthy committal hearing, the risk is that the Crown Court would instead find its time being wasted by weak cases which are dismissed after the end of the prosecution evidence.

Once the case has been committed for trial, the defence in particular will commence preparation of their case in earnest. In complicated cases there may be a pre-trial hearing before a judge to decide on procedural matters (such as how long the actual trial will last). Dwight's solicitors will interview all relevant witnesses, obtain any other relevant evidence (e.g., forensic reports), and brief the barrister who will be representing Dwight at the trial. They can seek disclosure of all evidence obtained by the prosecution, but this is now limited by the Criminal Procedure and Investigations Act 1996. The prosecution must first disclose all evidence which they feel might undermine the prosecution case and which has not already been disclosed ('primary disclosure'). The defence must then send the prosecution a written statement setting out in general terms the nature of the defence, and explaining the matters on which they take issue with the prosecution case, and why. Dwight will also have to give notice to the prosecution if he intends to produce alibi evidence at his trial (i.e., a witness who will testify that Dwight was elsewhere when the crime was committed), together with details of the name and address of the witness. If any of this is not done, or not done properly or within any time limits which apply, or if Dwight's defence at trial differs materially from that which is set out in the statement, the court is allowed to draw adverse inferences. It is vital, therefore, that Dwight's solicitors draft the statement carefully, as otherwise his defence at trial could be regarded as fabricated. After receiving the defence statement, the prosecution are obliged to disclose any other evidence in their possession which could be relevant to the defence case ('secondary disclosure'). In due course the Crown Court office will notify both prosecution and defence of the date of the trial, and it will be the duty of the Crown Prosecution Service and Dwight's solicitors to ensure that all witnesses turn up for the trial. If necessary Dwight's solicitors can ask the court formally to summon a witness, so that failure to attend would amount to contempt of court.

When the day of the trial arrives, the jury will be selected from those people who have been summoned as potential jurors. The case will be called and the charge formally read out to Dwight (who will be standing in the dock). Dwight must then plead guilty or not guilty. As his plea will be 'not guilty', the prosecution barrister will outline the prosecution's case before calling all their witnesses in turn. Each witness will be examined by the prosecution barrister and then cross-examined by Dwight's barrister. After cross-examination the prosecution barrister may re-examine briefly, by picking up on any new points introduced by the defence. At the end of the prosecution case, the defence may ask the judge to rule that there is insufficient evidence to justify the case going any further. If the case is to continue, the defence will now call each of its witnesses in turn, who again can be cross-examined, this time by the prosecution barrister. Re-examination may also take place, as before. At any time during the trial, either prosecution or defence may ask to address the judge on a point of law, in the absence of the jury. This may be in order to try to exclude certain evidence, for example. If it is excluded, it would obviously defeat the object of excluding it if the jury were to have heard all about it during argument! At the end of the defence case, the prosecution barrister will address the jury, seeking to emphasise the strength of the prosecution case. Dwight's barrister may then also address the jury, to convince them that Dwight should be acquitted. The judge will then sum up the evidence for the jury and give them directions on the law, so that they know exactly what it is that they have to decide. This summing up can be vital, as the judge can make suggestions to the jury as to how they should view certain evidence. The jury will then retire to come to a decision. This must usually be unanimous, but the judge may allow a majority verdict if the jury have been unable to reach an unanimous decision after several hours. If the jury convict Dwight, the judge will then pass sentence upon him. Rape carries a discretionary sentence of life imprisonment, but it is more likely that the judge would fix a definite term.

(b)   A defendant convicted after a trial on indictment can appeal to the Court of Appeal (Criminal Division), under the terms of the Criminal Appeal Act 1968, as amended by the Criminal Appeal Act 1995. The grounds of appeal were amended and simplified by the 1995 Act so that the Court of Appeal 'shall allow an appeal against conviction if they think that the conviction is unsafe; and shall dismiss such an appeal in any other case'. There is no other guidance as to the circumstances in which a conviction might be deemed 'unsafe', and the pre-1995 Act case law presumably still applies. In cases such as *R* v *Cooper* [1969] 1 QB 267, the Court of Appeal referred to 'some lurking doubt in our minds', and it seems clear that this intuitive approach will still form the basis of most successful appeals.

It is possible, although rare, for the trial judge to grant a certificate that the case is fit for appeal. This would usually happen only where there is a clear element of doubt about a point of law, and the ground of appeal must be identified in the certitificate. More typically the defendant will have to apply for leave to appeal to the Court of Appeal itself. This will entail setting out the grounds of appeal in a formal document and submitting it within 28 days of the conviction. The application will be heard in the first instance by a single judge and, if leave is refused, the defendant may 'renew' the appeal by notice within 14 days. This means that the full court will then consider the appeal in open court, but there is a danger that they will agree with the single judge and order that the time that the defendant has spent in custody awaiting their decision will not count towards the sentence of imprisonment imposed at the original trial. Dwight should be made aware of this possibility, as otherwise he might be tempted to appeal for the sake of it. A defendant is treated as an unconvicted prisoner while awaiting the outcome of the appeal process, and can therefore receive certain benefits in prison which are not available to a convicted prisoner. The rules are therefore an attempt to ensure that the court will only have to hear realistic applications, by discouraging defendants spinning out the appeal process for as long as possible.

At the appeal (if leave is granted) the defendant (now known as 'the appellant') is entitled to be present unless the appeal is purely on a point of law, when specific leave is necessary. Three judges (Lords Justices of Appeal) will hear argument from counsel for the appellant and the prosecution, but only rarely will oral evidence be given. This will usually happen only when a new witness is available who could not give evidence at the trial for some reason.

The Court of Appeal may quash the conviction, order a re-trial, substitute a conviction for an alternative charge (e.g., Dwight could be convicted of indecent assault instead of rape) or dismiss the appeal altogether. If the appeal is dismissed, the Court may certify that a point of law of public importance is involved and grant leave to appeal to the House of Lords. Again this is unusual, and it is more likely that an application for leave to appeal will have to be made to the House of Lords itself. Usually five judges (Lords of Appeal in Ordinary) will hear the appeal, and the House of Lords can dispose of the appeal in the same ways as the Court of Appeal.

If this standard route of appeal fails, there are two other possibilities. If a point of European Community law is involved, any court (but usually the House of Lords) can refer the matter to the European Court of Justice. It is unlikely that Dwight's case will give rise to such a point, as they usually occur in commercial disputes in the civil courts. Otherwise, the new Criminal Cases Review Commission, set up by the Criminal Appeal Act 1995, is a possible way for Dwight to have his case re-opened at some future time, if (for example) fresh evidence turns up, such as a witness who could prove that Dwight was elsewhere at the time of the rape. This Commission has the power to investigate alleged miscarriages of justice, and to refer the case back to the Court of Appeal for further consideration. The ultimate decision will still be made by the Court of Appeal, however.

QUESTION 5

Surinder lives next door to Winston and Joanna, a young couple with two children aged five and seven years. Winston is confined to a wheel-chair because of a serious road accident some years ago. Relations between the two households are strained because Winston and Joanna often play loud music until the early hours. Surinder has also on several occasions found rubbish in her garden, and suspects that the children have thrown it over the fence. One day, after a night when music had been playing next door until 4.00 am, Surinder was in her back garden when she heard Winston joking with his children about them throwing an empty bottle over the fence. In a flash of temper Surinder picked up the bottle, jumped over the fence and hit Winston over the head with the bottle. Winston suffered several small cuts to his scalp, but no other injuries.

Surinder has pleaded guilty at Billingham magistrates' court to a charge of 'assault occasioning actual bodily harm'. This offence is triable either way and carries a maximum penalty of five years' imprisonment. Advise Surinder how the court might deal with her, discussing the approach that the magistrates will take.

Commentary

This type of problem question may occasionally be encountered as a full question in its own right. It is more likely, however, that you would come across a shorter version as part of a question involving the criminal process generally (e.g., AEB paper 2), or several different aspects of criminal procedure. The facts provided may be more straightforward and shorter, but the approach should be the same, setting out the different options available and the framework provided by legislation before considering exactly what the court might do. Even then, it is more important that you show an awareness of the relevant aggravating and mitigating factors described in the problem (a matter of commonsense, really), rather than try to guess what a sentencer would do. It is not even essential that you know the relevant Magistrates Association guidelines, but if you do, that should be the icing on the cake. The structure of your answer, and the key points which should be covered, are:

- brief outline of sentencing options and procedures

- the magistrates' powers of sentencing

- decision-making structure under Criminal Justice Act 1991

- identify and discuss aggravating and mitigating factors

- discuss specific sentences (especially custody).

Suggested Answer

As the offence can be tried by the magistrates, and carries a possible penalty of imprisonment, the court has the full range of possible sentencing options to choose from in dealing with Surinder. Apart from a sentence of immediate imprisonment, they could suspend a sentence of imprisonment, so that it would come into effect only if Surinder committed another imprisonable offence within a specified period (e.g., two years). The magistrates are, however, restricted to a maximum sentence of six months' imprisonment for one offence, or 12 months in total for two or more offences. If they feel that their powers are insufficient to deal with a particular offender, they can commit the case to the Crown Court for sentence.

There are also various 'community sentences' which could be imposed. The most serious of these is probably a community service order, whereby Surinder would be ordered to do a specified number of hours unpaid work for the community (up to a maximum of 240 hours) within the next 12 months, under the supervision of the Probation Service. Another possibility would be a probation order. This again would be for a fixed period of time (maximum three years), during which Surinder would be supervised generally by the Probation Service. The court could also make a combination order, whereby Surinder is put on probation but also has to do work in the community for a fixed period of up to 100 hours. A less likely community sentence option would be a curfew order, including electronic monitoring if that option is available to magistrates in the area where Surinder lives (pilot schemes for such orders were started in 1995 in certain areas). This would involve the court ordering Surinder to stay inside her house (including the garden) during specified times. As that is where the trouble is occurring, it would not seem to be a suitable option!

If the court did not think a community sentence was appropriate, they could fine Surinder up to a maximum of £5,000, or impose a discharge. A conditional discharge would not involve any punishment as long as Surinder did not offend again within the currency of the order, typically two years. An absolute discharge would involve no punishment at all, as it recognises that the offender is morally blameless although technically guilty. That would also be an unsuitable option in this case, as it is clear that Surinder has been morally wrong in doing what she did. If the magistrates are unable to decide on a penalty, they may defer sentence for up to six months. This is usually done where the defendant's circumstances are about to change, e.g., by gaining employment or getting married. When the case comes back to court, the court can consider how the defendant has reacted to the changes in his or her life, the implication being that constructive changes in attitude will merit a lenient sentence. No such circumstances seem to be relevant to Surinder, and it would be unwise to specify 'getting on with your neighbours', because that would depend as much upon Winston's family as upon Surinder! Lastly, the court may, without registering a conviction, require Surinder to be bound over to keep the peace. This would mean that she would enter into an undertaking, for a specified sum of money (e.g., £50) and for a specified period (e.g., 12 months). If she were to be guilty of another incident, the court could forfeit all or part of the sum specified. This would usually occur in a minor assault case, with the prosecution dropping more serious charges. As injury has been caused in this case, it is perhaps not a realistic possibility.

As well as imposing a sentence, under the Powers of Criminal Courts Act 1973, s. 35, the magistrates are bound to consider compensation where personal injury has occurred, and must give reasons if they do not do so. This is obviously applicable in this case, and the court must have regard to Surinder's means, to ensure that she is able to pay such an order to compensate Winston for the cuts to his head.

The court must chose carefully between the various options. The effect of the Criminal Justice Act 1991 is that the choice is restricted to sentences other than community sentences or sentences of imprisonment unless conditions based on 'seriousness' or 'protection' can be met. Thus, a community sentence should not be passed unless the offence is 'serious enough to warrant such a sentence' (s. 6). Similarly, a custodial sentence cannot be passed unless the court feels that 'the offence was so serious that only such a sentence can be justified', or 'only such a sentence would be adequate to protect the public from serious harm' (s. 1(2)). The length of a custodial sentence must be 'commensurate with the seriousness of the offence' (s. 2(2)), and a community sentence must be 'the most suitable for the offender' (s. 6(2)). In deciding these issues, the court must look at aggravating and mitigating features of the case. These may include (under s. 29) any previous convictions, a failure to respond to previous sentences, and the fact that the offence was committed while on bail. None of these applies to Surinder. The court is assisted by guidelines issued by the Magistrates Association for the most common offences, and occasionally by special judgments passed by the Court of Appeal dealing with a certain offence. In Surinder's case, there are relevant Magistrates Association guidelines. The magistrates could also ask for a pre-sentence report to be prepared by the Probation Service. This would take some weeks to prepare and would involve interviews with Surinder and her family, and Winston and his family, and would detail Surinder's personal circumstances and all the circumstances of the case that could be discovered. As this seems a fairly straightforward affair, it is perhaps unlikely that the court would require such a report.

In order to assess the 'seriousness' of the offence, and to determine the exact sentencing option that is appropriate, the court will take into account aggravating and mitigating factors. In this case, possible aggravating features would be: that Surinder came onto Winston's property to commit the offence; that Winston was disabled and therefore particularly vulnerable; and that Surinder used a weapon (the bottle). Mitigating factors could be: that there was provocation, both in the past, because of Winston's family's behaviour, and immediately before the attack, because of Winston's actions in condoning his children's misbehaviour. Surinder's actions were also impulsive rather than premeditated, and the injuries caused to Winston were at the lower end of the scale for 'actual bodily harm'. It is also important that Surinder pleaded guilty. Under the Criminal Justice and Public Order Act 1994, s. 48, the court must take into account the stage at which a guilty plea was indicated by the defendant, and the circumstances in which this indication took place. The courts have developed a system of giving up to a third off the normal sentence for a plea of guilty (it is explicitly recognised in the Magistrates Association guidelines), and this statutory provision is meant to support that principle. The 'one-third' discount is not automatic, however, as sometimes a guilty plea will be inevitable, and the discount is meant to show approval for remorse and for saving the court time and the victim the unpleasantness of giving evidence. Surinder would certainly be given credit here for pleading guilty.

After considering these factors, the court would pass sentence. A community penalty could be regarded as the usual punishment for this type of offence. As the aggravating factors do not outweigh the mitigating factors, it is unlikely that the court would consider a sentence of imprisonment. It may be that, because of the mitigating factors, they would regard the incident as sufficiently minor to impose a fine, allowing Surinder time to pay according to her income and outgoings. The aggravating and mitigating factors, however, seem to cancel each other out, and therefore there would need to be some mitigation relating to Surinder's personal circumstances to justify the magistrates in departing from the usual penalty of a community order. They would certainly have to award compensation to Winston, however, or give reasons why not. There do not appear to be any reasons here why a compensation order should not be made.

4 Criminal Law

INTRODUCTION

The JMB/NEAB and Oxford syllabuses require an extensive knowledge of the criminal law, whereas the AEB syllabus is limited to a few basic principles, the general defences, and the specific crimes covered by the law of homicide. As with other case law subjects, such as contract and tort, the emphasis in criminal law papers is on situation-based or problem questions. The usual style for problem questions in criminal law is for the candidate to be asked to 'consider the criminal liability of ...', without any guidance as to what crime or crimes may have been committed. In every board's examination papers, however, problem questions tend to be restricted to one distinct area so that (for example) a particular question will not include both homicide *and* property offences. This means that AEB candidates can usefully study not only the question which has been specifically designed in the AEB style, but also all those problem questions which concern offences of homicide. They are easy to spot — somebody has been killed! On the other hand, candidates for the other boards can also attempt those questions which are broken down into smaller questions in the AEB style, as useful revision of particular points of law.

There is a wide range of crimes and defences covered in these seven questions, but it has not been possible to cover every aspect of the typical A level criminal law syllabus. Use these questions and answers to improve your exam technique therefore, rather than just as a test of your knowledge. Answers to criminal law exam questions are particularly prone to the 'street-wise' method of bluff! Unfortunately, the general knowledge picked up from TV programmes and newspapers is inadequate, even when properly understood and not based on

United States law. Criminal law is a technical subject at this level, and is handled much better if it is treated as such. In fact, problem-type questions in criminal law require an *extra* degree of method in addition to that suggested in Chapter 1 of this book. Follow this pattern, therefore:

(a)   You must begin by stating the crime that you are going to discuss (ignore general defences for the time being, as they are relevant only if the defendant has actually committed a crime!).

(b)   Every crime has a specific, detailed definition. This must be stated right at the very beginning, and the source for the definition given (i.e., common law or statute).

(c)   The offence will be defined by reference to an *actus reus* and *mens rea*. Every offence therefore has two separate elements, and your answer should follow that pattern. Furthermore, it is important to discipline yourself to deal with the *actus reus* of the crime first, no matter how obvious it is that the defendant's *mens rea* is a relevant issue. The defendant's mental state is relevant only if he or she has done something 'wrong' in the first place; and often the offence in question (and therefore the exact definition of the *mens rea* required) can be determined only by analysing the defendant's act. For example, the degree of harm caused by an assault will determine whether the relevant charge is 'actual bodily harm' (s. 47 of the Offences Against the Person Act 1861) or 'grievous bodily harm' (s. 20 or s. 18 of the Offences Against the Person Act 1861). The *mens rea* required for a conviction is different for each of those offences, and you will get into real difficulties if you have not sorted out which crime is relevant before you begin your discussion.

(d)   Having discussed the crime in full, now go on to consider any general defences which may apply.

QUESTION 1

Joshua is walking along the street when he sees a new MG motor car parked by the kerb. While leaning through the window to admire the interior he accidentally knocks the handbrake off, and the car starts to roll down the street. Joshua realises that the car is heading for Martin, who is lying on the grass at the bottom of the hill, but he does nothing. Joshua is still upset because Martin has shouted rude remarks at him on several occasions in the past few weeks, merely because they support different football teams. The car carries on running down the hill and hits Martin, causing him serious injuries.

Samson, a passerby, tries to rescue Martin from beneath the car, but becomes trapped when the suspension collapses. Another bystander telephones Delilah, a garage owner who is an expert in moving cars after an accident. Delilah has just got in from an all-night party where she had been drinking heavily, but she comes out to the scene of the accident anyway. She fails to check her jacking equipment properly, however, and the car falls back onto Samson, crushing and killing him.

Samson's sister, Ruth, is extremely distressed by the events, and approaches Joshua to see if he knows anything about what has happened. Ruth is unaware that Joshua had been involved, but Joshua assumes that she is going to attack him and knocks her to the ground before running away.

(a) Explain the different ways in which an omission to act can amount to the *actus reus* of a crime. (10 marks)

(b) Discuss whether Joshua could be guilty of Martin's murder if Martin died from injuries caused by the car hitting him. How might Joshua seek to have his liability reduced? (15 marks)

(c) Outline the elements of the different types of 'involuntary' manslaughter. (10 marks)

(d) Analyse the facts relating to Samson's death to show whether Delilah could be guilty of manslaughter, considering any defences which she may raise. (10 marks)

(e) Discuss any defence which Joshua may have to the attack upon Ruth. (5 marks)

Commentary

This question is in the style of AEB paper 2, which covers the 'Liability in English Law' part of the syllabus. Such a question would also usually raise specific points on general issues of criminal liability and procedure (see, for example, Chapter 2, Question 3, Chapter 3, Questions 3 and 4) and/or questions on sentencing (see, for example, Chapter 3, Question 2). Students of other boards should note that points **(a)**, **(b)**, **(c)** and **(d)** could all be encountered as one element in a two-part question on their 'Criminal Law' option paper. Even point **(e)** involves issues which are often included, and could form part of a question if more detailed coverage and discussion of the law were required, or as part of an Oxford four-part question.

The question as a whole requires a good working knowledge of the law of homicide in particular, but also some understanding of the principles of the *actus reus* of a crime and the general defences available to a defendant. As is typical with this type of question on the AEB paper 2, some of the issues are clearly stated for you. Furthermore, as the question is broken down into separate, smaller questions, there should be little difficulty in structuring your answer. Allow yourself 90 minutes to answer the whole question, or a proportionate time for each part, using the marks allocated as a guide to the amount you should write. Point **(e)**, for example, could be covered more fully, with more detailed examination of the facts of the cases cited, but that would not be appropriate in view of the fact that it carries only 5 marks. The key points which should be covered are:

Question 1(a)

- basic principle — no liability. Exceptions:

- statutes

- crimes involving a 'state of affairs'

- duty arising under a contract

- after a duty has been assumed

- parent and child

- creating a dangerous chain of events.

Question 1(b)

- definition of murder

- *actus reus* — omission by starting dangerous chain of events

- *mens rea* — Define 'malice aforethought'

- explain 'intention'

- was serious injury 'virtually certain'? Did Joshua know that?

- provocation as a partial defence

- define provocation

- was there a 'sudden and temporary loss of self-control'?

- was it reasonable for Joshua to lose self-control?

Question 1(c)

- manslaughter by unlawful and dangerous act defined

- 'unlawful act' explained

- 'dangerous' explained — harm, objective test

- other elements?; 'directed at' discussed

- discuss courts' attitude to the crime

- manslaughter by gross negligence — brief history

- concepts of 'duty' and 'breach of duty' explained

- 'gross breach' explained

- problems with the definition.

Question 1(d)

- manslaughter by gross negligence — define it

- Delilah's duty to Samson — she was an expert

- breach of duty — failure to check equipment

- breach 'gross' — risk of death

- possible intoxication at time — the scope of the defence

- partial intoxication not relevant

- voluntary and involuntary intoxication discussed

- full voluntary intoxication — manslaughter 'basic intent' crime.

Question 1(e)

- self-defence as a defence

- subjective test 'honest belief'

- reasonable force issue — retreat, heat of moment, defendant's beliefs.

Suggested Answer

(a) The basic principle in English law is that nobody is obliged to act, in any situation, unless there is a positive duty to act imposed by the law. Therefore an adult will not be guilty of a criminal offence merely by watching a child drown in a shallow pond, even though it would be simple to rescue the child. Thus, in *R v Ahmad* [1986] Crim LR 739 the defendant landlord was acquitted of an offence under the Protection from Eviction Act 1977 although he had deliberately failed to rectify damage to the property in order to make the tenant leave. The Act made it an offence if a landlord 'does acts likely to interfere with the peace or comfort of the residential occupier', and the Court of Appeal ruled that this required a positive act rather than an omission.

Certain exceptions to this rule are governed by statute. Thus, for example, it is an offence to fail to stop and report an accident if you were involved in it (Road

Traffic Act 1978). There is also a peculiar category of crimes involving a 'state of affairs'. These are rare, however, and the cases are of questionable authority. In *R* v *Larsonneur* (1933) 24 Cr App R 74, for example, a woman was convicted of 'being' in the country when she was a previously excluded alien, even though she had been brought into England by the police! Of more importance, perhaps, are those situations where a duty arises at common law. First, a contract may give rise to a positive duty to act. In *R* v *Pittwood* [1902] 19 TLR 37, it was held that a signal-man was liable for deaths caused by his failure to shut the level-crossing gate when a train was due, because his contract of employment imposed that duty on him. It did not matter that, at civil law, the basic obligation under the contract was to his employer, and it is assumed that any contractual duty to act could give rise to a similar liability. It is also possible to assume a duty voluntarily. Thus in *R* v *Stone & Dobinson* [1977] QB 354, the defendants were held to be guilty of manslaughter because an old woman in their care had died from lack of nutrition and medical attention. They had started to look after her when she became bedridden, but had gradually given her less and less attention. The Court of Appeal ruled that they had a duty at least to call in medical or social services, because they had taken on the responsibility for her care and therefore had a duty to keep caring for her. It is also accepted that parents have a duty to look after their children (*R* v *Gibbins & Proctor* (1918)), although it is uncertain whether this derives from common law, or from statutory provisions making 'wilful neglect' of a child a specific criminal offence. This would mean that, in the example given above of an adult watching a child drown, the adult would be under a duty to act if the child was his or her own. It is uncertain how far this duty extends, in the sense that there are no cases imposing a duty on (for example) step-parents or spouses. It is likely that most of those situations would be covered by the rule in *Stone & Dobinson*, but that need not necessarily be the case. It is unclear, for example, at what stage in *Stone & Dobinson* the defendants' duty arose. Was it when the old lady fell sick, or was it necessary for them to have cared for her for a while? If the latter, then presumably they could have let her die without incurring liability if they had merely done nothing at all.

Lastly, it seems that the categories of duty may not be closed. In *R* v *Miller* [1983] 2 AC 161, a tramp was asleep in a derelict house. He woke up to find that his cigarette had accidentally started a small fire. Instead of putting it out, he merely went back to sleep in another part of the house, with the result that considerable damage was caused to the property. The House of Lords upheld his conviction for criminal damage, stating that he had a duty to act because he had created the dangerous chain of events in the first place. This gives rise to further uncertainty, as it is not clear exactly what the tramp should have done to discharge his duty, nor whether he would be judged by a standard which is purely objective or partially subjective. He could only be expected to take reasonable steps, such as putting out a small fire, or calling the fire-brigade for an extensive blaze. But would it be reasonable to expect a drunken, confused and generally inadequate old tramp to do any of those things? Perhaps the greatest difficulty with these examples of liability by omission is that the full extent of liability has not been clarified by the courts, and therefore future defendants could find themselves at risk of a criminal conviction in situations which have never arisen before.

(b)   The definition of murder derives from common law, and can be stated as the 'unlawful killing of a human being under the Queen's Peace, with malice aforethought, death occurring within a year and a day'. The final element has been changed by the Law Reform (Year and a Day Rule) Act 1996, but still applies to deaths resulting from an injury incurred on or before 16 June 1996. In this case there is no doubt about most of the elements of the definition. Martin is clearly a 'human being'; the death takes place within the jurisdiction of the English courts ('the Queen's Peace'); and Martin dies (we can assume) within a year and a day of the incident. The existence of the *actus reus* of murder — 'unlawful killing' — depends therefore upon whether Joshua 'acted'.

As explained in **(a)** above, there is no obligation in English law to act to save another person from harm unless a special duty is imposed under one of the exceptions to the general rule. It could be argued, however, that Joshua had a duty to act under the principle in *Miller*, as explained above. By accidentally knocking off the handbrake of a car on a slope (we are told that the car started to 'roll down the street', and that Martin was 'at the bottom of the hill'), Joshua started a chain of events as dangerous as the fire started by the tramp in *Miller*. He was therefore under an obligation to take steps to undo what he had started, perhaps by trying to put the brake back on, or even by shouting a warning. At first sight he is therefore responsible in law for the result, which in this case is the death of Martin.

Committing the *actus reus* of a crime is not sufficient for guilt, though, unless the *mens rea* for that crime was also present at the time — '*actus non facit reum nisi mens sit rea*'. The *mens rea* for murder is described by the phrase 'malice aforethought'. This was defined as 'intention to kill or cause grievous bodily harm' in *R* v *Cunningham* [1982] AC 566, where the defendant had beaten another man to death with a chair during a pub brawl, and this decision was confirmed by the House of Lords in *R* v *Moloney* [1985] AC 905. 'Grievous bodily harm' has never been defined any further than 'really serious harm':

DPP v *Smith* [1961] AC 290. 'Intention' does not necessarily require 'purpose' or 'desire' (*R* v *Hancock and Shankland* [1986] AC 455) and may be inferred if the defendant knew that death or grievous bodily harm was 'virtually certain' as a result of his actions. Thus, in *R* v *Nedrick* [1986] 1 WLR 1025, the defendant had poured paraffin through the letterbox of the house of a woman against whom he had a grudge and set fire to it, with the result that the woman's child died in the blaze. The Court of Appeal quashed his conviction for murder and ruled that a jury are not entitled to infer intention unless they feel sure that death or grievous bodily harm was a virtual certainty and that the defendant appreciated that such was the case. They went on to say, however, that in such a situation the inference that the defendant 'intended' the result 'may be irresistible'. In this problem, therefore, the first question is whether Joshua wanted seriously to injure Martin. We are told that he was 'upset', but otherwise there is no clear evidence of purpose or desire here. The second question must therefore be whether the car was 'virtually certain' to cause Martin serious injury. This may depend upon how steep the hill was, how far the car had to run before it would hit Martin, whether the road was straight or had a bend in it, and any other circumstances (such as Martin's awareness of the car) which would affect the likelihood of it hitting him. Even if serious injury was virtually certain, Joshua could still claim that he just did not realise the risk to Martin, and the jury must acquit him unless they are certain beyond reasonable doubt that he is lying. In that situation, the jury are entitled to look at how obvious it was that injury would result, and use that fact as evidence in deciding whether Joshua is telling the truth or not. Only if there was no possibility of Martin escaping serious injury, and Joshua knew that to be the case, could a jury infer that Joshua 'intended' to kill or seriously injure Martin.

Lastly, if Joshua had the *mens rea* for murder, he could ask for the charge to be reduced to manslaughter on the grounds of provocation. This is a common law defence, put into a statutory framework by the Homicide Act 1957. If Joshua pleads this defence, the prosecution must disprove it. The defence relies upon a twofold test. First, the subjective test requires the defendant to have suffered a 'sudden and temporary loss of self-control' (*R* v *Duffy* [1949] 1 All ER 932) because of 'things done or things said or by both together' (Homicide Act 1957). As a result the defendant must have been 'not master of his mind'. Evidence that the defendant had time to 'cool down' after the provocation could be enough to defeat the defence. Thus in *R* v *Thornton* [1991] NLJ 1223, a woman who had suffered years of abuse at the hands of her husband stabbed him while he was asleep, a few minutes after the last assault upon her. As her actions showed evidence that she was in control of herself at the time, the defence of provocation failed and she was convicted of murder. Similarly in

R v *Ahluwalia* [1992] NLJ 1159, the Court of Appeal explained that a delay would not automatically defeat the defence, but that 'the longer the delay and the stronger the evidence of deliberation on the part of the defendant, the more likely it will be that the prosecution will negative provocation'. It is unclear here how long ago Martin had shouted abuse at Joshua, but in view of the fact that he has had time to fall asleep at the bottom of the hill, it seems unlikely that Joshua could still be out of control in the sense required by the courts. Joshua's actions, like Thornton's, also suggest control and deliberation on his part.

If Joshua can surmount this first hurdle of the subjective test, the jury would then have to decide upon the objective test, i.e., if the 'reasonable man' would have reacted to Martin's abuse (we do not know exactly what it was) in this way. The jury are entitled to take into account any characteristics of Joshua. In *R* v *Camplin* [1978] AC 705 the House of Lords ruled that the defendant's age and sex could be relevant, as in that case the defendant was a young boy who had been taunted by the victim, a much older man who had just sexually assaulted him. In *R* v *Newell* [1980] Crim LR 576, it was explained by the Court of Appeal that any characteristic which is significant and of a permanent nature may be taken into account, but only insofar as it is relevant to the provocation in question. In that case the jury were not allowed to take into account the facts that the defendant was intoxicated, suffering from the after-effects of a drug overdose and upset because his girlfriend had left him. They would have been able to take into account his alcoholism, but only if it was connected to the provocation (and it was not connected). Therefore, the exact nature of Martin's abuse, and any characteristics of Joshua which may have increased its effect upon Joshua, must be ascertained.

(c)   There are now two types of manslaughter. The first is known as 'constructive manslaughter', or 'manslaughter by unlawful and dangerous act'. This requires the accused to have committed a 'dangerous' criminal offence which resulted in a person's death. There must have been a crime committed regardless of the death. Thus in *R* v *Lamb* [1967] 3 WLR 888, a boy was acquitted of manslaughter after he accidentally shot his friend with a revolver. The boys had been playing with the gun and misunderstood that the barrel revolved as the trigger was pulled and not afterwards. The victim had not been in fear when Lamb pointed the gun at him, because he thought (like Lamb himself) that there was no bullet in the chamber opposite the barrel. The only crime that Lamb could have committed was assault, but there was no assault (or any other crime) because the offence of assault necessitates at least putting the victim in fear of unlawful violence. The crime must also have been one that requires *mens rea* of recklessness or intention, so that a crime which can be proved by establishing merely negligence would not suffice (*Andrews* v *DPP* [1937] AC 576). The word 'dangerous' implies that the act was capable of causing some harm, albeit slight harm (*R* v *Church* [1965] 2 All ER 72 (CA)). The harm must be of a physical nature, so that 'fright' will not be enough unless it amounts to shock sufficient to cause an actual medical condition (*R* v *Dawson* (1985) 85 Cr App R 150). This requires an objective test, so that the question is whether the 'reasonable person' would have known that some injury could be caused by the crime. In *DPP* v *Newbury* [1977] AC 500, a young boy had thrown a stone from a bridge at a passing train. It went through a window and killed the guard. The court ruled that it was irrelevant that the boy himself did not appreciate the risk, as long as a reasonable person would have anticipated the possibility of causing harm to someone.

These rules show how the courts have progressively restricted the scope of the crime during the twentieth century. There have also been attempts to add a further restriction. In *R* v *Dalby* [1982] 1 WLR 621, the accused was charged with manslaughter after supplying drugs to a friend who subsequently died from an overdose. He was acquitted as the Court of Appeal ruled that the act (supplying the drugs) was not 'directed at' the victim in a harmful way. This decision has since been doubted (e.g., in *R* v *Goodfellow* (1986) 83 Cr App R 23) on the grounds that the issue is merely one of causation — i.e., in *Dalby* the victim had 'broken the chain' of causation by taking too much of the drug, so that Dalby's act in supplying the drugs was not a direct cause of the death. The debate continues, but this shows how dissatisfied the courts are with this type of manslaughter. Indeed, in *Scarlett* (1994) 98 Cr App R 290 the Court of Appeal said that it was 'an antiquated relic' and recommended its abolition.

The second type of manslaughter is manslaughter by 'gross negligence'. This was first stated in *R* v *Bateman* (1925) 94 LJ KB 791, but has now been restated by the House of Lords in *R* v *Adomako* [1995] 1 AC 171. The case of *Adomako* (following the Court of Appeal decision in *Sulman and Prentice* (1994)) overruled cases such as *Seymour* [1983] 2 AC 493 and *Kong Cheuk Kwan* (1985) 82 Cr App R 18, which suggested that the only test was one of 'recklessness'. The cases in the Court of Appeal concerned different charges of manslaughter against various doctors, an anaesthetist and an electrician, all of whom had caused a death because of negligence in the course of their work. The anaesthetist was Adomako, and he appealed to the House of Lords. The elements of gross negligence manslaughter, as defined in *Adomako*, are: existence of a duty of care by the accused towards the deceased; breach of that duty by the accused; and the breach to be 'gross', so that a jury consider it to be a criminal matter rather than a matter that can be settled by compensation in the civil courts. The first two elements are the same as those required for civil liability in the tort of negligence. The third element is the factor which converts liability to pay damages into liability under the criminal law. The House of Lords merely stated that this is 'supremely a jury question', meaning that the jury will simply be asked to decide if the facts of the case are bad enough to justify a criminal, rather than just a civil, sanction. Very little other guidance has been given by the House of Lords, apart from mention that the 'risk of death' is an important factor in deciding whether the breach was 'gross' or not.

(d)   As explained above, there are two possible types of manslaughter. Constructive manslaughter requires an unlawful and dangerous act resulting in the death. Disregarding the death of Samson, Delilah does not appear to have committed any criminal offence here, and thus constructive manslaughter could not apply to her (see *Lamb* at (c) above). The only head of manslaughter which could be relevent, therefore, would be manslaughter by gross negligence. As explained above, in *Adomako* (1995) the House of Lords defined this as requiring the existence of a duty of care by the accused towards the deceased; breach of that duty by the accused; and the breach to be 'gross', so that a jury consider it to be a criminal matter rather than a matter that can be settled by compensation in the civil courts. The issue of 'duty of care' usually involves judging actions according to the standards of the 'reasonable person' (*Donoghue* v *Stevenson* [1932] AC 562). In this case, Delilah owed a duty to Samson to a higher standard, as it is stated that she is a garage-owner and an expert in this type of matter. She would therefore be expected to show the skill and expertise of a reasonable person in that position. She appears to have been in breach of that duty by her failure to check the equipment, although we would perhaps need to know the normal, expected routine that such procedures involve. The final issue therefore is whether her breach of duty was 'gross'. As stated above, in *Adomako* the House of Lords stated that the risk of death would be a factor in deciding this point. Where a man is trapped under a car, there is a high risk of death by crushing should the car fall onto him from even a few feet, unless perhaps he is trapped only by his legs. We would therefore need to know exactly what situation Samson was in, but it is likely that a jury would indeed find Delilah guilty of manslaughter in this case.

Delilah may wish to explain that she did not take her usual care because she was intoxicated at the time. This would first depend on whether she was so drunk that she did not know what she was doing ('full' intoxication); or merely drunk so that she would not normally behave in this way ('partial' intoxication). Partial intoxication can never be a defence. In *R* v *Kingston* (1994) a man committed an indecent assault upon a boy. He admitted that he knew what he was doing, but explained that he was usually able to control his impulses. On this occasion he had been trapped by another man into drinking a laced drink, so that he was involuntarily intoxicated, and then put into the position where he would be tempted to commit an offence. The Court of Appeal were persuaded to acquit him, but the House of Lords restored his conviction as partial intoxication is not a defence, even if it was involuntary. The first issue here, therefore, would be whether Delilah was so drunk as not to know what she was doing. This seems unlikely, as otherwise she would not have been able to perform such complicated manouevres, and therefore the fact that she was partially intoxicated would be relevant only to sentence, if at all. If she was fully intoxicated, however, she would be able to use it as a defence only if the intoxication was involuntary. This could apply here if Delilah had drunk something at the party which had been spiked with alcohol or drugs, so that the drink had the unexpected effect of rendering her completely intoxicated. This principle is strictly limited, however, so that even a mistake as to the strength of the alcohol she was drinking would not prevent the effect of the drink amounting to voluntary intoxication. In *R v Allen* (1988), the defendant had thought he was drinking ordinary wine when in fact he had been given a strong home-brewed wine. The court ruled that he was voluntarily intoxicated.

Voluntary intoxication can only be a defence to a crime of 'specific intent' (*DPP v Majewski* [1977] AC 443). As manslaughter is a crime of basic intent (*R v Lipman* [1970] 1 QB 152), under the rule in *Majewski* voluntary intoxication is irrelevant to liability. If Delilah were voluntarily intoxicated, therefore, she would have no defence to the charge of manslaughter.

(e)   Joshua may wish to plead self-defence as a defence to his attack upon Ruth. This defence allows the infliction of violence upon another person if there is an 'honest belief' that it is necessary for self-protection or to protect somebody else, and only reasonable force is used. The belief does not have to be reasonable as long as it is honestly held (*R v Gladstone Williams* (1984) 78 Cr App R 276). As Joshua 'assumed that she was going to attack him', he was entitled to defend himself from Ruth. There is no requirement in English law that the victim of an attack has to try to escape before using violence as a means of self-defence, as in the case of *R v Bird* [1985] 1 WLR 816. The defendant in that case was a woman in a public house who hit a man with a glass as soon as she thought he was about to attack her, and the court ruled that her failure to try to retreat was not necessarily fatal to her defence. Accordingly, the fact that Joshua hit Ruth 'before running away' does not automatically negative his defence. It may, however, be a factor in deciding whether the force he used was reasonable or not. The only issue therefore is whether his action in knocking her to the ground was 'reasonable force', as the defence is completely invalidated by the use of unreasonable force, i.e., the defence fails completely, with no reduction in the charge (*R* v *Clegg* [1995] 1 AC 482). The court will take into account the 'heat of the moment' in assessing both Joshua's reaction and the amount of force used (*R* v *Palmer* [1971] AC 814), and therefore Joshua will not be judged too harshly for failing to try to escape, or for knocking Ruth to the ground when, with the benefit of hindsight, he could have merely pushed her away. He is judged on the facts as he believed them to be, as in *R* v *Scarlett* (above), where a landlord used unnecessary force to eject a drunken customer, but only because he thought that the man was strong and less drunk than he actually was. Joshua's version of events, and his particular beliefs at the time of the attack, must be carefully considered, therefore; but it is unlikely that Joshua would be convicted of an assault upon Ruth in this case.

QUESTION 2

Is the law allowing intoxication as a defence to a criminal charge in a satisfactory state?

Commentary

This is typical of the more traditional type of essay question found on the Oxford or JMB/NEAB papers, but a shorter version could easily appear as part of an AEB type of question, perhaps by concentrating on one aspect out of three, namely:

(a) the law;

(b) defects in the law;

(c) possible reforms.

If you divide your answer into those three aspects you will have a simple structure for your answer, and should allow yourself 45 minutes for the whole question, or 15 minutes for each section.

Essay questions asking for a critical analysis of an issue also require a succinct statement of the relevant law as a starting point. You should not underestimate how difficult it is to state the law clearly and simply, however, and should plan your answer so that you allow yourself at least as much time for criticism as for a statement of the law. You should therefore aim to outline the structure of the law, and should avoid the temptation to detail every case you can think of. The key points you should cover are as follows:

- what is meant by 'intoxication'?

- distinguish 'full' and 'partial' intoxication

- distinguish 'voluntary' and 'involuntary' intoxication

- outline the rules on crimes of basic and specific intent

- outline some defects in the law — underlying clash of principle and policy; unrealistic division into 'full' and 'partial'; inconsistent categorisation of 'involuntary' intoxication; illogical reasoning for basic/specific intent division

- outline Butler Committee and Law Commission's initial proposals; abolition of *Majewski* rule; Law Commission final Report

- discuss sentencing difficulties with Butler/Law Commission proposals

- give your own conclusions.

Suggested Answer

Intoxication can arise through the consumption of alcoholic drinks or many types of legal or illegal drugs, and may become relevant to criminal liability if an accused committed a crime while under the influence of a particular intoxicating substance. The basic structure of the law is in three parts. First, intoxication can be a defence to a charge only if the accused was fully intoxicated. Secondly, if the intoxication was involuntary, this will be a complete defence to any charge. Thirdly and lastly, if the intoxication was voluntary, the accused will be guilty of a crime of 'basic intent', but not guilty of a crime of 'specific intent'. Each of these stages must now be looked at in turn.

First, the intoxication must be 'full' rather than merely 'partial' before there can even be the possibility of it amounting to a defence. In *R v Kingston* [1994] 3 WLR 519 the House of Lords ruled that a man who had committed an indecent assault on a boy had no defence if he knew what he was doing at the time, even though it was accepted that he would not have given in to temptation had not his will-power been weakened by a drug put into his drink by another man. This was so even though the defendant had been 'set up' by the other man, who had both drugged his drink surreptitiously and arranged for the victim to be present. The intoxication must therefore be such as to prevent the accused from forming the *mens rea* for the crime in question. The difficulty here is that the terms 'full' and 'partial' do not have much meaning in practice, as it would surely be impossible to decide objectively if and when a person crossed the boundary between the two. In reality the courts almost always have to rely upon the accused's own statements to determine his state of mind at the time of the offence, although certain observable behaviour may give a clue as to what was happening inside his head.

Secondly, if the accused was fully intoxicated in this sense, there will be a defence to a criminal charge if the intoxication was 'involuntary'. Typically this would mean that food or drink consumed by the accused had been 'spiked' with a drug or strong alcohol by another person. The courts have extended this principle to cover other situations, however. An unusual reaction to medically prescribed drugs, if taken properly, will be classed as involuntary intoxication. In *R v Quick* [1973] QB 910, the defendant claimed that he was acting unconsciously when he assaulted another man, because of the effect of the insulin he had taken for his diabetes, and he was acquitted on that basis. Even non-prescribed drugs may come into this category. In *R v Hardie* [1985] 1 WLR 64, it was held that a man who set fire to his former girlfriend's flat could have a defence to a charge of criminal damage. He claimed that he had taken several tranquillisers, but that instead of falling asleep, he had committed the crime unconsciously. The key element seems to be the unpredictable effect of the drug in question. In *Quick* the defendant's intoxicated state was accepted as involuntary even though the insulin had an unusual effect because he had not eaten properly. In *R v Bailey* [1983] 1 WLR 760, on similar facts, the Court of Appeal suggested that there would be no defence if the prosecution could prove that the defendant was reckless, in that he knew that his actions were 'likely to make him aggressive, unpredictable or uncontrolled with the result that he may cause injury to others'. They acquitted Bailey, however, on the basis that it was not common knowledge among diabetics that failure to eat properly would have such an effect. Presumably neither Quick nor Bailey would be able successfully to plead intoxication in the same circumstances again. This lenient approach by the courts contrasts with their attitude towards alcohol. In *Bailey*, the Court of Appeal noted that it is assumed to be common knowledge that alcohol can make a person unpredictably violent, and it seems unlikely that the court would allow a person to claim that he or she had never had such an experience when drunk in the past. In *R* v *Allen* [1988] Crim LR 698, the court ruled that the defendant was voluntarily intoxicated where he had drunk wine thinking it was ordinary table wine, when in fact it was a strong home-brew. This raises the interesting problem of how the court would react were a person to have become intoxicated after drinking low-alcohol lager which had been spiked with vodka by a 'friend'. The basic principle developed in *Quick*, *Bailey* and *Hardie* would suggest an acquittal; whereas *Allen* would seem to call for conviction. It cannot be right that the law should be so uncertain, and this shows how the courts can become confused by entrenched attitudes when attempting to develop a principled approach to an issue.

Thirdly, if the accused became intoxicated voluntarily, it will only be a defence to a crime of 'specific intent', and not to a crime of 'basic intent'. This principle was established in the case of *DPP* v *Majewski* [1977] AC 443, where it was held that an assault contrary to s. 20 of the Offences Against the Person Act 1861 was a crime of 'basic intent' (i.e., it only requires a *mens rea* of recklessness), and that therefore the defendant's intoxication at the time was irrelevant. It would, however, have been relevant to a crime under s. 18 of the same Act, as that requires a specific *mens rea* of 'intention'. The result will often be that the accused is acquitted of a serious crime (e.g., murder) but convicted of a less serious offence (e.g., manslaughter). In some cases, however (e.g., offences of theft), the accused will escape liability completely.

The rule in *Majewski* appears to be an attempt by the courts to reconcile principle with policy. It is a fundamental principle of English law that a person should not be convicted of a criminal offence without *mens rea*, with only a few exceptions for crimes of strict liability. It would be unrealistic, however, to allow people to escape liability because they had got drunk or taken drugs before committing the crime, as this could encourage anti-social habits. The rule is therefore a compromise, in that it follows the principle of *mens rea* so far (i.e., it will allow acquitttal of a crime requiring intention), but draws a line at crimes requiring recklessness so that the defendant may be convicted of something, in most cases. This rule is illogical and unfair in many respects, however. First, as already mentioned, it is not always possible to say exactly when a person has become fully intoxicated, and yet the effects of partial intoxication may be just as pernicious, as Mr Kingston found out. Indeed, in Kingston's case, he was acquitted by the Court of Appeal before subsequently having his conviction restored by the House of Lords. Secondly, the courts have used the idea of 'involuntary' intoxication to deal with policy issues. In *Allen*, for example, the accused was not allowed the defence of intoxication because the drug in his case was alcohol, yet his was a similar problem to that suffered by the defendants in *Quick* and *Hardie*. Lastly, the House of Lords in *Majewski* reasoned that voluntary intoxication should not be a defence to a crime of basic intent because the *mens rea* of recklessness is supplied by the initial 'reckless' drinking or drug taking. Yet that could have happened hours beforehand, with no particular crime in mind; and being 'reckless' in a general sense is not the same as the technical requirement of 'recklessness' for a criminal offence. Neither were the court able to supply a convincing definition of the term 'specific intent', and in effect we have to rely upon successive decisions of the courts to know into which category a particular crime will fall.

The real need is for the law to focus on the dangerous behaviour of *getting* intoxicated. The Butler Committee in 1957 proposed a new crime of 'dangerous intoxication'. A person who committed a 'dangerous' crime (e.g., an assault) while fully intoxicated would be entitled to be acquitted, but instead would be convicted of the new offence. This idea was taken up by the Law Commission in 1993 in their Consultation Paper No. 127, and an offence of 'criminal intoxication' was proposed. Thus, intoxication would always be a defence (if 'substantial'), but for certain listed offences a conviction for the new offence would be substituted. A final possibility would be that adopted by the courts in Australia and New Zealand. They have refused to follow *Majewski*, and instead always allow full intoxication as a defence.

The main difficulty with the Butler Committee/Law Commission proposals is that of sentencing. If the crime is 'getting intoxicated', the punishment should be only slight (the Butler Committee proposed a maximum of one year's imprisonment for the first offence, and three years for subsequent offences). But it is unrealistic to ignore the gravity of the crime committed, especially if it has resulted in a death. The Law Commission therefore suggested that the maximum sentence should be two-thirds of the usual maximum (10 years for crimes usually carrying life imprisonment). The result of this compromise is that there would be little practical difference in sentencing, as maximum sentences are a lot higher than the sentences usually imposed by the courts for a specific offence. The only clear way of overcoming these conflicting principles and policies is to follow the line taken by the Australian and New Zealand courts. It is rare that an accused will be able to establish full intoxication, as this would normally render a person incapable of doing anything, let alone committing a crime! The only problem would be whether this would be acceptable to public opinion initially, before the reality became apparent. It would need a strong-willed and highly principled Government to take that course of action, and the Law Commission have perhaps recognised that this is unlikely to happen (and given in to pressure from the judiciary) by abandoning the proposals in their Consultation Paper and, in their final Report No. 229 in 1995, reverting to a mere 'tidying up' of the law as it is at present.

QUESTION 3

Rebecca is a member of a pressure group opposed to factory farming. She decides to set free the chickens kept in cages by Fresh Eggz Ltd, a company notorious for its intensive farming methods. Rebecca borrows a crow-bar from Winston, the leader of the pressure group, and tells him that she is going to use it to 'take direct action'. Taking advantage of a special open day at Fresh Eggz Ltd, when visitors are allowed to look at the cages, Rebecca goes in intending to open as many cages as possible. Using the crow-bar to force a lock, she successfully opens a cage so that several chickens escape. Joseph is another visitor who, coincidentally, has the same idea as Rebecca. Joseph is stopped and arrested while standing in front of a cage, holding a carrier bag containing a hack-saw. Rebecca is arrested later, and says that she believes that everyone thinks that factory farming is wrong.

Advise Winston, Joseph and Rebecca of their criminal liability.

Commentary

As is usual in A level law papers, a problem question will concentrate on one area of law in respect of the specific crime(s) involved, but with perhaps one or two other points concerning the 'general part' of the criminal law. Here, the crimes to be considered are offences against property, but there are also issues concerning attempts and liability as an accomplice. The main crime is that of theft. If you can remember the definition, and the structure of the Theft Act 1968, you can make any answer to a theft problem look very impressive. Start your plan by jotting down the five elements (defined in s. 1). Each element is then further defined, in turn, by the next five sections of the Act. You should be able to work out which, and jot the section number down next to the relevant phrase in your plan. You now have some useful material with which to impress the examiner! Lastly, note that this question is typical of the 'problem' style of question found on the Oxford or NEAB paper 2. Allow yourself 45 minutes in total to answer it. The specific points to be considered are:

- Rebecca's liability for theft — statutory definition

- appropriation by assuming a right of the owner

- dishonesty under the *Ghosh* test

- Winston's liability as an accomplice — statutory definition

- *mens rea* where crime unknown to accomplice

- Rebecca's liability for criminal damage — statutory definition

- 'lawful excuse' defence

- Joseph's liability for attempted theft — statutory definition

- the *actus reus* for an attempt.

Suggested Answer

The main criminal offence to be considered in this problem is the crime of theft, as not only might Rebecca be guilty of this crime, but Winston might be an accomplice to her offence, and Joseph could be guilty of attempted theft. Theft is defined in the Theft Act 1968, s. 1, as follows: 'A person is guilty of theft if he dishonestly appropriates property belonging to another with the intention of permanently depriving the other of it ...'. The *actus reus* of the offence is therefore 'appropriates property belonging to another', and the *mens rea* requires the two elements of 'dishonesty' and 'intention permanently to deprive'. Each element of the definition is further defined and explained in other sections of the Act.

I will first consider Rebecca's liability for theft of the chickens from Fresh Eggz Ltd. The chickens are clearly 'property belonging to another'. 'Appropriates' is defined under s. 3 of the Act as 'any assumption . . . of the rights of an owner'. In *R* v *Morris* [1984] AC 320, the House of Lords ruled that this included *any* of the rights of an owner, and therefore covered a person who had changed labels on some goods in a supermarket. The defendant had 'appropriated' the goods without him needing actually to take them out of the supermarket, because he had done something which only the owner was entitled to do — put price labels on the goods. By releasing the chickens, therefore, Rebecca has assumed the right of the owner to keep them locked up, and has therefore 'appropriated' them. The *mens rea* for theft requires two elements, as already explained. Rebecca intended the owner to be 'permanently deprived' of the chickens, because she wanted them all to escape. It is more doubtful, however, whether she was being 'dishonest'. This word is not defined further in the Act, although s. 2 sets out certain situations which are deemed *not* to be dishonest. None of these applies here, but in *R* v *Ghosh* [1982] QB 1053, the Court of

Appeal set out a two-stage test which the jury should apply in other situations. First, were the defendant's actions dishonest according to the standards of ordinary people? Secondly, did the defendant know that her actions were contrary to those standards? If it is assumed that 'ordinary people' would regard Rebecca's actions as dishonest, the question remains as to whether Rebecca knew that to be the case. When arrested, she says that 'she believes that everyone thinks that factory farming is wrong'. She could therefore argue that she thought that ordinary people would approve of her actions, and accordingly would not think that she was being dishonest. On the other hand, even though ordinary people may disapprove of factory farming, they could still accept that it is dishonest to steal the animals concerned. On balance, it is likely that a jury would convict her despite her statement to the police, unless she could raise more convincing doubts in evidence at her trial.

Winston assisted Rebecca by lending her a crow-bar. Under the Accessories and Abettors Act 1861, whosoever shall 'aid abet counsel or procure' a criminal offence is liable to be charged and convicted of that offence. Winston is therefore liable to be convicted of theft of the chickens in just the same way as Rebecca. Lending her the crow-bar is probably 'counselling', as it involves assistance prior to the crime being committed. The *mens rea* for an accomplice requires the accused to have known about the crime for which the implement was to be used. In *R* v *Bainbridge* [1960] 1 QB 129 the defendant had lent some cutting equipment to another man, who had used it for a bank robbery. The defendant claimed that he thought it was to be used to cut up stolen cars. The Court of Appeal ruled that he would be entitled to be acquitted if that were the case, as it is not enough for the accused to know that he is assisting in criminal activity in general; he must at least know the type of crime to be committed. Criminal damage is not the same type of crime as robbery. It is, however, sufficient if the accused knows the range of crimes that may be committed. In *DPP for Northern Ireland* v *Maxwell* [1978] 3 All ER 1140, a man drove known terrorists in his car, after they told him they were going to 'do a job'. The court ruled that Maxwell was guilty as an accomplice, as he knew that the phrase 'do a job' meant that the men were going to do something in connection with their terrorist activities. As he also knew the sorts of crimes that terrorists commit, it did not matter that he did not know the exact crime in this case. Therefore to convict Winston of theft, as an accomplice, the jury would need to be satisfied that either he knew that Rebecca was going to use the crow-bar to steal something; or that theft was one of a list of possible crimes that he knew Rebecca would be going to commit. The first principle does not seem to be applicable here, but the second one might be. Both Rebecca and Winston are members of the same pressure group. If that group has a history of criminal offences, including releasing caged animals, then Rebecca's words 'take direct action' might have been understood by Winston to mean that she was going to commit one of those offences. In that case, the principle in *Maxwell* would apply, and Winston would be convicted. There would have to more evidence to that effect, however.

Joseph would also be liable to be convicted of theft, in the same way as Rebecca. He, however, has done nothing at the time he is arrested, except stand suspiciously near to one of the cages with an implement which could have been used to break into a cage. Under the Criminal Attempts Act 1981, a person is guilty of an attempt if he does an act which is 'more than merely preparatory' to the commission of a crime. There are no strict rules as to when the line has been crossed between preparation and attempt. In the case of *R* v *Gullefer* [1987] Crim LR 195, the defendant had gone onto the track during a greyhound race and stood there waving his arms about. He admitted that he wanted to have the race stopped and declared void, because he could see that 'his' dog was going to lose anyway, and he would then be able to recover his stake money from the bookmaker. The Court of Appeal acquitted him of attempted theft from the bookmaker. There was insufficient evidence that he had gone beyond 'mere preparation', and 'embarked on the theft itself'. [*Note*: cite your favourite case on attempts instead of this one, e.g., *R* v *Campbell* [1991] Crim LR 268 or *R* v *Jones* [1990] 1 WLR 1057. They are all good illustrations.] In this case it seems that Joseph has 'merely' prepared to open the cage, and has done nothing to actually start on the crime itself (e.g., by trying to force or pick the lock, or use the hack-saw to cut a padlock).

Lastly, in damaging the lock of the cage with the crow-bar, Rebecca may also be liable to be convicted of criminal damage under the Criminal Damage Act 1971. This is defined as a crime for any person who 'without lawful excuse damages or destroys property belonging to another'. The *mens rea* is intention or recklessness. Rebecca has clearly damaged the lock on the cage deliberately, but she may wish to claim 'lawful excuse'. Under s. 5(2) of the Act there are only two specific situations which can amount to lawful excuse — belief that the owner would have consented, or belief that it was necessary in order to protect other property. The first point clearly does not apply here. Rebecca may attempt to argue under the second point, perhaps to the effect that direct action of this nature can eventually turn opinion against factory farming and therefore protect other chickens from damage caused by intensive farming methods. In *R* v *Hill and Hall* [1989] Crim LR 136, the defendants had tried a similar argument when they were prosecuted for cutting a fence surrounding a United States naval base. They argued that the existence of nuclear weapons at the base would make it a prime target for attack should a war break out with the USSR, and that in that event surrounding homes would be destroyed. By their action, the USA might be persuaded to withdraw, thus nullifying the threat. The Court of Appeal ruled that it was a question of law whether the damage in question would actually have the effect of protecting property, and upheld the trial judge's ruling that, in this case, it would not. It seems unlikely, therefore, that such an argument would be accepted from Rebecca. No other general defences apply, and consequently Rebecca would be convicted of criminal damage.

QUESTION 4

Bill and Helen live together as husband and wife, although they are unmarried. They enjoy a particularly active physical relationship; and one night, while engaging in their usual games, Bill allows Helen to scratch her name on his back with her finger-nails. The next day Bill tells his friend Alan about the incident. Alan is so concerned for Bill that he reports the matter to the police, who immediately visit Helen in order to interview her about the incident. Bill is incensed by Alan's action and he visits Alan's house in a fury to remonstrate with him. When Alan opens the door and sees Bill, he thinks that Bill is about to attack him, and responds by punching Bill in the stomach. Bill falls down the steps and suffers a broken leg.

Advise Helen and Alan of any offences that they may have committed and of any defences available to them.

Commentary

Allow yourself 45 minutes to answer this question. It focuses on non-fatal assaults, but with an additional element relating to general defences. In your plan, compile a brief outline of the structure of the different assaults, especially those contained in the Offences Against the Person Act 1861. A short introduction to your full answer can explain this structure, thus making an immediate good impression on the examiner. You can also take this opportunity to make your answer more fluent, by preventing the necessity for constant repetition. Note, for example, how you can indicate that you are going to use a short-hand form of the full title of the Offences Against the Person Act 1861 by putting it in brackets after the first full citation (i.e., 'OAP'). Although the Law Commission has issued proposals for reform in this area of the law, you must base your answer simply on the law as it is. The key points you should refer to are:

- Helen — common assault or s. 47 assault, definitions

- consent as a defence to assault — outline the law

- issues — extent of Bill's injuries, the nature of their 'usual games'?

- Alan — s. 20 or s. 18 assault, definitions

- self-defence — honest mistake and reasonableness of response.

Suggested Answer

Both Helen and Alan may have committed offences under the law relating to non-fatal assaults. There is a minor offence known as 'common assault' under the Criminal Justice Act 1988. There are also three offences set out in the Offences Against the Person Act (OAP) 1861, of increasing severity as far as punishment is concerned. Under s. 47, 'assault occasioning actual bodily harm' is punishable by five years' imprisonment; under s. 20 it is an offence to 'wound or inflict grievous bodily harm', punishable by five years' imprisonment again (but considered a more serious offence); and under s. 18 it is an offence to 'wound or cause grievous bodily harm' with intent, punishable by life imprisonment.

Helen appears to have committed an assault under s. 47, OAP. The *actus reus* for this crime requires some harm to have been caused to the victim. This need not be serious harm, as long as it is of a physical nature. In *R* v *Miller* [1954] 2 QB 282, the court ruled that a 'nervous disorder' lasting for two days would suffice, although more recently in *R* v *Chan-Fook* [1994] 1 WLR 689, the Court of Appeal made it clear that it must be a recognised psychological disorder with medical evidence to that effect. The scratches on Bill's back would therefore seem to be sufficient to count as 'actual bodily harm', although if they were little more than a temporary reddening of the skin, there might be some doubt about it. The *mens rea* for the s. 47 offence requires that the accused intended or was reckless as to an assault or battery (*R* v *Parmenter* [1991] 4 All ER 698). These are terms deriving from the common law. An assault is committed when a person is put in fear of an immediate battery; and a battery is merely an unlawful application of force to the victim. The word 'assault' in s. 47, OAP would therefore cover both situations, although it was ruled by the Divisional Court in *DPP* v *Little* [1992] 1 All ER 299 that each should be charged separately and specifically if a basic offence under the Criminal Justice Act 1988 is being alleged. It is not necessary, therefore, that Helen knew that her actions would or might cause damage to Bill's back, merely that she knew that she would be applying force to his body. Depending on the extent of the scratches, therefore, Helen would have committed the main elements of either battery, or assault under s. 47, OAP.

The remaining issue is whether the force used by Helen was 'unlawful', as this is an element of the definition of assault (*R* v *Gladstone Williams* (1984) 78 Cr App R 276). It states that Bill was consenting to the actual harm in question, in that he allowed Helen to scratch her name on his back. The law allows force to be used in various situations where there is consent, but these are limited. In *R* v *Brown*, the House of Lords considerd the question at some length in a case involving a group of men who had inflicted harm on each other for their sexual pleasure. All the men had been consenting, but the House of Lords ruled that this was not relevant where actual bodily harm was being caused for sexual reasons. Such harm was permissible, however, where it occurred accidentally during a recognised sport or non-violent 'horse-play'; during an authorised boxing match; and during other socially acceptable activities such as tattooing or ear-piercing. According to this judgment, if Helen and Bill were indulging in 'games' where physical harm was being caused for sexual pleasure, Helen would therefore be liable to be convicted of assault under s. 47, OAP but not for battery under the Criminal Justice Act 1988. If, however, the 'games' were more in the nature of 'horse-play', Bill's consent to the activity would render it lawful, and therefore Helen would not be guilty of any offence. The position has been clouded by the case of *R* v *Wilson* [1997] QB 47. In this case the defendant had carved his name on his wife's buttocks with a hot knife, with her consent (indeed, at her insistence!). He was acquitted, apparently because it was felt by the Court of Appeal that the law had no right to interfere in activities of a private and personal nature between husband and wife. It was also noted that the couple mistakenly thought that what they were doing amounted to tattooing. Helen and Bill are not married, but it must be presumed that the courts would not allow this fact to prevent the *Wilson* principle being applied to them. In that case, the material difference could be that Helen was committing her assault for sexual pleasure, whereas Mr Wilson was merely doing something as a mark of love and affection. If the court were to follow this distinction, Helen would be liable to be convicted of s. 47 assault.

Alan's attack on Bill may amount to an offence under either s. 20 or s. 18, OAP. Both offences require the victim to have suffered either a wound, or 'grievous bodily harm'. A wound necessitates the breaking of the inner and outer skin of the victim's body, whereas 'grievous bodily harm' is merely defined as 'serious harm' (*R* v *Saunders* [1985] Crim LR 230). As Bill has suffered a broken leg, this would clearly bring the harm done within the category of grievous bodily harm. The *mens rea* for s. 18, OAP is intention to wound or cause grievous bodily harm. By punching Bill in the stomach, Alan has not indicated that he intended serious harm, and therefore it is unlikely that he could be convicted under s. 18, OAP. The *mens rea* required for a conviction under s. 20, OAP is 'maliciously'. The use of this word denotes intention or subjective recklessness (*R* v *Cunningham* [1957] 2 QB 396). It need only be intention or recklessness as to the inflicting of some harm, no matter how slight (*R* v *Mowatt* [1968] 1 QB 421). Therefore the prosecution would have to prove that, by punching Bill in the stomach, Alan intended to cause Bill some harm, or knew that there was a risk of some harm resulting from his actions. Causing bruising would therefore be sufficient, and it does not matter that the actual injury suffered by Bill was unforeseen and much more serious. As far as the issue of 'recklessness' is concerned, it is obvious that there was at least a risk that Alan would cause some bruising. That in itself is not sufficient, however, as the prosecution must prove that Alan knew the risk existed. He might claim, for example, that he was so upset or annoyed that he did not think about what he was doing. The risk is so obvious, however, that a jury are unlikely to believe such a story.

Alan may wish to plead self-defence as a defence to his attack upon Bill. This defence allows a person to inflict violence upon another person if there is an 'honest belief' that it is necessary to protect himself, and he uses reasonable force. The belief does not have to be reasonable, as in the case of *R* v *Gladstone Williams* (above). In that case, the defendant had seen two men struggling on the ground, and had attacked the man who appeared to be the aggressor. The 'aggressor', however, was actually restraining and attempting to arrest a mugger! Although the circumstances were such that Williams should have known what was going on, the Court of Appeal ruled that he should be judged according to what he actually believed, rather than by what he should have known. As Alan 'thinks that Bill is about to attack him', he was entitled to defend himself no matter how stupid or unreasonable he may have been. The only issue therefore is whether his action in punching Bill in the stomach was 'reasonable force', in the light of what he believed was happening. It could be argued by the prosecution that Alan should have tried to retreat into his house and shut the door, before he resorted to punching Bill. This failure to retreat does not automatically negative his defence, however, as there is no requirement in English law that the victim of an attack has to try to escape before using violence as a means of self-defence, as in the case of *R* v *Bird* [1985] 1 WLR 816. The defendant in that case was a woman in a public house who hit a man with a glass as soon as she thought he was about to attack her, and the court ruled that her failure to try to retreat was not necessarily fatal to her defence. It may, however, be a factor in deciding whether the force used was reasonable or not. If Alan's action in punching Bill in the stomach amounted to 'unreasonable force', the defence is completely invalidated, i.e., the defence fails completely, with no reduction in the charge (*R* v *Clegg* (1995)). The court will take into account the 'heat of the moment' in assessing both Alan's reaction and the amount of force used (*Palmer* v *R* [1971] AC 814), and therefore Alan will not be judged too harshly for failing to try to escape, or for punching Bill when, with the benefit of hindsight, he could have merely reasoned with him or pushed him away. He is judged on the facts as he believed them to be, as in *Scarlett* (1994), where a landlord used unnecessary force to eject a drunken customer, but only because he thought that the man was strong and less drunk than he actually was. Alan's version of events, and his particular beliefs at the time of the attack, must be carefully considered, therefore, but it is unlikely that Alan would be convicted of an assault upon Bill in this case.

QUESTION 5

Answer *both* questions.

(a)   Jasvinder is a teacher and is invited to attend a presentation at a local company's headquarters. The company manufactures equipment for the arms industry, and wishes to improve its image by influencing anybody who is involved with young people. On the day of the presentation, Jasvinder has to wait in the reception area while the receptionist goes to the toilet. Looking over the top of the reception counter, Jasvinder sees that the receptionist has been typing a document headed 'A New Anti-personnel Bomb'. Jasvinder goes round to the other side of the counter intending to take the document, but is surprised by the receptionist returning. When questioned by the police, Jasvinder says that she was going to photocopy the document and then return it. Advise Jasvinder of her liability for criminal offences under the Theft Act 1968. (15 marks)

(b)   Discuss the issue of dishonesty in the English law of theft. (10 marks)

Commentary

This question is concerned with the offences of theft and burglary, and requires a good knowledge of the appropriate statutory definitions. Your preliminary plan should therefore start with a simple outline of the elements for each crime, but note that each part of the question requires a different style and length of answer. This means that you should plan differently for each part, while at the same time apportioning your time carefully according to the marks available. The first part calls for a problem-style answer, concentrating on the law as it is, and applying it to the facts of the given case. The second part is an essay-style question which therefore requires critical comment as well as a clear statement of the law. Do not get carried away, however, as part **(b)** carries fewer marks than part **(a)** and you should therefore spend less time on it (approximately two-fifths of the available time, i.e., 18 minutes). You should cover the following specific points:

Question 5(a)

- define burglary, distinguishing s. 9(1)(a) from (b)

- entering 'part of a building'?

- 'trespasser' — relevance of consent for the entry

- *mens rea* — intention to steal

- statutory definition of theft

- *actus reus* — 'property', information or document itself?

- *mens rea* — intention of permanently depriving?

Question 5(b)

- statutory provisions (Theft Act 1968, ss. 2(1) and 2(2))

- two-part *Ghosh* test and associated cases

- criticisms of each part in turn

- possible alternative test(s).

Suggested Answer

(a)   Under the Theft Act 1968, Jasvinder may be liable for burglary because of her intention to take the document 'A New Anti-personnel Bomb'. Burglary is defined in s. 9, Theft Act 1968, the definition covering two different ways of being guilty of the offence. Under s. 9(1)(a), the crime is defined as entering 'a building or part of a building as a trespasser and with intent' to commit any one of the offences listed in s. 9(2). There are four such offences (theft, rape, causing grievous bodily harm, and criminal damage). Section 9(1)(b) covers the situation where the accused entered a building innocently but as a trespasser, but then committed (or attempted to commit) theft or grievous bodily harm. It would appear that s. 9(1)(a) is the appropriate section here, and that the relevant offence is that of theft.

The *actus reus* requires entry as a trespasser into a 'building or part of a building'. 'Part of a building' covers those areas of a building which are marked off in some way. In *R* v *Walkington* [1979] 2 All ER 716, the Court of Appeal ruled that this could extend to part of a department store behind a three-sided counter. By going behind the reception counter, therefore, Jasvinder is entering 'part of a building'. She is a trespasser if she has not received the permission of the occupier to go there. There would clearly be implied permission by the company for people to enter the reception area, as otherwise there would be little point in having such an arrangement! Even if Jasvinder could argue that she has implied permission to enter every part of the reception area, however, she would certainly not have permission to go there in order to steal something. In *R* v *Jones & Smith* (1976) 63 Cr App R 47, it was held by the Court of Appeal that a young man who entered his father's house to steal a television was a trespasser, even though his father had given him permission to enter the house at any time. That permission clearly did not extend to entry for the purpose of stealing the contents, and therefore entering outside the scope of the authority given will amount to a trespass. Consequently, Jasvinder has entered part of a building as a trespasser, and will be guilty of burglary if she had the intention to steal at the time she entered, regardless of whether she stole or attempted to steal anything thereafter. It is stated that she was 'intending to take the document' and therefore the next issue is whether this would have amounted to theft. Under s. 1, Theft Act 1968, theft is committed if a person 'dishonestly appropriates property belonging to another with the intention of permanently depriving the other of it'. By taking the document Jasvinder would clearly have committed the *actus reus* of theft (i.e., she 'appropriates property belonging to another'). The *mens rea* for theft is indicated by the two requirements of 'dishonestly' and 'with the intention of permanently depriving'. Again, it seems clear that Jasvinder was being dishonest, as all ordinary people would consider her actions dishonest, and there is no suggestion that she thought otherwise (*R* v *Ghosh* [1982] QB 1053). It is stated, however, that she intended to return the document after photocopying it. Therefore she would not have had the requisite intention to be guilty of theft of the document unless her actions could be said to be covered by s. 6, Theft Act 1968, which extends the concept of 'permanently depriving' to situations where 'borrowing' is 'for a period and in circumstances making it equivalent to an outright taking or disposal'. This is to cover situations where an object is to be returned, but after its value has been diminished (*R* v *Lloyd* [1985] QB 829). Thus taking and using a train ticket and then returning it would amount to intention permanently to deprive. Therefore only if the company can demonstrate that the document (i.e., the actual paper) is now worthless, will Jasvinder's actions amount to theft. This seems unlikely, as in *Oxford* v *Moss* (1978) 68 Cr App R 183 it was held that a student was not guilty of theft by obtaining an exam paper, as he returned it after he had read the contents. Although the paper could no longer be used for an examination, it still had some value as the questions could be used for other purposes (e.g., as coursework or seminar questions). The final possibility is that the 'property' that Jasvinder was stealing was not the document itself but the information contained in it. This cannot be theft, however, as this argument was also turned down in *Oxford* v *Moss*.

To conclude, therefore, it would seem that Jasvinder is not guilty of burglary as she had no intention to 'steal' within the meaning of the Theft Act 1968. This would also rule out the possibility that she could be convicted of attempted theft.

(b) 'Dishonesty' is part of the *mens rea* for theft along with 'intention permanently to deprive'. The Theft Act 1968 covers the issue in two places. First, there is a short provision under s. 2(2), where it states that a person who has appropriated property may be dishonest 'notwithstanding that he is willing to pay for the property'. This is meant to cover situations where the accused had taken an item but intended to pay for it, or perhaps even left the correct sum of money. The section merely enables the magistrates or jury to consider the behaviour as dishonest, as there may be situations where the accused could give a convincing explanation. On the other hand, such behaviour would clearly be dishonest if, for example, the owner had already refused to sell the item in question. Secondly, there are more complicated provisions under s. 2(1). This sets out three situations which do not amount to dishonesty. These apply to people who appropriate property where they believe:

(a)   that they have the right in law to do so;

(b)   that they would have the owner's consent; or

(c)   that the owner cannot be found by taking reasonable steps.

The important point to note here is that liability depends upon the accused's honest belief in each situation, and therefore an honest but unreasonable mistake would be sufficient to enable the accused to avoid conviction for theft. The first situation is particularly unusual, as it allows a defendant to escape liability where the mistake was one of law rather than fact. This is contrary to the established general principle in English law that such a mistake cannot be a defence (*R* v *Esop* (1836) 7 C & P 456). Nevertheless, if (for example) the accused was owed money and had taken the property in the belief that she was entitled to seize goods to cover the debt, this would be a valid defence to a criminal charge of theft. The second situation is perhaps not controversial, but the third again allows an accused to escape conviction in unusual circumstances. It is meant to cover the situation where a person finds something of value but cannot discover to whom it belongs. But s. 2(1)(c) allows that person to avoid a conviction for theft although there was an obvious and reasonable way of discovering the owner, as long as he himself did not consider it reasonable. Thus, in theory, the more unreasonable a person is, the easier it would be for him to establish a defence to a charge of theft!

These statutory provisions are not a full definition of 'dishonesty', however, as they merely give examples of what is (s. 2(2)) or is not (s. 2(1)) dishonest. There are many other situations, and these would all have to be judged according to a more general test. The courts have developed such a test, but only by clarifying what the jury have to decide. In *R* v *Feely* [1973] QB 530, a manager of a betting shop borrowed some money from the till despite the fact that his employer had specifically prohibited such a practice. The Court of Appeal quashed his conviction for theft as the trial judge had ruled that his actions were dishonest. Instead the judge should have left the issue to the jury. This decision was followed, and developed, in the case of *Ghosh* (see **(a)** above). Here the Court of Appeal ruled that the test was a two-part one. The first question is: 'Was what was done dishonest according to the standards of ordinary reasonable people?' If so, then the second question is: 'Was the accused aware that what he was doing was contrary to those standards?' The second question need be dealt with only if the issue is specifically raised by the defence (*R* v *Roberts* (1987) 84 Cr App R 117).

The Court of Appeal have thus decided that the issue of dishonesty is a matter for the jury, and not a question of law upon which the judge can give directions. This approach gives rise to a number of problems. The first question in itself ('Was what was done dishonest according to the standards of ordinary reasonable people?') can receive different answers according to the make-up of the jury, as there is an almost infinite number of different situations which could arise. Such decisions of fact are very difficult to appeal against, unlike a decision by a judge on a point of law, so that the Court of Appeal cannot even provide an element of consistency by giving guidelines. This means that inevitably there will be inconsistency in the application of the law by magistrates and juries around the country. The second question ('Was the accused aware that what he was doing was contrary to those standards?') seems logical, bearing in mind the tests under s. 2(1). Those three situations all allow a successful defence where the accused had an honest but mistaken belief, and therefore depend upon a purely subjective test of dishonesty. The *Ghosh* test, however, seemingly allows an accused to be acquitted who has eccentric beliefs of his own, or is simply out of touch with the normal standards of his community. Smith (*The Law of Theft* (1997)) has said: 'The law fails in one of its purposes if it does not afford protection to a person against what he quite reasonably regards as a straightforward case of theft'. Indeed, the *Ghosh* test appears to overlook that the situations under s. 2(1) are not based upon a mistake as to other people's opinions, but upon a mistake as to a fact (e.g., that the owner would consent). As explained above, however, even those situations can give rise to unmeritorious defences. Smith has suggested that dishonesty could be defined as 'knowing that the appropriation will or may be detrimental to the interests of the owner in a significant practical way', in the sense that taking someone else's property prevents that person from using it. This would help to remove the possibility of inconsistent decisions, and make the law much more understandable and in tune with common conceptions of what 'theft' is.

QUESTION 6

Leila has her own business as a builder and makes a living from small extensions and repairs to private homes. Over the past four years she has done several small jobs for an elderly couple, John and Janet. Recently John and Janet have been having trouble with their roof, which has been leaking during periods of heavy rain. They telephone Leila and ask her to repair their roof to stop the leaks. Leila spends 20 minutes on the roof replacing one tile, and presents a bill to John and Janet for £860.

Before paying the bill, John and Janet are told by their nephew (who is an architect) that the work is worth only £50, and they complain to the police. When she hears about the complaint, Leila is so angry that she goes round to John and Janet's house and throws rubbish into their garden, over their eight-foot high garden wall. Some of the rubbish consists of half-bricks, and one of these smashes a window in the greenhouse. When she hears the crash, Leila panics and goes home to set fire to her own garden shed, in the hope that this will confuse the police and deflect suspicion from her. The shed is very close to her neighbour's house, and it is only prompt action by the Fire Brigade that prevents the fire spreading to it.

Leila has now been charged with attempting to obtain property by deception. Advise her in connection with that charge, and also as to any other offences she may have committed. (25 marks)

Commentary

This is a typical problem-style question, in that it appears to be one scenario but in fact can simply be broken down into two separate questions. The first part relates to the incident with the excessive bill, and is slightly easier because the crime which you need to consider has been specified ('attempting to obtain property by deception'). The second part perhaps requires more careful thought because there are two offences, albeit covered by the same area of law. Plan your answer along those lines, therefore, so that you are dealing with three elements separately and one at a time. You should cover the following specific points:

- statutory definition — 'obtaining property by deception'

- *actus reus* — 'deception'

- *mens rea* — 'dishonestly'

- statutory definition — 'attempting'

- *actus reus* — 'more than merely preparatory'

- statutory definition — criminal damage

- *mens rea* — recklessness

- statutory definitions — aggravated offences of criminal damage

- damage to own property where life endangered?

- *mens rea* — recklessness as to endangering life.

Suggested Answer

The offence of obtaining property by deception is set out in s. 15(1), Theft Act 1968. It states that a person will be guilty of the offence if he or she 'by any deception dishonestly obtains property belonging to another, with intention of permanently depriving the other of it'. The *actus reus* of the offence is therefore to obtain property belonging to another by deception. If John and Janet had paid the bill, Leila would have 'obtained property belonging to another' (the money, amounting to £860), but it is not clear if any deception took place. A deception requires a false statement of fact 'by words or conduct' (s. 15(4)). The only possible falsehood here would be that the work was worth £860, when in fact it was worth only £50 (assuming that the nephew's assessment is correct). There is no suggestion that Leila ever stated this directly to John and Janet in order to persuade them to pay the bill. There would have been a deception, therefore, only if Leila's conduct could be said to have suggested this. In *R* v *Silverman* [1987] Crim LR 574, the accused had done work for two elderly sisters for many years before charging an exhorbitant price for a particular job. The Court of Appeal ruled that in normal situations the seller of goods or services can charge whatever price the buyer will accept. In that case, however, a relationship of mutual trust had developed between the sisters and the workman. This meant that the workman was now implying that he was continuing the arrangement which they had had for some time (i.e., that he would render a bill which would fairly reflect the work actually done) and that therefore his bill was a fair price for the job. If it was in fact unfair, this would be contrary to their previous arrangement and he would be deceiving the sisters. The crucial issue in Leila's case is therefore whether she had a relationship of mutual trust with John and Janet which could amount to the type of arrangement between Silverman and the sisters. It is stated that 'over the past four years she has done several small jobs'. This suggests that the situation may be in the same category as the *Silverman* case, but it would be necessary to ascertain how close was the relationship between Leila and John and Janet. If they had negotiated each and every contract, by obtaining an estimate in advance, for example, that would suggest that there was no real element of trust involved but merely a normal business arrangement from time to time. If John and Janet neglected to obtain an estimate in this case, or if the estimate was grossly excessive, this would not constitute deception without that important element of trust.

The *mens rea* for the offence comprises the two elements of 'dishonestly' and 'intention of permanently depriving'. There is no doubt that Leila intended to keep the money representing the excessive profit, but the prosecution would still have to prove that she was acting 'dishonestly'. In *R* v *Ghosh* [1982] QB

1053, the Court of Appeal stated that the test of dishonesty was in two parts. First, was the behaviour of the defendant dishonest according to the standards of ordinary reasonable people? If so, the second question must be was the accused aware that what she was doing was contrary to those standards? There is no indication here that Leila had any specific views on how ordinary people would view this sort of behaviour, and therefore only the first question need be dealt with (*R* v *Roberts* (1987)). This is a matter of fact for the jury, and their opinion would certainly be coloured by the nature of Leila's previous relationship with John and Janet.

Because Leila did not actually obtain money from John and Janet, she has been charged with an attempt. Under the Criminal Attempts Act 1981, a person is guilty of an attempt if he does an act which is 'more than merely preparatory' to the commission of a crime. In cases such as *R* v *Gullefer* [1987] Crim LR 195, CA, the accused was acquitted because he had only gone part of the way towards committing the crime. As Leila had gone as far as she could to obtain payment (she 'presents a bill'), it is clear that she has gone past the stage of preparation, and embarked on the act itself.

Leila's behaviour after she learns of John's and Janet's complaint may render her liable to convictions for criminal damage. Under the Criminal Damage Act 1971, the basic offence is committed when a person 'without lawful excuse destroys or damages any property belonging to another intending to destroy or damage any such property or being reckless as to whether any such property would be destroyed or damaged'. Leila has clearly committed the *actus reus* of the offence, in that she has damaged a glass pane in the greenhouse. The *mens rea* of the offence is either 'intending' or 'being reckless'. Leila's intention seems merely to have been to fill the garden with rubbish. 'Intention' can have an extended meaning in the sense that a jury may infer intention where the defendant knew that the results of her actions (i.e., damage) were 'virtually certain' (*R* v *Nedrick* [1986] 1 WLR 1025). This would apply only if Leila knew that the stone she was throwing would land on the greenhouse and damage it, and the facts imply that she was surprised by the result. It is more likely therefore that the prosecution would have to prove that she was reckless. In *R* v *Caldwell* [1982] AC 341, the defendant had set fire to a property, and the House of Lords stated that the test was whether 'he does an act which in fact creates an obvious risk that the property will be damaged and when he does the act he either has not given any thought to the possibility of there being any such risk or has recognised that there was some risk involved and has none the less gone on to do it'. Leila could not see over the wall (it is eight feet high) and we do not know if she was aware that there was a greenhouse in the garden. It could be argued, however, that throwing stones over a high wall creates an obvious risk of causing some sort of damage, and that therefore she was 'reckless' by failing to give thought to that possibility.

Leila's subsequent actions in setting fire to her shed could render her liable for more serious charges. Under s. 1(2) of the Criminal Damage Act 1971, it is an offence to commit criminal damage 'intending by the destruction or damage to endanger the life of another or being reckless as to whether the life of another would be thereby endangered'. The key differences between this offence and the basic offence of criminal damage are that, first, it applies to damage to 'any property' and not just to 'property beonging to another'; and, secondly, the maximum punishment is life imprisonment as opposed to 10 years' imprisonment for the basic offence. The elements of the *actus reus* are otherwise the same, so that, by setting fire to her own shed Leila would clearly be destroying or damaging property. The *mens rea* requires intention or recklessness both as to damaging property (which Leila clearly had), and as to endangering life. It seems clear that Leila had no intention to endanger life, but she may nevertheless have been reckless. It is irrelevant that life was not actually endangered, as in *R* v *Dudley* [1989] Crim LR 57, where the defendant had set fire to a house because of a grievance against the occupiers, but the fire was extinguished very quickly before any danger was actually caused. Accordingly, the fact that the Fire Brigade was able to prevent the spread of the fire will not in itself relieve Leila of liability for this offence. Even the fact that, with hindsight, there was no risk at all may not affect liability. In *R* v *Sangha* [1988] 2 All ER 385, the defendant set fire to an unoccupied flat, and at his trial produced expert evidence that the construction of the flats was such that the fire could not have spread to the occupied part of building. The Court of Appeal ruled that the relevant time to assess the danger was when the fire was started, and that the danger at that time would be what an 'ordinary prudent bystander' would appreciate. The test for recklessness here is the same objective standard as for the basic offence, extending even to the risk of endangering life (*Caldwell* (above)). Therefore, if Leila created an obvious risk of endangering the life of another person when she set fire to the shed, she will have been 'reckless' if she gave no thought to that risk. The shed was 'very close to her neighbour's house', which suggests that there was a clear risk of the fire spreading to it. Indeed, 'it is only prompt action by the Fire Brigade that prevents the fire spreading', and therefore there seems to have been a real risk of that happening. On the basis that the 'ordinary prudent bystander' would think there was a risk in such circumstances of people in the house being in danger of their lives from the fire, Leila would seem to be guilty of the offence.

QUESTION 7

Answer *both* questions.

(a) Explain and discuss the definition of murder in English law. (13 marks)

(b) Brian, who is an alcoholic, is taunted by Floyd, who calls him 'a useless drunken bum'. Brian immediately attacks Floyd with a chair and beats him to death. Advise Brian as to any defences he may have to a charge of murder. (12 marks)

Commentary

This two-part question focuses on the crime of murder by asking for an outline of the definition and consideration of the partial defence of provocation. It needs to be approached with care, however, as it would be easy to spend a long time on the first part and then deal with the second part too simply. The division of marks indicates that you should not stray into peripheral matters in the short essay, and that the problem also requires you to touch on one or two possible general defences. You should therefore aim to spend about 20 minutes on each part (45 minutes in total, with some planning time included). The following points should be covered:

Question 7(a)

- the definition and statutory elements

- *actus reus* — explain each element

- *mens rea* — explain 'intention' and *Nedrick* formulation

- problems — 'oblique intention', grievous bodily harm rule, mercy killing?

Question 7(b)

- general defences — intoxication, insanity

- outline partial defences (voluntary manslaughter)

- provocation — statutory and common law definitions

- subjective test — time lapse?

- objective test — characteristics, alcoholism.

Suggested Answer

(a)   The crime of murder derives from common law, although the penalty is fixed by the Murder (Abolition of Death Penalty) Act 1965, and there are certain special defences under the Homicide Act 1957 which can reduce the charge to manslaughter. It can be defined as the unlawful killing of a human being under the Queen's Peace, with malice aforethought, and the victim's death occurring within a year and a day. Each of the elements of this definition needs further explanation.

'Unlawful' means that not every killing will necessarily amount to murder — executions in the normal course of justice, or killing in self-defence would not be unlawful, for example. Similarly, the phrase 'the Queen's Peace' means that killing an enemy during the course of a military action in time of war would also not be murder. It also refers to the limits on the jurisdiction of the English courts, in that they can only deal with killings either inside Britain, or outside Britain by a British subject. This limitation gave rise to the War Crimes Act 1990, which allowed the courts to deal with charges against British citizens who were guilty of war crimes on the continent of Europe during World War II, but who were not British citizens at that time. Even the phrase 'human being' needs further explanation. A foetus still in its mother's womb, or a child which is in the process of being born but which is not yet independent of its mother, cannot be 'murdered' (there are other crimes which cover such acts). In *Attorney-General's Reference No. 3 of 1994* [1997] 3 WLR 421, however, the House of Lords ruled that, where the accused had injured the foetus while it was in its mother's womb, it could amount to murder if the child dies from its injuries after it has been born. Lastly, death must occur within a year and a day, so that if the victim takes longer than that to die, the defendant can be convicted of an assault only, or possibly of attempted murder. This provision has caused much controversy of late, as modern medical practice enables doctors to keep alive seriously injured people when there is little immediate prospect of their recovery. It will occasionally become apparent only after two years or more that it is inevitable that the victim is going to die as a result of the injury suffered. The rule was probably adopted by the courts in the seventeenth century when medical knowledge could not determine the cause of death if more than a few months had elapsed after an injury. In modern times it has been seen more as a time limit by way of procedural protection, to prevent prosecutions after too long a period and thus causing injustice to a defendant. There is no reason why this should always cause a defendant injustice, however, and therefore the Law Commission recommended that the rule be abolished. Under the Law Reform (Year and a Day Rule) Act 1996, the rule will now apply only to cases where the injury was incurred on or before 16 June 1996. In all other cases, the only restriction is that the Attorney-General's consent will be required before commencing a prosecution in two situations:

(a)   where the death occurred more than three years after the injury;

(b)   where the accused has already been convicted of a crime arising out of the incident (e.g., for causing grievous bodily harm under s. 18, Offences Against the Persons Act 1861).

The phrase 'malice aforethought' refers to the *mens rea* necessary for a homicide to amount to 'murder', and which will distinguish it (for example) from 'manslaughter'. The phrase '*mens rea*' means the mental element of the crime, or the extent to which the accused must have been aware of his or her actions. In the case of murder, this must be an intention to kill or cause grievous bodily harm to the victim, as in *R v Cunningham* [1982] AC 566, where the accused had beaten another man to death with a chair during a pub brawl, which decision was confirmed by the House of Lords in *R v Moloney* [1985] 1 AC 905. 'Grievous bodily harm' means really serious harm (*R v Saunders* [1985] Crim LR 230), and therefore an accused may be guilty of murder even if she actually wanted the victim to live. This could occur where the victim was being 'punished', for example, and where death was not even anticipated as a possibility, let alone desired. Some critics regard this rule as amounting to 'constructive crime', and the Law Commission has suggested restricting murder to situations where there is an intention 'to cause really serious personal harm being aware that he may cause death'.

Intention usually means 'purpose', in the sense that the defendant desired the result of his actions. This basic meaning of intention is sometimes known as 'direct intention', to distinguish it from the concept of 'oblique intention'. The concept of oblique intention means that intention can also be inferred in situations where people know that their actions will result in serious injury to another person, whether that result is desired or not. It was decided in the case of *R v Hancock and Shankland* [1986] 1 AC 455, that if the injury was a highly probable result of the defendant's actions, that would be evidence that he foresaw that result; and that if it was decided therefore that he did foresee it as highly probable, and was willing for the injury to happen to the victim, then it could be inferred that he intended it. The formulation was later clarified by the Court of Appeal in *R v Nedrick* [1986] 1 WLR 1025 as requiring knowledge that it was 'virtually certain' that death or serious injury would occur. The Lord Chief Justice also went on to say that in such circumstances an inference of intention 'may be irresistible'. The problem with this formulation is that it is unclear what the definition of intention actually is. The House of Lords said only that foreseeing the result as 'highly probable' (which seems to mean the same as 'virtually certain') is evidence that the result was intended, without going on to explain what other circumstances could be relevant to the decision. The jury are therefore left to make up their own minds, without any proper guidance. The Lord Chief Justice in Nedrick was bound by the House of Lords' decision in *Hancock and Shankland*, and was therefore going as far as he could to 'tidy up' the formulation when he said that the inference of intention 'may be irresistible' in such a situation. It seems clear that the defendant's motive would not affect liability. This causes problems in cases of so-called 'mercy-killings', where the victim is suffering from an incurable medical condition with no quality of life, or perhaps also in great pain. It is settled that doctors cannot kill, but that they can give pain-killing drugs in such quantities that they have the effect of shortening the patient's life (*R v Adams* [1957] Crim LR 365). The courts are even prepared to allow the doctors to stop giving nutrition and medicine to patients in a 'persistent vegetative state' so that they die (*Airedale NHS Trust* v *Bland* (1993) *The Times*, 5 February). Both these situations should, strictly speaking, amount to murder, as in both situations the doctors will know that their actions (or inactions) will be virtually certain to cause the death of the patient.

Both the Lord Chief Justice's *dictum* in *Nedrick* and the avoidance of the effects of the 'oblique intention' rule in medical cases show the courts adopting a pragmatic approach to the definition of murder, but it is hardly satisfactory that the most serious crime in English law is dealt with in this way. The time is therefore ripe for a proper statutory definition of murder, as in the Law Commission's draft Criminal Code.

(b)   As it is clear from the given facts that Brian caused the death of Floyd and intended at least to cause him grievous bodily harm, both the *actus reus* and *mens rea* of the crime of murder are present. Brian can therefore escape being convicted on a murder charge only if he can establish one of the general defences, or one of the special defences to murder.

Of the general defences available, only intoxication or insanity would appear to be possible in this case. Intoxication is a defence if the defendant was so drunk that he did not know what he was doing, i.e., he did not have the *mens rea* for the crime (*Kingston* [1995] 2 AC 355). However, if the intoxication was voluntary (i.e., the defendant had knowingly consumed alcohol), it can be a defence only to a crime of 'specific intent', i.e., a crime which requires a particular intention to have been formed by the defendant before he can be convicted (*DPP* v *Majewski* [1977] AC 443). Murder *is* a crime of specific intent, and therefore if Brian can establish that he was so drunk at the time of the attack upon Floyd that he did not form the intention to kill or cause him grievous bodily harm, he will be entitled to be acquitted. If he was voluntarily intoxicated he could, however, be convicted of manslaughter instead, as that is a crime of basic intent. There is no specific mention in this case of the extent to which Brian was drunk at the time of the attack on Floyd, and indeed only a suggestion (from Floyd) that Brian was drunk at all. There would need to be more detailed evidence of the extent and manner of his intoxication, therefore, before definite advice could be given, but it would seem unlikely that Brian would have a defence based on drunkenness.

Alternatively, if Brian could prove that he was insane at the time of the attack, because of a disease of the mind brought on by his alcoholism, and in accordance with the *M'Naghten* Rules, again he would be entitled to be acquitted of murder (*Attorney-General for Northern Ireland* v *Gallagher* [1963] AC 349). He would, however, be found 'not guilty by reason of insanity' and sent to a mental institution, to remain there at the discretion of the Home Secretary under the Criminal Procedure (Insanity and Unfitness to Plead) Act 1991. The burden of proof is on the defendant under the *M'Naghten* Rules, and therefore Brian would have to produce medical evidence of the effects of his alcoholism.

It appears more likely in this case that Brian could use one of the special defences to a murder charge. These are the defences of diminished responsibility and 'suicide pact' under the Homicide Act 1957; and provocation, which was a common law defence put into statutory form, again by the Homicide Act 1957. If successfully pleaded, these defences have the effect of reducing the charge to one of manslaughter, said to be 'voluntary manslaughter' because the defendant had the *mens rea* for murder (i.e., 'voluntarily' killed the victim). Thus the defendant escapes the mandatory penalty of life imprisonment for murder (Murder (Abolition of Death Penalty) Act 1965), and the trial judge has complete discretion as to what sentence to pass. However, there is no suggestion that Brian was suffering from an 'abnormality of mind' within the meaning of the Homicide Act, nor was this a 'suicide pact'! Thus the only possible defence here would be that of 'provocation'. Under the Homicide Act

1957, s. 3, for this defence to be available, the defendant must have lost his self-control at the time of the attack because of 'things done or things said or both together', and his reaction must have been that of a reasonable man. Here, Brian must first establish the 'subjective' test, i.e., that he actually lost his self-control at the time that he was hitting Floyd with the chair. This is a matter of fact for the jury, but as Brian attacked Floyd 'immediately' there would be no difficulty in accepting that he lost control. He must then go on to convince the jury that a 'reasonable man' would have lost self-control, i.e., the 'objective' test. In considering this, the jury are allowed to take into account certain characteristics of the defendant, because certain words (for example) would be 'provoking' only to a particular person. This was established in the case of *DPP* v *Camplin* [1978] AC 705, overruling the earlier pre-Homicide Act case of *Bedder* v *DPP* [1954] 1 WLR 1119. In *Bedder*, a prostitute had taunted Bedder with his impotence, as a result of which he killed her. It was held that the jury would have to consider Bedder's actions in the light of the behaviour of an ordinary (i.e., sexually potent) man, despite the fact that it was Bedder's impotence that made the prostitute's taunts so offensive that he lost his self-control. In *Camplin*, the House of Lords decided that the jury could take into account the accused's age and sex, together with 'such of the accused's characteristics as they think would affect the gravity of the provocation to him' (*per* Lord Diplock). However, in *R* v *Newell* [1980] Crim LR 576, the Court of Appeal held that Newell could not ask the jury to take into account the fact that he was intoxicated, suffering from the after-effects of a drug overdose and depressed by the fact that his girlfriend had left him, as these were all only temporary conditions and therefore not 'characteristics'. The Court of Appeal also ruled that the characteristic must relate to the provocation before it is relevant. Therefore Newell's alcoholism would not be a relevant characteristic, as it had nothing to do with the provoking insults and suggestions.

In this case, therefore, Brian would want the jury to take into account the fact that he is an alcoholic, as this clearly would make Floyd's taunts more serious to him. The Court would have to decide if alcoholism was a permanent feature, amounting to a characteristic. It was suggested in *Newell* that it could be a characteristic, and it is likely that this *dictum* would be followed, because of the case of *R* v *Morhall* [1995] 3 WLR 330. In this case the House of Lords ruled that addiction to glue-sniffing could be a 'characteristic' for this purpose, thus overruling the trial judge who had decided that it should not be taken into account as a matter of public policy because it was a self-induced problem. The jury would therefore have to decide if a reasonable alcoholic would have reacted as Brian did, before Brian's defence of provocation could be successful.

5   Law of Tort

INTRODUCTION

Tort is not covered on the NEAB syllabus and its treatment by the other boards varies. Tort enjoys its own paper with both AEB (two papers from tort, criminal and contract) and Oxford (one paper from criminal, or contract or tort). The Oxford board has the widest coverage including defamation, trespass and *Rylands* v *Fletcher*. The AEB covers the main torts apart from defamation and trespass. The London (now EDEXCEL Foundation) and Welsh boards include some tort in their papers on individuals and their rights. Oxford and AEB have both problem and essay questions on tort, whereas the other boards have problem questions based on tort. Both problem and essay questions require knowledge and understanding to be shown. However, the two types of question require a different approach in answering. Problem questions need some explanation of the law, but the main emphasis should be on how the law applies to the question. Essay questions also need an explanation of the law along with an evaluation or critical appraisal of the law.

It is important to read the question carefully and to identify the issues it raises. Many candidates then take the opportunity to regurgitate all they can remember on a particular topic while ignoring the question. Although this approach may achieve a pass, it will not obtain a good mark. It is also important to provide a clear structure to the answer, almost like a story with an introduction, a middle and a conclusion. Using case law and statutes to back up points made is central to any answer in tort. Explanations of cases should be kept brief — it is the understanding of the legal principle and its application to the question which is most important.

QUESTION 1

Alan, Bill and Chris were all prisoners at HMP Parkhurst, a maximum security prison on the Isle of Wight. The prison was under the supervision of the Home Office. During an exercise session in the prison gym, which was supervised by only two officers, Alan, Bill and Chris slipped away and scaled the prison wall. They changed into civilian clothes they had taken with them and went their separate ways. This was only the third escape from inside the prison in 20 years.

The next day Alan stole Dot's car, which she had left unlocked on her drive with the keys in the ignition. As Alan was speeding away, he knocked down Erica and badly injured her. Bill tried to jump on to a ferry, which was leaving for the mainland, but fell into the sea and he was injured. Meanwhile Chris, who unknown to the prison authorities was a qualified pilot, managed to start a small plane at a local airport. He flew to the outskirts of London, before running out of fuel and crashing onto Fiona's house.

Advise Bill, Erica and Fiona about any claims they may bring in civil law.

Commentary

The answer requires a knowledge of the basic principles of negligence, including new intervening acts and the actions of third parties. It is typical of the problem questions on the Oxford paper, but could also be a part of a larger question from the AEB paper. The key points which need to be covered are:

- the three requirements for a duty of care to arise

- the three requirements to establish liability in negligence

- factors relevant to determining the standard of care

- consideration of whether Bill has committed a new intervening act

- identify the claims by Erica against the prison, the Home Office, Dot and Alan

- identify the possible claims by Fiona.

Suggested Answer

This question involves giving advice to Bill, Erica and Fiona about whether they are owed a duty of care in the tort of negligence and by whom, whether there is a breach of duty and whether damage is suffered as a result. Bill's claim involves issues of how the Home Office exercise their powers and causation; Erica's involves consideration of the acts of third parties; and Fiona's covers matters of proximity and remoteness of damage.

To establish whether the prison owe a duty of care to Bill, to prevent him escaping, the requirements laid down in *Marc Rich* v *Bishop Rock Marine* [1995] 3 WLR 227 have to be met. The House of Lords set out a three stage test of foreseeability, proximity and just and reasonableness. It is foreseeable that if a prisoner escapes he may be injured in doing so, particularly if he takes risks, which he is very likely to do. As regards proximity between the prison authorities and Bill, they are physically very close and there is a close relationship between them, as the prison are responsible for Bill 24 hours a day. The third factor is whether it would be just and reasonable to make the prison liable. Although it can be argued that the prison authorities should not be made liable because of the large number of prisoners and the fact it would fetter the actions of prison governors, as in *Home Office* v *Dorset Yacht Co.* [1970] AC 1004 (HL), one of the purposes of prisons is to keep prisoners from escaping, and it is reasonable to make the prison authorities liable for not preventing the escape.

In determining if the prison are in breach of their duty, the courts apply the objective test of the 'reasonable man'. Although the likelihood of escape is low, this is a maximum security prison and a higher standard is expected. With only two prison officers in a busy gym, this would seem to be a breach of duty, depending on the number of prisoners, the number of exits, previous practice etc. Has the breach caused Bill's injuries? Even if it is accepted that the prison authorities have been negligent, it is Bill's own action, in trying to jump on the ferry, which causes his injuries. In *McKew* v *Holland & Hannon* [1969] 3 All ER 1621 the defendant had negligently injured the plaintiff's leg, which caused it sometimes suddenly to give way. But later the plaintiff fell and injured himself while going down some steep stairs, and this was held to be a new intervening act for which the defendant was not liable. This may be applied here, so the prison authorities would not be responsible for Bill's injuries.

Erica may have a number of claims against the prison authorities, the Home Office, Dot and Alan. First, in dealing with the prison management, the three requirements from *Marc Rich* (above) need to be applied to establish if the prison authorities owe a duty of care to Erica. It is foreseeable that if the inmates of a maximum security prison escape they may cause harm to members of the local population. As regards proximity, we are not told that Erica and the prison authorities are known to each other, but there is a certain physical proximity in Erica being on the island, which is probably sufficient to create a duty as there is a limited number of potential plaintiffs living on the island. One other issue here is public policy, and it can be argued that the prison authorities should not be hampered in carrying out their job by worries over incurring liability in negligence for the acts of escaped prisoners. But this should not be a blanket immunity; following arguments in *Swinney* v *Chief Constable of Northumbria Police* [1996] 3 All ER 449 that the police should not enjoy a blanket immunity from claims in negligence. However, the number of people on the island is small, and they should be protected from dangerous prisoners from a maximum security prison, As regards the just and reasonable requirement, it could be claimed that there is an existing system, through insurance, to protect the victims of road traffic accidents, but this situation can be distinguished as Alan, as an escaping prisoner, is unlikely to have valid insurance.

The prison authorities owe a duty to Erica and are in breach of this duty in letting Alan escape, but is there a break in the chain of causation, by either Dot or Alan? Dot's omission (not locking her car) and her negligent act of leaving the keys in the ignition could be a new intervening act, but it does not seem to be as overriding as the police inspector's negligence in *Knightley* v *Johns* [1982] 1 WLR 349. Does Dot owe a duty of care to Erica? It is certainly foreseeable that if Dot leaves the keys in the car it may be stolen, and it may even be argued that it is foreseeable the car could be used to knock someone down. But is there sufficient proximity between Dot and Erica? It may be argued that as Erica was knocked down as Alan was speeding away, this is fairly close to Dot's house and this fulfils the requirement of proximity. But Alan's theft of the car is likely to be seen as a new intervening act which overrides Dot's negligence. In *Topp* v *London Country Bus Ltd* [1993] 1 WLR 976, the defendants were not liable for the acts of a third party who stole the defendant's bus which was left with the keys in it and knocked someone down. Alan, however, owes a duty of care to other road users, including Erica, and is in breach of that duty by speeding and causing the injury to Erica. Erica could successfully sue Alan although he may not be able to pay damages.

Does Alan's act override the original negligence of the prison authorities? The difficulty with this argument is that the prison authorities are responsible for Alan. In *Home Office* v *Dorset Yacht Co.* (above), the Home Office were made liable for the actions of borstal boys, who escaped and damaged a yacht. It would seem that the prison authorities would remain liable here. The Home

Office take overall responsibility for prisons in the public sector and they will be vicariously liable for the negligence of the prison management.

Fiona's possible claims would be against the prison authorities and Chris. To be successful she would have to establish that she is owed a duty of care, that this has been broken and that she has suffered damage. In establishing that she is owed a duty of care by the prison, she would first have to prove that it was foreseeable that damage would be caused. It is foreseeable that an escaped prisoner would cause damage of some sort. The exact sequence of events does not have to be foreseen (*Hughes* v *Lord Advocate* [1963] AC 837). As regards proximity, Fiona lives physically far away and has no close relationship with the prison, so this requirement is not satisfied. In *Bourhill* v *Young* [1943] AC 92, the plaintiff was 45 feet away from the road accident caused by the defendant and was outside the area of foreseeable risk. Fiona could insure her house against such damage and this would go against imposing liability on the prison authorities. An alternative argument against making the prison authorities liable is to say that the damage is too remote and that it was not foreseeable that a prisoner would steal a plane and fly 100 miles and crash onto someone's house. Even though Fiona could establish that Chris was in breach of a duty of care by continuing to fly if he knew or should have known he was running out of fuel, Chris is unlikely to be insured and it would be fruitless pursuing a claim against him.

In conclusion, although Bill may appear to have a strong claim against the prison authorities, it is likely to fail on the issue of causation, as he caused his own injuries. Erica initially has strong claims against Alan, Dot and the prison authorities but would be advised to pursue the claim against the prison authorities. Fiona is unlikely to succeed against the prison authorities, and although she is likely to succeed against Chris, she is unlikely to obtain any damages from him.

QUESTION 2

The *Lady Luck* is a pleasure cruiser owned by Kevin. She was cruising along the River Thames one afternoon under the command of the captain, Mick, when (due to poor maintenance) the steering mechanism broke and the cruiser went out of control. It collided with another boat being steered by Norma, and a fire started which quickly engulfed both vessels. A nearby BBC radio car broadcast live coverage of the incident. Mick was not physically injured but suffered nervous shock. Norma was badly burned. Olive, who was walking along the bank, dived into the river to help in the rescue. The following day Olive was prescribed tablets by her doctor, to calm her nerves. Pauline, Norma's sister, arrived at the local hospital six hours after the incident and saw Norma lying on a stretcher heavily bandaged. Pauline suffered nervous shock. Queenie, Norma's mother, nursed Norma back to health but then suffered a nervous breakdown from the strain. Mick's wife, Rose, heard the broadcast of the incident on her car radio and, fearing for her husband's safety, she too suffered nervous shock.

Advise Mick, Olive, Pauline, Queenie, and Rose about any claims they may have against Kevin.

Commentary

Answering this question needs a sound knowledge of the principles of negligence and the requirements for claims relating to nervous shock. It is important to be aware of recent developments in this area to produce a good answer.

The key points which need to be covered are:

- basic requirements for establishing a duty of care, including that the defendant could foresee personal injury, and the need to suffer a recognised psychiatric injury

- proving breach of duty

- distinction between primary and secondary victims

- particular requirements set out in *Alcock* and *Page* v *Smith*

- position of employees and rescuers.

Suggested Answer

All the potential plaintiffs are making claims for 'nervous shock'. They must all establish that a duty of care is owed to them, that there is a breach of this duty and that they suffer injury as a result. In establishing that a duty of care is owed, the three factors set out in *Marc Rich* v *Bishop Rock Marine* — i.e., foreseeability, proximity and the just and reasonable requirement — must be fulfilled. The other matters the plaintiffs must prove will depend on whether they are primary or secondary victims, as established in *Page* v *Smith* [1995] 2 WLR 664, or whether they are in the special position of employees or rescuers. The phrase 'nervous shock' is not a medical term but a legal one, and is now more commonly known as 'psychiatric injury'. A plaintiff has to prove that he or she has suffered from a recognised psychiatric injury before he or she can claim. These matters must now be examined in relation to the particular claims made by each party.

Mick has to prove that Kevin owes him a duty of care and that Kevin's omission to maintain the boat properly is negligent. It is foreseeable that if Kevin is negligent in not maintaining the boat, the boat may cause an accident and that someone in Mick's position — the captain and an employee — would suffer personal injury. In *Frost* v *Chief Constable of South Yorkshire Police* [1997] 1 All ER 540, a claim was made by police officers who suffered nervous shock arising from their involvement in the disaster at the Hillsborough football ground. It was said that in the master–servant relationship the duty of care arose from that relationship, and the chief constable was liable in negligence because he had created the dangerous situation. Applying this to the incident arising from the defective steering, Kevin, as the employer, owes a duty of care to Mick to take reasonable care not to expose Mick to unnecessary risk of personal injury. Assuming that Mick is someone of normal fortitude and that he feared for his own safety, Kevin is in breach of this duty and liable to Mick. Kevin may have a partial defence if he can show that Mick was contributorily negligent, in that he knew or should have known that the steering was defective or had not been properly maintained, but carried on using the boat. If this was the case then under the Law Reform (Contributory Negligence) Act 1945, Mick's damages would be reduced to the extent the court deemed fit.

Does Kevin owe a duty of care to Olive, who is a rescuer? It is foreseeable that someone may go to the rescue if Kevin is negligent and the boat crashes into another one, and it is foreseeable that that person would suffer personal injury. There may be close physical proximity here, depending on how far away Olive is from the accident. But has Olive accepted the risk, or has she acted unreasonably? If there are people in the water, which seems likely, Olive's action will be reasonable, but it has been held by the courts that a rescuer is not accepting the risks of rescuing someone. In *Chadwick* v *British Railways Board* [1967] 1 WLR 912, the defendants were liable to the plaintiff who went to help at a train crash. In *Frost* (above) the court said that a rescuer was in a primary relationship with a tortfeasor and not subject to the limits imposed on secondary victims. One difficulty Olive faces is establishing that she has a recognised psychiatric injury. Merely being distressed is not sufficient, and it would seem that Olive is suffering from a temporary attack of nerves which is unlikely to be classed as a psychiatric injury. Consequently her claim would fail.

Does Kevin owe a duty to Pauline? If Norma is injured through Kevin's negligence, it is forseeable that Norma's relatives will suffer nervous shock. Pauline is a 'secondary victim', as she is not directly involved in the incident but suffers from what she sees or hears. With secondary victims, injury through shock must be foreseeable. Pauline must also be someone of normal fortitude. To have a valid claim the four factors set out in *Alcock* v *Chief Constable of South Yorkshire Police* must be established.

(a)   there must be a relationship of love and affection between the plaintiff and the victim. There is a presumption of such a relationship between spouses and between parents and children;

(b)   the plaintiff must be at the accident or the immediate aftermath;

(c)   the plaintiff must see or hear the event or its aftermath;

(d)   the plaintiff must suffer a sudden shock.

As she is Norma's sister, Pauline must show a relationship of 'love and affection' between them. This will depend on how close the sisters, are and the fact that Pauline came to the hospital could indicate that they are reasonably close. Pauline must either be at the scene of the accident or present at the 'immediate aftermath'. In *McLoughlin* v *O'Brian* [1983] AC 410, the plaintiff saw her family at the hospital two hours after the car accident, and this was treated as being within the definition of 'immediate aftermath'. However, in *Alcock* those who identified bodies eight hours after the tragedy were not treated as being present at the immediate aftermath. Pauline may argue that if this is a major tragedy the aftermath could be regarded as extending to the hospital, as in a sense the tragedy is still going on. But as Pauline saw Norma six hours after the accident in a different place, this is unlikely to be sufficient to be classed as the 'immediate aftermath'. If the hospital is regarded as part of the aftermath, then she has seen her sister in the aftermath but because Norma is heavily bandaged, this may be regarded as less traumatic than the plaintiff seeing her family covered in blood and oil (*McLoughlin*). The final requirement was that the shock is a sudden assault on the nervous system, which is met here by actually seeing the victim. Pauline will not be able to establish proximity.

Queenie's claim for nervous shock again depends on meeting the factors set out in *Alcock* (above). It is foreseeable that if Norma is injured, her relatives will suffer nervous shock. Queenie's relationship to Norma is that of mother and so raises a rebuttable presumption of love and affection. There is no evidence to rebut this presumption. Queenie will also have to show proximity to the accident, and this would depend on when she saw her daughter. As we are not told that Queenie went to the scene or the hospital, it may be that she cannot satisfy this requirement. The means by which the nervous breakdown was caused is by caring for Norma over a period of time, and this does not meet the criterion of seeing or hearing the event, neither can it be regarded as 'sudden'. In *Sion* v *Hampstead Health Authority* [1994] 5 Med LR 170, the plaintiff suffered nervous shock after sitting at his son's bedside for 14 days, watching him die but failed in his claim for nervous shock. It is likely that Queenie's claim will fail.

There is a rebuttable presumption of 'love and affection' between Rose and Mick, who are husband and wife. As regards proximity to the incident, is Rose nearby or does she drive there on hearing about the accident ? If she cannot show that she was at the scene or present at the immediate aftermath her claim will fail. In *Alcock* (above) the court said that seeing the events on television was not sufficiently proximate, but one of the reasons for this was that the code of ethics prevented the broadcasters showing indentifiable individuals. Although individuals cannot be recognised on the radio, as such, Rose does not need to show that she recognised her husband because she knows that her husband is the captain of the pleasure cruiser involved in the accident. An analogy may be drawn with Nolan LJ's example in *Alcock* of the balloon carrying children, which is being shown live on television when the balloon bursts. The parents watching television could recover for nervous shock. Similarly Rose could claim here. Even if this argument is accepted, the shock resulting might not be regarded as 'sudden' in the same way as viewing a television picture, although it could be argued that it is worse hearing something on the radio, for the very reason that one cannot see what is happening.

Mick, as an employee, has a strong claim for nervous shock. Olive, the rescuer, would have a claim apart from the fact that she has not suffered a recognised psychiatric illness. Pauline will have difficulty proving proximity to the incident. The claims of Queenie and Rose will also fail because of difficulty showing proximity and proving that the shock was sudden.

QUESTION 3

Examine the defences of *volenti non fit injuria* and contributory negligence and assess their importance in the law today.

Commentary

This type of essay question is mainly found in the Oxford board examinations, but could be part of a larger question found in the AEB examinations. Most essay questions require an explanation of the relevant law plus appropriate comment or analysis, as called for by the particular question. The key points which should be covered include the following:

- explain the principle of *volenti*

- outline the three requirements for *volenti*

- explain contributory negligence

- outline the need for carelessness and causation

- outline problems with and limitations on the defences

- conclusion summarising the current position.

Suggested Answer

The principle of fault plays an important role in the law of tort, and the plaintiff invariably has to prove that the defendant is at fault. The plaintiff may also be at fault, though, and this fact is recognised by the defences of *volenti non fit injuria* and contributory negligence. *Volenti* means that if the plaintiff has consented to the risk of injury, he or she cannot claim compensation for it: contributory negligence means that the plaintiff is partly responsible for the damage. Although they can be seen as separate defences, it should be recognised that both of them developed from contract terms used to limit the liability of employers and occupiers in the nineteenth century. There is still a relationship between the two defences and they are often used together, since if *volenti* cannot be proved the defendant may be able to establish contributory negligence. The defence of *volenti* has become less important than previously for a number of reasons, and a defendant is more likely to rely on contributory negligence.

The phrase *volenti non fit injuria* means that no wrong is done to one who consents. It is sometimes loosely known as 'consent', but it is important to distinguish between intentional torts and unintentional torts. With intentional torts, like trespass to the person, for example, if a patient consents to medical treatment that patient cannot later sue the doctor for trespass. But this does not mean that the plaintiff has consented to the doctor acting negligently. With unintentional torts like negligence, the defendant has to show that the plaintiff consents to the risk and waives his or her own legal rights, and thus exempts the defendant from legal liability.

It is generally recognised that to establish consent three requirements must be met: first, the plaintiff must have full knowledge of the risk; secondly, the plaintiff must consent to the risk; thirdly, the consent must be given freely. The first requirement is that the plaintiff must know about the nature of the risk. In the nineteenth century, knowledge was treated as consent, so that an employee carrying out a dangerous task was treated as consenting. Following *Smith* v *Baker* [1891] AC 325, knowledge on its own was not treated as consent and the plaintiff had to act in an unreasonable way. Smith was an employee in a quarry and knew that a crane swung rocks overhead in a net. A rock fell on him but his knowledge did not mean he consented to the risk. Secondly, the plaintiff must not only know of the risk but consent to it. For example, if someone gets into a car with a learner driver, can that be regarded as consent to the driver being negligent because the passenger knows that the driver is inexperienced? In *Nettleship* v *Weston* [1971] 2 QB 691, the plaintiff was teaching the defendant, a friend, to drive. The defendant negligently drove into a lamp post and the plaintiff was injured. The evidence showed that the plaintiff had checked to see if he was covered on the defendant's insurance and it was held that he was not regarded as consenting to waiving his legal rights against the defendant. Problems have arisen in 'drinking' cases. If the plaintiff is drunk, can he or she consent? If he or she was treated as unable to consent, this would put a sober plaintiff in a worse position. In *Morris* v *Murray* [1991] 2 QB 6, it was suggested that being drunk would not exclude the defence. What if the defendant has been drinking: can accepting a lift be treated as consent by the plaintiff? In *Dann* v *Hamilton* [1939] 1 KB 509 the passenger and driver set out on a social trip during which both of them had a number of drinks. On the way home the driver negligently crashed and the passenger was injured. It was held that the passenger had not consented to giving up her legal rights against the driver. This case was distinguished in *Morris* v *Murray* (above), where the plaintiff and defendant spent the afternoon drinking before going flying in the defendant's plane, which crashed, injuring the plaintiff. The court said that the plaintiff had consented to waiving his rights against the defendant, as the plaintiff had taken an active part in going to the aerodrome, knew the defendant was extremely drunk, knew that flying had been suspended and that in all the circumstances flying was dangerous. Thirdly, the plaintiff's consent must be given freely. In *Smith* v *Baker* (above) the plaintiff worked for the defendant in a quarry and had complained about cranes swinging rocks overhead. Later a rock fell from a crane and injured the plaintiff. It was held that merely continuing to work was not consent, as the plaintiff had no real choice if he wished to keep his job. If the defendant manages to establish consent, the effect is that it provides a complete defence and the defendant is not liable for the plaintiff's injury.

Originally at common law, if the plaintiff was partly to blame for the damage the defendant was not liable. This can be illustrated by the old case of *Butterfield* v *Forrester* (1809) 1 East 60, in which the defendant left a pole in the road. The plaintiff rode his horse into the pole and fell off. But the plaintiff's claim for negligence failed as he was riding too fast and not looking where he was going. This rule was unjust and the law was changed by the Law Reform (Contributory Negligence) Act 1945, s. 1(1), which provided that if someone suffers injury partly through their own fault and partly through someone else's fault, the damages payable will be reduced by what the court thinks is just and equitable.

In order to establish contributory negligence the defendant must show that the plaintiff acted carelessly and that the plaintiff's act caused some damage. The defendant does not need to show that he was owed a duty of care by the plaintiff and that the plaintiff broke that duty; it simply has to be shown that the plaintiff acted carelessly. In *Jones* v *Livox Quarries* [1952] 2 QB 608, the plaintiff was standing on the back of the defendant's dumper truck when it was hit from behind by another vehicle. The plaintiff was injured. The Court of Appeal held that the plaintiff was careless and had been contributorily negligent, and his damages were reduced by 20%.

The standard applied to the plaintiff is that of the 'reasonable man' and so is an objective one; but in some circumstances subjective factors are taken into account. With children, the test used is a 'child of that age', which is partly subjective. In *Yachuk* v *Oliver Blais Ltd* [1949] AC 386, a nine-year-old boy bought petrol from the defendant and was subsequently burned by it. It was held that a child of that age could not be treated as contributorily negligent. With employees, the employer is under both a common law and a statutory duty to ensure that employees are safe. If an employer could claim contributory negligence by the employee, the employer would be able to avoid some of its liability. Although employers can use the defence, the courts are reluctant to find employees to be contributorily negligent. With emergency situations, in which the plaintiff is put in a dilemma, the courts apply a test of 'reasonableness' rather than a strict objective standard. In *Sayers* v *Harlow UDC* [1958] 1

WLR 623, the plaintiff was locked in a public toilet due to the negligence of the defendants and tried to climb out, but fell and was injured. It was held that trying to climb out was reasonable, but standing on the toilet-roll holder was not, and the plaintiff was found to be 25% contributorily negligent.

The second important factor is that the plaintiff's act must have caused some damage. In *Froom* v *Butcher* [1976] QB 286, Lord Denning made an important distinction between the cause of the accident and the cause of the damage. The plaintiff was a passenger in the defendant's car, and due to the defendant's negligent driving an accident was caused. The plaintiff, who was not wearing a seat belt, was injured. The injuries were caused partly by the bad driving and partly because the plaintiff was not wearing a seat belt. The plaintiff was found to be 20% contributorily negligent. It may be, though, that the plaintiff's act was a cause of the accident, as in *Stapley* v *Gypsum Mines* [1953] AC 663, in which it was held that the plaintiff's action in going into the mine against orders was a cause of his death. Damages to his widow were reduced by 80%.

If the defendant has been drinking (as mentioned above), the courts are reluctant to find that the plaintiff has consented, but an alternative defence is that the plaintiff has been contributorily negligent. In *Owens* v *Brimmell* [1977] QB 859, the plaintiff and defendant had been out drinking. On the way home, due to the defendant's negligence, the plaintiff was injured. It was held that the plaintiff had been contributorily negligent in getting into a car with a driver he knew to be drunk, and his damages were reduced by 20%. The effect of establishing contributory negligence is that the plaintiff's damages are reduced by the court, by an amount the court considers just and reasonable.

How important are these defences in the modern law? If the defendant can prove consent by the plaintiff, the defendant is not liable. This is a fairly drastic result and the courts will not accept such a defence easily. The defendant must prove that the plaintiff consented not just to the risk of injury, but also to giving up his or her legal rights against the defendant, which is a heavy burden.

The development of the law of consent has not always been clear and logical. There is disagreement over whether there needs to be an 'agreement' for consent to operate. In the case of players and spectators at sports events, they are regarded as consenting to the normal risks of the game but not to negligent acts by players. In *Murray* v *Harringey Arena Ltd* [1951] 2 KB 529, the plaintiff was a six-year-old boy who was watching an ice hockey match and who was injured by a puck going into the crowd. It was held that the defendant organisers were not liable. However, it can hardly be regarded as a consent to the risks by a six-year-old. Some writers, for example K. M. Stanton, *The Modern Law of Tort* (1994), have argued that such instances should not be treated as consent by the spectators but that the defendant does not owe a duty in negligence.

The use of the defence of consent has been limited by a number of factors. Under the Road Traffic Act 1988, the defence is not available against victims of road traffic accidents. The Unfair Contract Terms Act 1977 prevents businesses excluding liability for death or injury arising from negligence and so stops plaintiffs consenting in such circumstances. The defence is not available against rescuers, unless the rescue is unnecessary (*Haynes* v *Harwood* [1935] 1 KB 146).

The defence of consent is now available only in extreme cases, such as *ICI* v *Shatwell* [1964] 2 All ER 999, where the two shotfirers took no notice of instructions. Because consent provides a complete defence, the courts favour contributory negligence, which enables liability to be shared. Contributory negligence is easier to establish than consent and has gained a more prominent role. One major criticism of allowing contributory negligence, however, is that in most negligence claims the defendant is insured and does not pay damages personally, but if a plaintiff is found to be contributorily negligent this directly reduces the damages he or she is paid. The relationship between the two defences can be seen in cases such as *Owens* v *Brimmell* (above). Even though the plaintiff was too drunk to consent when he accepted the lift home, because he had started the evening with the defendant he was treated as being contributorily negligent and damages were reduced by 20%.

The courts have moved away from the nineteenth century view that individuals could consent to harm, and they continue to restrict the use of consent. Contributory negligence is seen as having a deterrent effect on the conduct of plaintiffs, but whether it does is questionable. It often operates unfairly against plaintiffs.

QUESTION 4

Ali bought a detached house in a small village and moved in with his wife Babs and his children. They soon discovered that one of their nextdoor neighbours, Cyd, who had been a 1960s pop star, practised from a studio in his house. Cyd had lived in the village for many years. Sometimes loud music continued until late at night. Ali's son, Danny, a quiet child, was disturbed by the noise and lost sleep, and his hearing has been irreparably damaged.

One weekend Cyd organised a 'Sixties Festival', which was held in a field which Cyd owned behind his house. The festival attracted over 1,000 people and the noise was virtually continuous for the whole weekend. Electronic equipment used at the event caused interference with television reception, and as a result Ali was unable to watch television. Smoke and grit from the campfires damaged Ali's washing which was hanging on the clothes line, including his wife's delicate satin underwear. Visitors to the festival parked their cars in the street and on pavements.

Ali complained to Cyd about the festival. Cyd replied that it had been held to raise money for charity and that he was going to hold another one next year.

Advise Ali, Babs and Danny.

Commentary

Problem questions like this one are found on the Oxford, London (EDEXCEL Foundation) and Welsh boards/papers and arise as part of the larger questions found in the AEB examinations. Although such questions mainly centre round a particular tort, the examiners will also give credit to candidates who identify possible alternative claims. This question requires a thorough understanding of the rules of nuisance, both private and public. You need to appreciate the two different forms which private nuisance can take and be aware of the differences between private and public nuisance. In nuisance claims both damages and injunctions are often requested. Although knowledge and understanding of the legal principles is required, the onus should be on the application of these principles to the problem situation. The key points which should be mentioned are:

- the definition of private nuisance and public nuisance

- identification of possible claims — Ali (noise from the festival — private/public; parking — public; washing on line — private; television reception — private); Babs (damage to washing — private/*Rylands* v *Fletcher*); Danny (noise — private; physical injury — negligence)

- factors relevant to deciding if use is 'reasonable'

- identifying who has the right to sue in nuisance

- explain the remedies available — damages and injunctions.

Suggested Answer

In advising Ali, Babs and Danny, the possible claims they may have in tort must be identified, especially in the tort of nuisance. It must also be determined whether their claims are valid, whether they have the legal right to sue and the remedies which are suitable in each case.

Ali's first claim is in respect of the noise from Cyd's festival. A private nuisance is any unlawful act which indirectly causes physical injury to land or substantially interferes with the enjoyment of land. Noise would be an interference with enjoyment of land and it is accepted that noise can be a nuisance. In *Tetley* v *Chitty* [1986] 1 All ER 663, noise from go-karting was held to be a nuisance. The law is trying to balance the interests of two landowners, however, and conduct like Cyd's will be a nuisance only if it is unreasonable. The test of reasonableness used by the courts is 'What is reasonable according to the ordinary uses of mankind living in society?' (*Sedleigh Denfield* v *O'Callaghan* [1940] AC 880 *per* Lord Wright). In determining this, certain factors are considered, the relevant ones here being the locality, the duration, the time of day and the public usefulness of the festival. A small village will be a fairly quiet place, so the noise from the festival would be seen as unreasonable. The general rule is that the longer an interference carries on, the more likely it will be classed as unreasonable. Although the festival is just for the weekend, that does not stop it being a nuisance. In *Andreae* v *Selfridge* [1938] Ch 1, the loss of one night's sleep was held to be a nuisance. The fact that the noise goes on day and night would point towards it being unreasonable. If something is for the benefit of the public, though, it may not be classed as a nuisance. Cyd could argue that the event is for charity and that raising money for charity is a benefit to the public. But this argument is unlikely to succeed as the interference outweighs any such benefit.

Although it seems that the noise is likely to be a private nuisance, one problem is that it may also be a public nuisance, and this would have an effect on Ali's claim. A public nuisance is an act 'which materially affects the reasonable comfort and convenience of life of a class of Her Majesty's subjects' (*Attorney-General* v *PYA Quarries* [1957] 2 QB 169 *per* Romer LJ). A public nuisance is a crime and a prosecution will be brought by the Attorney-General. The noise from the festival could constitute a public nuisance. In *Attorney-General of Ontario* v *Orange* (1971) 21 DLR 3d 257, a pop festival which caused noise and traffic congestion was held to be a public nuisance. Parking cars in the street may also be a public nuisance, as obstruction of a public highway clearly affects the public. In *Attorney-General* v *Gastonia Coaches* (1976) *The Times*, 12 November, coaches parked in the street were held to be a public nuisance. Consequently the parking of cars in the village would be a public nuisance.

To bring a prosecution for public nuisance it must be established that the public at large or a 'class' of the public have been affected by the particular activity. Although there is no English authority on the number of people needed to constitute a 'class', it was said in *Attorney-General* v *PYA Quarries* (*above*) that the activity must be such that it would be unreasonable for one person to take action. A Canadian case has held that seven families are sufficient to form a 'class'. In the present situation it would depend how many people lived in the village and how many complained about the noise and cars, whether a public nuisance had been committed. It would seem here that there were sufficient to form a 'class' and that it would not be reasonable to expect one villager to take action. A similar situation occurred in *R* v *Shorrock* [1993] 3 WLR 698, where an 'acid house party' in a small village attracted 3,000 people and the noise, which continued for 15 hours, was held to be a public nuisance.

If a public nuisance is established, then anyone who can show that they have suffered damage over and above the public, may bring a claim for private nuisance. This will have an impact on Ali's claim for private nuisance. Unless Ali has suffered 'special damage' over and above that suffered by the public he cannot claim. We are not told the noise affects him more than others so he could not claim in private nuisance for this. Neither are we told that the parking has affected him more than others. However, an injunction could be sought in the prosecution to prevent a festival the following year. The injunction may be refused, as the festival is only for two days, or it may be granted on terms limiting the times during which music can be played (*Kennaway* v *Thompson* [1980] 3 WLR 361).

Will Ali have a claim because he is unable to watch television due to the electrical interference from the festival? In *Bridlington Relay* v *Yorkshire Electricity Board* [1965] Ch 436, the court said that receiving television for recreational purposes was not protected by the tort of nuisance. In *Hunter* v *Canary Wharf* [1997] 2 WLR 684, the House of Lords said that no claim could be made in nuisance for interference with televison reception by a tall building. The question is left open whether activity on the defendant's land causing interference could be a nuisance. Ali could argue that interference from the equipment was a nuisance, although he would have a weak case if he watched television only for fun. If Ali went ahead with his claim, he would have difficulty identifying the creators of the nuisance — everyone using electricial equipment at the festival? It would be better to take the action against Cyd as the owner of the land.

The damage to Ali's clothes may also be a private nuisance, as nuisance protects interests in land, including chattels on the premises. In *St Helens Smelting Co.* v *Tipping* (1865) 11 HL Cas 642, damage caused to plants by fumes was held to be a nuisance. If the damage to Ali's clothes is sufficient to amount to a 'sensible material injury' then nuisance is established. One difficulty faced by Ali is deciding who to sue. Although the creator of the nuisance is liable, Ali would face difficulties of causation and proof of who was responsible for the smoke and grit which affected his clothes. It would be better to sue Cyd as the landowner, as Cyd has presumably given permission for visitors to light campfires and he would therefore be liable as he has control over the visitors.

Babs may have a claim in respect of the physical damage to her underwear, which could amount to a private nuisance. If property is abnormally sensitive, no claim may be made if the particular activity would not have damaged normal property of that type. In *Robinson* v *Kilvert* [1884] 41 ChD 88, heat from the defendant's manufacturing activities would not have damaged normal paper, so the plaintiff was unable to claim in nuisance for damage to his sensitive paper. As regards Babs's claim, assuming Ali's clothes are normal and they suffered damage, then Babs may claim for her delicate clothes. The authority is *McKinnon Industries* v *Walker* [1951] WN 401 (PC), where the plaintiff could recover for damage to delicate orchids, as the fumes from the defendant's factory would have damaged ordinary flowers. Traditionally someone suing in nuisance had to have an interest in land, and this often meant that a wife had no claim because the property was owned by her husband, as in *Malone* v *Lasky* [1907] 2 KB 141. In *Khorasandjian* v *Bush* [1993] QB 727 the Court of Appeal accepted that a child living in her parents' house could sue in nuisance even though she had no proprietory interest in land. But in *Hunter* v *Canary Wharf* (above) the House of Lords said that action in private nuisance may be taken only by a person with a right to the land affected, overruling *Khorasandjian* v *Bush*. If Babs is the joint owner of the house she will have the legal right to sue in nuisance; but we are told that Ali bought the house and so it would seem that she would not be able to sue. An alternative claim for Babs would be under *Rylands* v *Fletcher* (1868) LR 3 HL 330 for the escape of a dangerous thing. To succeed, Babs would have to prove that:

(a)   she had suffered damage;

(b)   that the damage was reasonably foreseeable;

(c)   that the damage was caused by something the defendant brought on to his land;

(d)   there must be a non-natural use of land; and

(e)   there must be an escape from land.

Babs *has* suffered damage to her clothes; the damage *was* reasonably foreseeable if smoke and grit escaped; the material for the fires *was* brought on to Cyd's land and there *was* an escape from that land (*Read* v *Lyons* [1947] AC 156). Cyd could argue that lighting fires was an ordinary use of land but Babs could say that lighting lots of fires was a non-natural use of land. In defence to the claim Cyd could say the damage was caused by the act of a stranger but this would not succeed as the visitors were invited. But Cyd would have a good defence that Babs clothes were extra sensitive.

Danny's possible claims for private nuisance are in respect of the noise and the physical injury to his hearing. In deciding if the noise from Cyd's practising is unreasonable, one relevant factor is 'abnormal sensitivity'. We are told that Danny is 'quiet', which may mean that he is sensitive. If this is the case then he would not be able to sue unless Cyd's practising would have disturbed a normal person. Although we are not told that anyone else has complained it is certainly possible that loud pop music would disturb a normal person. Another factor is the duration of the nuisance. If Cyd practises regularly, this would seem enough to constitute a nuisance. Although the music carries on at night only sometimes, this would not prevent it being a nuisance. If Cyd has been practising for 20 years he may have acquired the right to do so by prescription. In *Sturges* v *Bridgman* (1879) 11 ChD 852, the defendant had not acquired a prescriptive right to make a noise because his activities became a nuisance only when the plaintiff doctor built a surgery next door. As regards the injury to Danny's ears, there is no case which says that a claim may be made in nuisance for personal injury. Danny does not have an interest in land and would not be able to sue (*Hunter* v *Canary Wharf Ltd*, above).

An alternative approach would be for Danny to establish that Cyd's practising was a public nuisance, when a claim for personal injury might be made, as Danny has suffered special damage, loss of sleep and injury. Although there is no evidence of other villagers complaining because the noise continues into the night, enough of them may be affected to establish a 'class' for public nuisance. Danny could consider a claim for negligence in respect of the damage to his hearing, but he would have to show that Cyd owed him a duty of care, had broken this duty and had caused damage, and there could be problems proving that it was the noise from the practising which caused the injury.

To summarise: Ali would have a good claim in private nuisance for the damage to his clothes on the washing line and would be entitled to damages. He would not be able to claim for the noise from the festival as he did not suffer special damage. A prosecution for public nuisance could be brought on behalf of the villagers, and they might be able to obtain an injunction to stop the festival being held next year. Interference with Ali's television viewing for a weekend is unlikely to be treated as a nuisance. Babs would not be able to claim in nuisance for her underwear unless she had an interest in land. Danny would not have the legal right to sue in private nuisance, but may be successful if a public nuisance was proved in respect of Cyd's practising.

QUESTION 5

Highshire Council owned a park with a river running through it, and the park was a popular attraction. Jane took her daughter Kate, aged nine years, to the park for a picnic. Jane gave Kate some money to buy ice-creams and Kate went off to the cafe, which was owned by Ian, in the middle of the park. On her way Kate saw a site which was being developed as a children's play area for the Council, by Leo Engineers Ltd, but which was unfinished. Kate squeezed through the flimsy fence and started to climb a climbing frame, which collapsed due to poor workmanship. She was badly injured. A notice on the fence stated in large red letters, 'WARNING — DANGER — KEEP OUT'.

Meanwhile, Jane was walking along the river bank in her high-heeled shoes when she decided to take a photograph of the park. As she focused the camera, Jane took a step backwards, slipped on the wet grass, fell into the river and was nearly drowned.

Maria climbed on to the roof of the cafe intending to gain access to the stockroom through a skylight and steal cigarettes. The roof was badly in need of repair and part of it collapsed, injuring Maria and ripping her leather jacket. This was the fourth time the cafe had been burgled in six months.

Advise Kate, Jane and Maria about any claims they may make under the Occupiers' Liability Acts.

Commentary

This type of question will be found in the problem section of the Oxford board examination paper, or as part of a scenario on the AEB paper. The question covers the area of occupiers' liability and requires knowledge and understanding of the requirements of the Occupiers' Liability Acts 1957 and 1984 and the common law. Once the issues have been identified, the emphasis should be on how the law applies to the problem. The key points should include:

- an explanation of who is a visitor and who is an occupier

- an explanation of the common duty of care under the 1957 Act

- liability to Kate — joint liability of the Council and Leo Engineering; children; independent contractors; warnings

- liability to Jane — the Council's duty to visitors; natural dangers

- liability to Maria — Ian's duties under the 1984 Act; illegality; consent.

Suggested Answer

Kate and Jane may have claims under the Occupiers' Liability Act 1957, as they are lawful visitors; but Maria is a trespasser and outside the 1957 Act, but may be within the Occupiers' Liability Act 1984. The meaning of the terms 'lawful visitor' and 'trespasser' will be explored further below.

Kate has implied permission to be in the park and as such is a lawful visitor. She does not have permission to go on to the play area site and thus could be classed as a trespasser there. But if a child is attracted to something which is classed as an 'allurement', the child will be treated as a visitor. Kate is therefore owed the 'common duty of care' under the Occupiers' Liability Act 1957, s. 2(1). This is a duty to take such care as is reasonable to see that the visitor is reasonably safe in using the premises for the purpose for which he or she is invited. With children this duty is modified by s. 2(3)(a), which provides that an occupier must be prepared for children to be less careful than adults.

Clearly a nine-year-old child may be attracted to a partly built play area. In *Glasgow Corporation* v *Taylor* [1922] 1 AC 44, the Corporation were held liable for a seven-year-old child who ate some poisonous berries in a public park and died. It may be argued that Highshire Council should have foreseen that children playing in the park would be likely to go into the play area site. Kate would be treated as a visitor on the site. One problematic issue is Kate's age. If children are very young the law expects their parents to look after them. In *Phipps* v *Rochester Corporation* [1955] 1 QB 450, parents were held responsible for a child of five years of age who was injured on a building site, where he had gone with his seven-year-old sister. Is Kate within this category of very young children, or is she mature enough to go off on her own? The cases have not clarified this distinction. In *Simkiss* v *Rhondda BC* (1983) 81 LGR 460, the defendant Council, who owned a hill, were held not liable for injury to a seven-year-old girl, who was allowed to slide down the hill by her father. If the father considered it safe, the defendants could not be held liable. Kate's mother, Jane, considers Kate old enough to go off to buy ice-creams, and it may be argued therefore that Highshire Council cannot be liable. But the courts favour children in such circumstances.

Even if Kate is a visitor, who will be liable for her injuries? Who is the occupier of the play area site? Although Highshire Council own the site, the law accepts that there may be more than one occupier. In *Wheat* v *Lacon* [1966] AC 552, both the manager and the brewery were treated as occupiers of a public house. The important factor is the control which a party has over the site, and it is possible for both Highshire Council and Leo Engineering to be occupiers in this sense. In *AMF International Ltd* v *Magnet Bowling Ltd* [1968] 1 WLR 1028, both the contractor and the owner of a building site were held to be occupiers.

Another relevant provision is the Occupiers' Liability Act 1957, s. 2(4)(b), which provides that if damage is caused due to faulty work by an independent contractor, the occupier will not be liable if he has acted reasonably in the circumstances. In deciding whether Highshire Council have acted reasonably the questions are asked whether it was reasonable to give the work to an independent contractor, whether they checked that Leo Engineering Ltd were competent, and whether they checked that the work had been done properly. It seems reasonable to give this type of work to an independent contractor rather than to Council staff, as the contractor provides expertise and it is now common practice for councils to contract out work. Leo Engineering Ltd may be a reputable firm and we are not told anything to the contrary. Presumably the Council carried out checks. As the work has not been finished the Council cannot carry out a final check that it has been done properly, but do they have to supervise the work in order to fulfil their common duty of care? Normally, if a competent contractor has been chosen then there will be no need to supervise the carrying out of the work, but here the Council know that the park is popular and that visitors may be going near the site so a duty to supervise the work could arise. It is unlikely that a court would impose such a high duty of care on the Council, however.

As regards the warning, s. 2(4) provides that if a visitor has been given a warning this will not avoid liability unless in all the circumstances it is enough to make the visitor reasonably safe. The courts apply a subjective test. Is saying 'DANGER — KEEP OUT' enough to make Kate safe? It is unlikely that a nine-year-old would appreciate the meaning of the warning. Neither is Kate likely to be regarded as consenting to the risk. The occupier would have to do more to fulfil its duty, and putting up a flimsy fence which a child can climb through is unlikely to be enough to satisfy this. Leo Engineering are therefore in breach of their common duty of care and liable for the injuries to Kate.

Jane has implied permission to be in the park and is a lawful visitor under the Occupiers' Liability Act 1957. Highshire Council own and control the park and are therefore the occupiers. Jane is owed the 'common duty of care' by the Council, which is a duty to see that she is reasonably safe for the purposes she is invited. Jane has suffered injury from falling into the river, but are the Council in breach of the common duty of care? In deciding this similar factors are taken into account as in deciding if there has been a breach of duty in negligence. For example, would the Council be under a duty to fence off the river? This may be required if there is a particularly dangerous stretch of water, but we are not told that it is dangerous. It would be too costly to fence the entire length of the river and it would seem unlikely that the Council would have to do this. Should the Council have erected warning notices to tell people that the river bank was dangerous? In *Cotton v Derbyshire Dales DC* (1994) *The Times*, 20 June the plaintiff was out walking on the defendants' hill and fell over a cliff. It was held that the defendants were not liable as they did not have to provide protection against obvious dangers. It can be argued here that Jane, as a responsible adult, should have realised the danger in stepping backwards on a river bank. Even if Jane did establish that Highshire Council were in breach of the common duty of care, Jane may be seen as being contributorily negligent by wearing high-heeled shoes, and her damages would be reduced depending on how much the court would deem her to blame by wearing unsuitable shoes while out walking (Law Reform (Contributory Negligence) Act 1945, s. 2(3)).

Maria would not be a lawful visitor under the 1957 Act, as she is going on to the premises to commit a crime. In *R v Smith and Jones* [1976] 3 All ER 54, Smith was deemed a trespasser even though he stole a television from his father's house, where Smith lived, because in doing so he was exceeding the permission he had been given. Consequently Maria is a trespasser.

The owner and occupier of the cafe is Ian, and the issue arises whether he owes a duty to Maria under the Occupiers' Liability Act 1984. Two questions need to be asked: Does Ian owe a duty to Maria? If he does, what must he do to fulfil that duty? The Occupiers' Liability Act 1984 provides that an occupier owes a duty if:

(a)   he is aware of the danger or has reasonable grounds to believe that it exists;

(b)   he knows or has reasonable grounds to believe that the other is near the danger; and

(c)   the risk is one against which he is expected to give protection.

In applying these requirements to Maria's situation, does Ian know of the danger or should he know of it? We are not told that he knows about the condition of the roof, but surely as the owner he should have noticed it. Given the fact of several recent burglaries, Ian may have reasonable grounds to believe that someone is near the danger. This would be more likely if the other burglars had climbed on the roof. Is the risk one against which Ian is expected to give protection? It may be more difficult for Maria to prove that this requirement is satisfied. Should occupiers have to keep their roofs repaired to prevent injury to burglars?! Some guidance may be obtained from *Revill* v *Newberry* (1995) 139 SJLB 244 (CA), where the plaintiff was breaking into the defendant's shed to steal when the defendant fired a shotgun through a hole in the door and injured the plaintiff. It was held that the plaintiff was not stopped from recovering damages because he was a trespasser, but his damages were reduced by two-thirds because of his contributory negligence. Ian's duty under s. 1(4) of the 1984 Act is to take reasonable care to see that Maria does not suffer injury by reason of the danger. The danger arises from the state of the premises. This raises an issue of causation. If the collapse of the roof was due to Maria's weight, then Ian will not be liable, as the injury was not caused by his breach of duty but by Maria's own act. But we are told that the roof is in poor condition and it was probably likely to collapse anyway. Ian may then be liable as it would create a risk of serious injury. The fact that someone is a trespasser does not mean they are owed no duty in civil law.

One possible defence to Maria's claim is that in going on the roof she accepts the risk of falling through it. In *Titchener* v *BRB* [1983] 1 WLR 1427, in interpreting the Occupiers' Liability (Scotland) Act 1960, which has slightly different wording, it was held that a 15-year-old girl had accepted the risks of injury involved in going on to a railway line through a broken fence. But Maria is not to be taken as accepting the risk of falling through a dangerous roof. Another possible defence that Ian could raise is that of *ex turpi causa*, i.e., that if a claim in tort is based on a criminal act, the claim will fail. Here the injury was suffered in the course of committing a criminal act, but in *Revill* v *Newbery* (above) the defendant was unable to rely on the *ex turpi causa* defence and the

Court said that burglars could not be treated as outlaws. If Maria succeeds in her claim she will be able to claim compensation under the 1984 Act for her injuries only, as the Act does not cover damage to property and so she cannot claim for her jacket.

To conclude: Kate in theory will have a claim against both Highshire Council and Leo Engineering, but is likely to succeed only against Leo Engineering, who are liable as independent contractors. Even though Jane is owed the common duty of care, the Council are not in breach of their duty and are not liable. Maria's claim for her injuries is weak but not impossible.

QUESTION 6

Sue works as a computer technician, diagnosing and solving problems for customers of Tom Ltd, Work is referred to Sue by Tom Ltd and Sue works from home and travels to customers' premises. She is paid according to the number of visits she makes. Sue works from 9am to 5pm, five days a week; Tom Ltd provide her with a van, which has the company name and logo on it, and with all necessary equipment. Her contract with Tom Ltd provides that she is an 'independent contractor'.

Sue was told not to give anyone lifts in the van. She was travelling to see a customer one day when she decided to go to her favourite cafe for a break. While in the cafe she met Una, and agreed to give her a lift. Realising that she was now late for her appointment, Sue started speeding. The van went out of control and crashed. Una was badly injured.

Advise Una.

Commentary

This type of question is found on the Oxford, London (now EDEXCEL Foundation) and Welsh board examination papers, or as part of a larger scenario on the AEB papers. It would take approximately 40 minutes to answer. It requires an understanding of the principle of vicarious liability and the circumstances in which it applies to the employer–employee situation. The key points which should be mentioned are:

- explain the principle of vicarious liability and its effect on Una's claim

- explain and apply the tests used to determine whether Sue is an employee or an independent contractor

- examine whether Sue is acting in the course of employment

- explain the legal effect of the prohibition not to give lifts

- outline the alternative claim in negligence by Una against Sue.

Suggested Answer

The first matter to determine is whether Sue is an employee of Tom Ltd or an independent contractor. If she is an employee, Tom Ltd may be vicariously liable for her actions. (Vicarious liability means that one person is made liable for the actions of another.) What effect, if any, does the ban on giving lifts have? Is Sue is acting in the 'course of employment' at the time of the accident? The answers to these questions will decide who is liable for the injuries to Una.

As a general rule an employer will only be liable for the torts of an *employee*. In determining whether someone is an employee or an independent contractor, the courts have used a number of tests. They ask whether the contract was a 'contract of service' or a 'contract for services'. An employee is employed under a contract of service, whereas an independent contractor has a contract for services. The traditional test is the 'control test', i.e., does the employer tell the person what to do and how to do it? Sue is a skilled person and, although she is told *what* to do since Tom Ltd tell her which customers to go to, it is unlikely she will be told *how* to do her work. Consequently this test of no use here. The 'multiple test' would prove more fruitful. This takes a wide range of matters into account and the court then makes an overall judgment, whether someone is an employee or not. The fact that Tom Ltd provide the van and equipment, and the fact that the van has the company name on it, would be evidence that Sue is an employee. She also works fixed hours, which again is indicative of her being an employee. Sue does not seem to take any business risks, which is further evidence that she is an employee. But other factors suggest that she could be an independent contractor. Working from home would suggest this, but travelling to customers would be the same even if she was an employee based at Tom Ltd's office. The fact she is paid per visit also suggests that she is an independent contractor, as they are paid on the basis of the work they do. But we are not told when Sue is paid, i.e., weekly, monthly etc., and payment at regular periods would suggest an employee. Her contract describes her as an independent contractor but this is not conclusive of that fact, although it will be taken into account by the court. In *Ferguson* v *Dawson* (1976) 8 Build LR 38, it was expressly agreed that a labourer on a building site would be self-employed, but he was held to be an employee as he was still treated in the same way as other employees.

There is evidence from the above that on balance Sue is an employee, as most factors point to that. Sue's position may be distinguished from that of the lorry driver in *Ready Mixed Concrete v Minister of Pensions and National Insurance* [1968] 2 QB 497, who was held to be an independent contractor, the important factors in reaching this decision being that he owned the lorry and took the risk of loss.

Sue crashed the van while speeding. As a driver she owed a duty of care in the tort of negligence to other road useres, which includes passengers (*Nettleship v Weston* [1971] 2 QB 691 (CA)). She has clearly breached this duty and caused injuries to Una, who could take action in negligence against Sue. An employer is vicariously liable for torts he has authorised, but there is no evidence here that Sue has been told to ignore speed limits when travelling to see customers. Employers are also vicariously liable for torts committed in the 'course of employment'. Was this accident in the course of Sue's employment? The courts adopt a test, that an act is within the course of employment if it is a way, although a wrongful way, of carrying out the authorised act. The fact that Sue has driven negligently does not mean the accident is outside the course of employment. In *Century Insurance v Northern Ireland Road Transport Board* [1942] AC 509, a driver who smoked while delivering petrol and caused an explosion, was held to be doing an authorised act in a negligent way and the employer was found to be vicariously liable.

Does the fact that Sue was expressly told not to give lifts mean that the employer cannot be liable? The law allows the employer to put limits on the sphere of employment, i.e., on the things the employee is employed to do, but not on the way of carrying out the work within the sphere of employment. This can be illustrated by the bus cases. In one the employer was held not liable for a bus conductor who drove a bus and caused an accident, which was treated as outside his sphere of employment (*Beard v London General Omnibus Co.* (1900) 2 QB 530). But in another case the employer was held vicariously liable for the actions of a bus driver who caused an accident while racing another bus, which was against instructions but was regarded as doing his job, driving, in a wrongful manner (*Limpus v London General Omnibus Co.* (1862) 1 H & C 526. Telling Sue not to give lifts may be seen as restricting the manner in which she carries out the work, rather than as limiting the sphere of employment. Some old cases like *Twine v Beans Express Ltd* (1946) 175 LT 131, though, have interpreted such restrictions as limiting the sphere of employment. Giving an unauthorised lift was classed as outside the course of employment, so that the employer was not vicariously liable. However, in *Rose v Plenty* [1975] 1 CR 430, the Court of Appeal held that a prohibition on a milkman not to give lifts did not affect the sphere of employment but simply the way of carrying out the job. The milkman paid a 13-year-old boy to help him with deliveries, and the boy was injured while riding on the milk float due to the negligence of the milkman. Consequently the employer was held vicariously liable. It may be argued that *Rose* v *Plenty* would be followed, as earlier cases are too restrictive against plaintiffs. Even though giving a lift to Una is against her instructions, Sue may still be regarded as acting within the course of her employment.

One other difficulty is that the accident happened after Sue had visited a cafe. This raises the issue of whether Sue was on a 'frolic of her own'? When she set out on the journey, travelling to a customer was within the course of employment, given the nature of Sue's work. But by visiting the cafe, does this take her out of the course of employment? The case law on this point is inconclusive and contradictory. The crux of the issue is whether Sue can be seen as embarking on an independent journey. We are not told whether the cafe is on her route or some miles off route. In *Harvey* v *O'Dell* [1958] 2 QB 78, going five miles for a meal during working hours was held to be within the course of employment. In *Smith* v *Stages* [1989] AC 928, Lord Lowry stated that a deviation or interruption of a journey undertaken in the course of employment, will take the employee out of the course of employment unless it is incidental to the journey. It can be argued here, that unless Sue has travelled a long way off route and stopped at the cafe for a long period of time, taking a short break is merely incidental to her journey and therefore she is still acting in the course of employment.

Una would be able to show that Sue is an employee, that she was acting in the course of her employment at the time of her negligent driving, and that Tom Ltd are therefore vicariously liable. They would have to pay damages to Una for her injuries. If an employer is made vicariously liable for the tort of an employee, the employer has a right of indemnity against the employee (*Lister* v *Romford Ice* [1957] AC 555. This is unlikely to happen here, as Tom Ltd will be insured. If Sue was seen as an independent contractor, Tom Ltd would not be vicariously liable and Una would have to claim against Sue for negligence.

QUESTION 7

Mrs Amanda Jones owns and runs the Waterhole Hotel which is situated in a small town in the south of England. Cybil was employed as a waitress at the hotel, but after a disagreement with Amanda, Cybil was dismissed. When Cybil was leaving she said to Amanda's husband, Brian, 'Amanda's no better than a prostitute and the food she cooks is poisonous'. Amanda Jones had often been seen by other staff, leaving the rooms of male guests early in the morning. The previous year Amanda Jones had been convicted of selling food which was unfit for human consumption after an outbreak of salmonella amongst guests staying at the hotel.

Cybil also wrote a letter to Don, the editor of the local paper, in which she set out the same allegations. The next edition of the paper contained an article on local hotels, in which the allegations were repeated under a headline 'Amanda — the most popular girl in town'.

A barmaid at another hotel in the town, Miss Amanda Jones, has complained that since the article appeared in the newspaper some of her friends believe it refers to her.

Advise both Mrs Amanda Jones and Miss Amanda Jones of any claims they may make for defamation.

Commentary

Problem questions based on defamation are found in the Oxford, London (now EDEXCEL Foundation) and Welsh board examination papers but not in AEB papers as the syllabus does not include defamation. This question requires a knowledge and understanding of the tort of defamation. It needs an explanation of the basic principles of defamation and their application to this question. It is also important to consider any relevant defences. Key points should include:

- the definition of defamation

- the distinction between libel and slander

- the three requirements to prove defamation — that the statement is defamatory; that it referred to the plaintiff; and that it was published.

- identification of the possible claims by Mrs Amanda Jones against Cybil and Don

- identification of the claims by Miss Amanda Jones against Don and possibly Cybil

- application of the defences of justification and qualified privilege, and offer of amends.

Suggested Answer

This involves a consideration of the tort of defamation, which protects a person's interest in their reputation. Defamation is the publication of an untrue statement which exposes a person to hatred, ridicule or contempt, or causes him or her to be shunned or avoided by right-thinking members of society. Here Mrs Amanda Jones has possible claims for defamation against Cybil and Don, while Miss Amanda Jones may claim against Don. Defences of justification and qualified privilege may be raised in the case of Mrs Amanda Jones, and an offer of amends may be made to Miss Amanda Jones. Each of these matters will be discussed in further detail below.

Mrs Amanda Jones's first claim would be against Cybil. Defamation takes two forms, libel and slander. Libel covers a statement in a permanent form, and slander a statement in a transient form. The oral statement made by Cybil to Brian could constitute slander, and it contains two possible defamatory statements: (i) that Amanda is like a prostitute, and (ii) that the food is poisonous. To prove defamation Amanda has to establish:

(a)   that the statement is defamatory;

(b)   that the statement referred to her; and

(c)   that the statement was published.

Normally slander is not actionable *per se* and actual damage must be proved. Exceptions to this rule include an imputation of unchastity in a woman and unfitness for a business being carried on, which are actionable *per se*. If Amanda could establish that these applied here she would not need to prove actual damage. Saying that Amanda is no better than a prostitute clearly imputes unchastity, and the statement about the food suggests that Amanda is unfit to run an hotel. Amanda therefore would not have to prove actual damage.

To determine whether the words are defamatory, they are given their ordinary and natural meaning. The test used by the courts is, 'Would the words tend to lower the plaintiff in the estimation of right-thinking members of society generally?' (*per* Lord Atkin in *Sim v Stretch* [1936] 2 All ER 1237). Would Amanda be lowered in the opinion of a right-thinking member of society by the allegation that she was no better than a prostitute? Although some people might not regard this as defamatory, in the eyes of a right-thinking member of society such an imputation would lower Amanda's reputation. Similarly the statement about the food suggests that Amanda is unfit to operate such a business, and again right-thinking members of society would tend to think less of her. The statements to Brian must refer to Amanda his wife, as we are not told of anyone else called Amanda at the hotel. The requirement that the statement is 'published' simply means that another person apart from the plaintiff is told about it, and telling the plaintiff's husband is sufficient.

As regards the letter written by Cybil to Don, this contains the statements in a permanent form and would be classed as libel. The statements are defamatory, as explained above, as they would tend to lower the reputation of Amanda. The second matter to prove is again that the statement referred to Amanda, and presumably in the letter Cybil identified Amanda by her surname or by reference to the actual hotel. The statement has been published by Cybil sending the letter to Don. When the article is printed in the newspaper, Don (the editor) and the reporter will both be liable to Amanda for libel. The statements are defamatory, refer to Amanda, and they have been published.

Normally, if a defamatory statement is repeated by someone else this would break the chain of causation, but here it is arguable that Cybil is liable for the later republication by Don. It was reasonably foreseeable that if she made a statement to a newspaper, it would be repeated by the newspaper. In *Slipper* v *BBC* [1991] 1 QB 283, the defendants were held liable for defamation in a television programme *and* for later newspaper articles which repeated the defamation.

The claim for defamation by Miss Amanda Jones will be against Don for libel, which is contained in the article written in the newspaper. It has been shown that the statements are defamatory and that they have been published to third parties, i.e., anyone who buys the newspaper. The third requirement is that they must be shown to have referred to the plaintiff. Miss Amanda Jones would have to prove that someone who knew her would believe that the article referred to her. It is immaterial that the editor did not intend to refer to Miss Amanda Jones. In *Hulton* v *Jones* [1910] AC 20 the defendants published a fictional article which defamed a character called Artemus Jones. By chance the plaintiff had the same name as the character, and he was able to prove that someone who knew him thought that the article referred to him. Miss Amanda Jones will be able to prove that some of her friends thought the article referred to her, and consequently she will have established libel.

The first defence open to Cybil against Mrs Amanda Jones is that the defamatory statement is true, which is known as justification. The burden of proof is on the defendant, Cybil, to prove that the statement is true. The statement may be treated as two separate ones. The statement about Amanda being like a prostitute could be shown to be true by Cybil bringing witnesses to relate Amanda's activities. It is sufficient to prove that the statement is substantially true and Cybil could do this. The statement that the food is poisonous refers to the present time and would be difficult to justify on the basis of the earlier conviction. The defence of justification is therefore likely to fail on this point. The fact that Cybil may have been motivated by malice because she was dismissed is immaterial to the validity of the defence of justification.

A second possible defence open to Cybil is qualified privilege. Cybil must show that she has a legal, moral or social duty to make the statements, and that Brian has a reciprocal interest in receiving them. In *Watts* v *Longsdon* [1930] 1 KB 130 the defendant showed a letter about Watts to Mrs Watts which alleged that Watts had had an affair with his housemaid. The defendant claimed qualified privilege. It was held that as a general rule it is not desirable to interfere between man and wife, and there was no moral or social duty on the defendant to tell Mrs Watts about these unsubstantiated allegations. It could be argued that this case can be distinguished from Cybil's situation, as the allegations about Mrs Amanda Jones leaving guests' bedrooms are more than rumour and could be proved. Cybil could argue that there is a duty to tell Brian and that he has an interest in knowing. As regards the statement about the food being poisonous, Cybil could argue that she was under a public duty to give information about unfit food to Brian, so that he could take appropriate action. One problem that Cybil would face is that the defence of qualified privilege only protects statements made without malice. Malice means making statements knowing they are false, or not caring or acting from personal spite. Cybil has just been dismissed by Mrs Amanda Jones and could be seen as acting from malice.

Don may have a number of defences open to him against Mrs Amanda Jones. Don cannot rely on the fact that someone gave him the information; it is up to Don to check the validity of such statements. Don's position is similar to Cybil's as regards justification, and the same arguments apply. But the defence of qualified privilege would not be available to Don for the statement about the food, as telling the public at large would be acting in excess of that privilege.

As regards Miss Amanda Jones's claim, Don may make an offer of amends under the Defamation Act 1996, s. 2. This would involve printing an apology and paying damages. If the offer was not accepted, Don would have a complete defence unless the plaintiff could show that Don knew or had reason to believe that the statement referred to her and that it was defamatory. However, Amanda would be unlikely to be able to prove that here.

In conclusion, Mrs Amanda Jones will have successful claims against both Cybil, for slander and libel, and Don, for libel, as regards the food. Miss Amanda Jones will be able to sue Don for libel over the statements made in the newspaper. The claims must be brought within one year of the accrual of the right of action (Defamation Act 1996, s. 5, amending the Limitation Act 1980).

QUESTION 8

Ron, an industrial chemist, lived alone for 20 years in a house in a docklands area, part of which was being redeveloped for private housing. He believed that a new fuel was needed to replace oil and spent much of his leisure time experimenting with chemicals in his garden shed, often working late into the night. Clouds of black, acrid smoke frequently drifted over nearby houses, and occasionally a loud bang could be heard coming from the shed. Tina owned the house next door and her father, Sid, who was an old man, had recently come to stay with her. Both Tina and Sid had their sleep disturbed by Ron's activities, and Sid had also developed a chest infection as a result of inhaling the smoke.

On one occasion an explosion blew a hole in the shed roof and injured Ron. Burning fuel from the explosion landed in Una's garden, which backed on to Ron's garden, and several of Una's prize rose bushes were destroyed. Ron was taken to Willow Hospital Trust casualty department, where he was examined by Dr Viv, a junior hospital doctor, and detained for a week for treatment.

While in hospital, Ron arranged for Tina to sort out his house ready for his return, but warned her to be careful in the garden as the debris from the explosion had not been cleared up. While preparing the house, Tina decided she would put an end to Ron's experiments and dispose of the remains of his equipment. As she walked towards the shed, she fell into a pit, which Ron used for his experiments. Tina was injured and her clothes were torn.

After returning home Ron was re-admitted to hospital, complaining of pain in his right eye. On examination, a splinter of glass from the explosion was discovered in his eye and surgery was needed to remove the glass.

(a) Discuss any claims which may be made in nuisance in the above scenario. (20 marks)

(b) Advise Ron of any claim he may have in negligence in respect of the splinter of glass. (10 marks)

(c) Discuss Ron's liability, if any, to Tina as regards her falling into the pit. (10 marks)

(d) Explain what is required to establish liability under *Rylands* v *Fletcher* and discuss whether the rule applies in the above scenario. (10 marks)

(e) Explain which courts would hear the cases arising from the above incidents, including any appeals which might be made. (10 marks)

Commentary

This question is similar to those found on the AEB examination paper, and it is wide-ranging in scope covering most of the tort syllabus. These questions may also cover matters from paper 1, such as the courts, precedent and statutory interpretation. Here the question contains a mix of problem and essay questions, and it would take approximately 90 minutes to answer them all. Individual parts would be similar either to a full tort question, or to part of such a question on the Oxford board paper. The key points which should be mentioned are:

Questio 8(a)

- definition of private nuisance and explanation of physical damage and interference with enjoyment

- explanation of factors relevant to determine if use reasonable — locality, duration, time of day, public utility and sensitivity

- the need for the plaintiff to have an interest in land

- the possible defences for Ron — public benefit and prescription

- explanation of public nuisance and application to the bangs and the smoke

- remedies of damages and injunctions.

Question 8(b)

- explain the requirements of negligence — duty, breach and damage

- explanation of the standard of care and the *Bolam* test

- consideration of the principle of *res ipsa loquitur*

- application of the principle of vicarious liability to the Willow Hospital Trust.

Question 8(c)

- explain the common duty of care owed to visitors under the Occupiers' Liability Act 1957 and who is an occupier

- consider the position of Tina as a visitor — going outside her permission, effect of warnings

- explain the requirements for liability under the Occupiers' Liability Act 1984 and how they apply to Tina

- consider the defences of consent and contributory negligence.

Question 8(d)

- explain the principle of *Rylands* v *Fletcher*

- outline the requirements for *Rylands* v *Fletcher* to apply

- application to Sid (the smoke) and Una (burning fuel).

Question 8(e)

- explain the circumstances in which the various civil claims may be made in the county court and High Court

- examine the grounds of appeal to the Court of Appeal and House of Lords

- criminal prosecution for public nuisance in the magistrates' court

- examine the grounds and routes of appeal in criminal cases.

Suggested Answer

(a)   Claims for private nuisance may be brought by Tina in respect of the
bangs and the loss of sleep, and possibly for the smoke; by Sid for loss of sleep
and his chest infection; and by Una for the damage to her roses. Ron may be
able to rely on the defences of prescription or public utility. There may also be
grounds to bring a prosecution for public nuisance as regards the smoke, and
for alternative claims in public nuisance by Sid for his chest infection and by
Una for her roses. Each of these points will be discussed in further detail below.

A private nuisance is an unlawful act which indirectly causes physical injury
to land, or substantially interferes with enjoyment of land and which is
unreasonable in all the circumstances. The smoke could constitute a private
nuisance by interfering with Tina's enjoyment of land, although we are not told
that Tina complains about this. Tina has had her sleep disturbed by Ron's
experiments, and the loss of sleep is treated as interfering with her enjoyment
of land. Whether Ron's activities amount to a nuisance will depend on how
'reasonable' they are in the circumstances, and this is judged by 'what is
reasonable according to the ordinary usages of mankind living in society'
(*Sedleigh-Denfield* v *O'Callaghan* (*above*), *per* Lord Wright). This is an
objective test and is not judged from the plaintiff's point of view but that of the
'reasonable man'. In determining this the courts take a number of factors into
account. The locality is important and the standard expected will vary. In
Sturges v *Bridgeman* (*above*), it was said that, 'what would be a nuisance in
Belgrave Square would not necessarily be so in Bermondsey'. As Ron lives in
a docklands area, one would expect a certain level of noise, but if the bangs
from the shed were above this level the noise could still be nuisance. If Tina
lives in the part being redeveloped for private housing, this will strengthen her
claim. The nature of an area may change, as in *Gillingham Borough Council* v
Medway Dock Co. Ltd [1992] 3 WLR 449, and loud bangs are less acceptable
in a residential area. Another factor is the duration of the interference, and as
a rule of thumb the longer the interference, the more likely it will be a nuisance.
Here the bangs happen only 'occasionally', but in *Andreae* v *Selfridge* (*above*)
it was held that the loss of one night's sleep amounted to a private nuisance, so
it could be argued a few bangs are sufficient. The fact that Ron worked late at
night would also point to it being a nuisance, as in a residential area the
reasonable man would be in bed late at night.

To be able to bring a claim in private nuisance the courts have traditionally
required the plaintiff to have an interest in land. In *Malone* v *Lasky* [1907]
2 KB 141, Mrs M was injured when vibrations from next door caused a toilet

cistern to fall on her. But her claim in nuisance failed as the tenancy was in her husband's name. In *Khorasandjian v Bush*, the majority of the Court of Appeal said that it was a sufficient interest if someone occupied premises as a home. But in *Hunter v Canary Wharf Ltd* (*above*), the House of Lords overruled *Khorasandjian v Bush* and held that an action in private nuisance may be taken only by a person with a right to the land affected. As Tina owns the house she has the right to sue Ron, the creator of the nuisance.

Sid's claim for loss of sleep involves consideration of the same factors as in Tina's claim, above. Ron may be able to argue that Sid is unduly sensitive because he is old and may be easily disturbed by noise. If this was established then the the bangs would not be a nuisance. However, if the noise levels would have disturbed the reasonable man, Sid may have a claim. In *Heath v Mayor of Brighton* (1908) 98 LT 718, buzzing from the defendant's electricity station was held not to be a nuisance to the vicar next door, as no one else had complained. Sid cannot claim compensation for his chest infection, as damages are not given for personal injury arising from nuisance. As mentioned above, to bring a claim in nuisance a person has to have an interest in land and this could be a stumbling block for Sid. If Sid is just visiting Tina this would not give him the right to sue; but even if he has moved into Tina's house permanently, Sid would not be able to show that he had exclusive possession and would not have the right to sue following *Hunter v Canary Wharf* (above).

In Una's case, her claim is for physical damage to land. Although this is a single escape, it arises from the activities carried on by Ron. The nuisance consists of physical damage to the roses, which are treated as part of the land. Locality is irrelevant in deciding if physical damage is a nuisance. In *St Helens Smelting Co. v Tipping* (1865) 11 HL Cas 642, the plaintiff successfully obtained compensation in nuisance for damage to his trees caused by fumes from the defendant's factory.

Ron could put forward two defences to the claims in nuisance. First, he could say that his activities are beneficial to the public. In *Adams v Ursell* [1913] 1 Ch 269, steam from a fish and chip shop was held to be a nuisance despite the defendant arguing that the shop was a benefit to the public. It is unlikely that such a defence would succeed here, particularly as any benefit seems speculative at this stage of development. Secondly, the defence of prescription might apply. This provides a complete defence if the nuisance has been carried on for 20 years. Although Ron has lived in the area for that time, it is important that the activity has been a nuisance throughout that preiod. This would depend on whether neighbours have lived nearby for the 20 years; and if the houses have been redeveloped only recently then the defence would not apply. In *Sturges* v *Bridgman* (above) the defendant cake maker had been operating for over 20 years. The plaintiff doctor then built consulting rooms next door. The defendant had not been committing a nuisance for 20 years but just from the time the consulting rooms had been built, and therefore the defence of prescription failed.

Some of Ron's activities may amount to a public nuisance. A public nuisance is a crime. It has been defined as an act or omission 'which materially affects the reasonable comfort and convenience of life of a class of Her Majesty's subjects' (Romer LJ in *Attorney-General* v *PYA Quarries* [1957] 2 QB 169). It is essentially an interference with public rights, and the prosecution is brought by the Attorney-General on behalf of the public. For action to be taken in public nuisance, there must be substantial harm to a 'class' of the public. For an individual to claim in tort based on a public nuisance, that person must show that he or she has suffered 'special damage' above that suffered by the public or class affected. The noise here may be substantial as it consists of loud bangs; it may be difficult to show that it affected a 'class' of people, though, as we are only told about Tina and Sid. If they are the only ones affected, public nuisance will not have been established. If sufficient people to constitute a 'class' have been affected, Tina and Sid may argue that they have suffered particular damage because of their loss of sleep. Similarly with the smoke, which seems to be substantial, but again the query is whether a 'class' of persons has been affected. In *R* v *Shorrock*, there were nearly 300 complaints about an 'acid house party' which went on for 15 hours. If only a few nearby houses are affected, then no public nuisance has been committed. As the area is being redeveloped, it may be that there are not many residents at the moment. If a public nuisance is established then Sid could bring a claim because he has suffered particular damage, as his chest has been affected.

A one-off explosion may also amount to a public nuisance, and Una would have a claim as she has suffered particular damage. However, she would not be able to claim twice in respect of the same loss.

The remedies available for private nuisance are damages and injunctions. Tina, Sid, and Una would be able to obtain damages as compensation for the nuisances. An injunction could also be obtained to stop Ron continuing with his experiments.

   (b)   Although Ron's initial injury was caused by his own act, he may have a claim in the tort of negligence against the Willow Hospital Trust as a result of the glass being left in his eye. He would have to prove that Dr Viv owed him a duty of care, that she broke that duty and that he suffered damage as a consequence. The rule of *res ipsa loquitur* could help Ron in these circumstances. His actual claim would be against Willow Hospital Trust, which would be liable under the principle of vicarious liability, as an employer is liable for torts of employees committed during the course of employment. All of these matters are discussed further below.

In *Donoghue* v *Stevenson* [1932] AC 562, the plaintiff became ill after drinking a bottle of ginger beer which contained a decomposing snail. The ginger beer had been made by the defendant. The court set out the three requirements for liability to arise in the tort of negligence: that the defendant owed a duty of care to the plaintiff; that the defendant breached that duty; and that the plaintiff suffered damage as a result. The hospital owes a duty of care to Ron when he is admitted, to examine and treat him. Has the hospital broken its duty? The law normally applies the standard of the 'reasonable man', but as the reasonable man does not have medical skills another test is used in such cases. In *Bolam* v *Frien HMC* [1957] 1 WLR 582, the court set out the test that the duty is to reach the standard of the ordinary skilled person with the particular skill under consideration. A doctor will not be negligent if he is following a practice adopted by a competent body of medical opinion. Dr Viv would have to reach the standard of a competent doctor in a hospital casualty department. If such a doctor would have identified the splinter and removed it, then Dr Viv is negligent by omission in failing to carry out a thorough examination. The fact that Dr Viv is a junior doctor would not be a defence, and the hospital would be under a duty to supervise her so that she reached the required standard. Ron has suffered pain as a result and there may be damage to his eye caused by the splinter being left in.

Rather than having to prove negligence, Ron could use the principle of *res ipsa loquitur*, which means 'the thing speaks for itself'. The three conditions for the principle to apply were set out in *Scott* v *London & St Katherine Docks Co.* (1865) 3 H & C 596:

(a)   there is no explanation for the accident;

(b)   the harm does not normally happen if care is taken;

(c)   the instrument causing the accident is in the defendant's control.

If there is an explanation for the failure to notice the glass — for example, the hospital was very busy — then the normal rules of negligence apply. Otherwise the first condition is met. Hospitals do not normally discharge patients with glass in their eyes when they have had a week to find it. The hospital has control over the actions of its staff. In *Cassidy* v *Minister of Health* [1951] 2 KB 343, the rule applied to the plaintiff, who went into hospital with two stiff fingers but left with four. In Ron's case it is likely that *res ipsa loquitur* applies unless the hospital can show there is some explanation for example, the splinter of glass was too small to detect.

Ron's action will not be against Dr Viv but against Willow Hospital Trust under the principle of vicarious liability. This principle holds one person liable for the acts of another, and an employer may thus be held liable for the acts of employees. For the principle to apply, a tort must be committed by an employee, in the course of employment. To satisfy the first requirement, it would have to be shown that Dr Viv was negligent, which may be established. Secondly, it needs to be shown that she was an employee, rather than an independent contractor. The courts have used a nember of tests to determine this question, and under the organisation test Dr Viv would be an integral part of the organisation and hence an employee, following *Cassidy* v *Minister of Health* (above). Lastly, the tort was committed during the course of Dr Viv's work. Consequently Willow Hospital Trust will be liable for the injury to Ron.

(c) Tina may be able to claim under the Occupiers' Liability Act 1957 if she is a visitor; or if she is a trespasser, under the Occupiers' Liability Act 1984. Ron can argue that he has given a warning and is not liable. He may also be able to rely on the defence of *volenti*, or on the partial defence of contributory negligence. Further details of all these matters are given below.

Under the Occupiers' Liability Act 1957, the occupier of premises owes the 'common duty of care' to lawful visitors. Ron is the occupier of the house even though he is not physically present. In *Harris* v *Birkenhead Corporation* [1976] 1 All ER 341, the Corporation were held to be the occupiers of an empty house because they had the right of control over it. Tina would seem to be a lawful visitor because she was given express permission by Ron to be on the premises. Under the 1957 Act, s. 2(2), the common duty of care is a duty to see that the visitor will be reasonably safe in using the premises for the purposes for which they are invited. The first query is over the extent of the permission. It would appear to cover the house and the garden, as Ron has warned Tina about the garden. The common duty of care may be fulfilled by giving a warning, although under s. 2(4) of the 1957 Act a warning in itself will not fulfil this duty unless it is sufficient to enable the visitor to be safe. The warning given by Ron is about the debris left by the explosion and does not mention the pit. The existence of the pit without a warning, leading to the injury to Tina could be a breach of the common duty of care by Ron, but it would depend on how big the pit was and how obvious it was. In *Cotton* v *Derbyshire Dales DC* (1994) *The Times*, 20 June, the court said that there was no duty to warn visitors of an obvious danger, in that case a cliff. A garden pit may not be classed as such an obvious danger. If the pit was clearly visible to someone going into the garden, perhaps they should have avoided it; but as Ron did not tell Tina about it and she suffered damage this could amount to a breach of the common duty of care.

Nevertheless, when Tina went towards the shed, intending to throw away Ron's equipment, it might be argued that she was acting outside her lawful purpose of sorting out the house. In *R* v *Smith and Jones* (1976), Smith burgled his father's house (where Smith lived) and he was treated as a trespasser. Similarly, Tina might be classed as a trespasser, and no duty would be owed to her under the 1957 Act. However, she might have redress under the Occupiers' Liability Act 1984 if she could prove the three requirements for liability:

(a)   that Ron is aware of the danger, which he is, as he uses the pit for his experiments;

(b)   that he would know that Tina is in the vicinity of the pit, as she is sorting out his house and may well go into the garden;

(c)   that the risk is such he should offer protection against it.

It will depend on how big and how deep the pit is, whether Ron should protect trespassers from it.

As regards Tina's claim under the 1957 Act, Ron has two possible defences. First, he could argue that Tina has taken the risk of injury by going near the pit. Under the 1957 Act, s. 2(5), the occupier is not liable for risks accepted by the visitor. Tina did not have to go into the garden, and in fact was going there for an unlawful purpose, so she could be regarded as taking the risk. If this defence was not successful Ron would at least be able to claim that Tina had been contributorily negligent, in going near enough to the pit to fall in. Her damages would then be reduced according to how much the court considered her to be responsible. If Ron was made liable under the 1957 Act he would have to pay compensation both for Tina's injuries and for the damage to her clothing. The defence of consent is also available under the 1984 Act.

Tina may have difficulty in establishing Ron's liability under the 1957 Act, as she could be treated as a trespasser. She may have more chance of success under the 1984 Act, but will be able to claim for her injuries only.

(**d**) The rule in *Rylands* v *Fletcher* imposes strict liability for damage caused by the escape of dangerous things from land. Strict liability means that the defendant is liable even though they have not been careless. The rule can be explained by examining the facts of *Rylands* v *Fletcher* (1868) LR 3 HL 330. The defendant engaged an independent contractor to build a reservoir on his land. When it was finished, water seeped through some disused mineshafts which no one realised were connected to the plaintiff's mine and flooded it. The House of Lords held that the defendant was strictly liable for the damage caused by the escape even though the defendant had not been negligent.

In order to establish liability under *Rylands* v *Fletcher*, the plaintiff must prove the following matters:

(a) the defendant has brought something dangerous on to his land;

(b) it must be something which is likely to cause damage if it escapes;

(c) the activity must involve non-natural use of land, so the defendant will not be liable if the escape is in the course of a natural use ('non-natural' has been interpreted by the courts to mean a use which is out of the ordinary. This will depend on all the circumstances, for example, making bombs in wartime could be a natural use of land);

(d) there must be an 'escape' from land. In *Read* v *Lyons* [1947] AC 156 the plaintiff munitions inspector was visiting the defendants' factory and was injured by an exploding shell. It was held that as there was no escape from land the defendants were not liable under *Rylands* v *Fletcher*;

(e) the damage must be reasonably foreseeable. Since the case of *Cambridge Water Co. Ltd* v *Eastern Counties Leather plc* [1994] 2 AC 264, it must be shown that the defendant knew or should have foreseen that damage would be caused. In the *Cambridge* case, no one could have foreseen that solvent spilt before 1971 would seep through the ground for over a mile and contaminate water in 1983, therefore the defendants were not liable under *Rylands* v *Fletcher*; and

(f) the thing must cause damage.

In the above scenario there are two incidents which may lead to liability under *Rylands* v *Fletcher*—the smoke and the burning fuel. The 'smoke' is brought on to Ron's land in the sense that it is produced from chemicals brought into his garden. Such acrid smoke is likely to cause damage if it escapes. Ron's carrying out experiments with chemicals is unlikely to be classed as a natural use of residential property. (In the *Cambridge Water* case (above), it was stated in the House of Lords that bringing chemicals into a factory in an industrial area was a non-natural use of land.) The smoke escapes from Ron's land and goes over nearby houses. It is reasonably foreseeable that damage will be caused, but one problem may be the type of damage. The smoke causes Sid to develop a chest infection. The law is unclear as to whether damages may be claimed for personal injuries under *Rylands* v *Fletcher*; but although it was not discussed in *Hale* v *Jennings Bros* [1938] 1 All ER 579, the plaintiff was able to recover compensation for injuries caused by the escape of the defendant's chair-o-plane. In applying that case here, Sid should be able to recover. There is no need for Sid to have an interest in land.

As regards the burning fuel, the same factors apply as above. Ron brings dangerous chemicals on to his land, and they are likely to cause damage if they escape. Experimenting with chemicals is likely to be seen as non-natural use of land, although it may be possible to argue that Ron's experiments are for the general benefit of the community. If this was established Ron would not be liable. There is an escape when the explosion occurs. It is reasonably foreseeable that damage will be caused, and in fact damage is caused to Una's roses. Ron will be liable to pay compensation to both Sid and Una.

(e)   The actions which would arise would be both civil and criminal. The civil claims for negligence, nuisance and *Rylands* v *Fletcher*, and under the Occupiers' Liability Acts would go to the civil courts; and any action for public nuisance would be dealt with by the criminal courts.

The civil claims by Tina and Sid for loss of sleep, by Sid for the chest infection, by Una for her roses and by Tina for her injuries in falling into the pit, would not seem to involve claims for large amounts of money. Consequently they would be heard in the county court, which deals with claims in tort under £25,000. In fact if personal injury claims are for under £1,000 they may be dealt with by a district judge under the arbitration procedure.

Ron's claim over the splinter of glass is also likely to be dealt with by the county court, as we are not told that there is any permanent damage. If Ron claims less than £1,000 for his injury the case would be automatically dealt with under the arbitration procedure.

Appeals from the county court may be made to the Court of Appeal (Civil Division) on points of law or fact. The court does not retry the case but acts on the notes from the court below. A further appeal may be made to the House of Lords on a point of law, with the permission of the Court of Appeal or the House of Lords.

If any claim was for over £25,000 it could go to the High Court (Queen's Bench Division), where a single judge tries tort claims. Appeals may be made to the Court of Appeal and appeal is by way of rehearing. A little-used procedure is the 'leapfrog' appeal direct to the House of Lords.

Any criminal case arising from the public nuisance would be tried in the magistrates' court. Appeal may be made to the Crown Court against conviction and/or sentence. An appeal on a point of law would go to the High Court (Queen's Bench Division). Appeals may be made to the Court of Appeal (Criminal Division). Further appeal to the House of Lords may be made if a point of law of general public importanace arises in the case.

6 The Law of Contract

INTRODUCTION

Contract is found in questions of the AEB, NEAB and Oxford boards, and as part of 'The Market' section of the London board (now EDEXCEL Foundation) and in 'The Consumer and the Law' section of the Welsh board papers. All the boards ask candidates to complete four questions in three hours, apart from the AEB where candidates have to answer one big question, with a number of sections, in one and a half hours.

Contract, like tort, is largely a case law subject, but there are now many Acts of Parliament to consider as well. The type of questions which are set are either problems or essays. Problem questions require identification of the issues and application of legal principles and cases to the facts. Essay questions usually require some explanation of the law, along with analysis or criticism of it. Like all law subject areas, it is important for candidates to focus on what the question requires rather than simply writing all they know on a particular topic. To score higher marks more application and analysis is needed.

QUESTION 1

'The courts do not need to look for a strict offer and acceptance in deciding if a binding contract has been made.'

To what extent is this statement true?

Commentary

This is a typical essay question, which requires you to examine the law on what is normally required to form a binding contract, to identify situations when the normal rules do not apply, and to comment on the above statement.

The key points which should be covered are:

- explain the doctrine of offer and acceptance

- identify exceptions to this approach, like acceptance by performance and unilateral contracts

- outline problems arising from the different approaches — artificially imposing offer and acceptance; uncertainty

- look at the actual practice of the courts

- comment on the quotation.

Suggested Answer

A contract is an agreement between two people which the law will enforce. The classical approach of contract law is to look for an *offer* by one party and an *acceptance* of that offer by the other party. An offer is a proposition which is made to someone and which is intended to be binding. The other party must accept that offer as it stands. The need for an offer and acceptance stems from the idea that a contract is a meeting of minds (*consensus ad idem*). In deciding if there has been an offer and an acceptance the courts take an objective approach. Rather than asking the parties what they intended, they take the view of the reasonable man of what the parties have said and done. This approach to forming a contract, of looking for an offer and acceptance, can be seen in such cases as *Pharmaceutical Society of Great Britain* v *Boots the Chemist* [1953] 1 QB 401, where, on the introduction of supermarkets, the question arose whether goods displayed on the shelf constituted an offer. It was held that the customer made an offer at the cash desk, which was accepted by the shop, thus forming a contract. Similarly in *Fisher* v *Bell* [1961] 1 QB 394, a display of flick knives in a shop window was held to be merely an 'invitation to treat', which means that the shop is inviting people to make offers. It is the customer going into the shop who makes the offer, and it is up to the shop whether to accept that offer.

The courts have accepted that this approach cannot cover all situations, and individual judges (notably Lord Denning) have criticised the traditional approach. In *Gibson* v *Manchester City Council* [1979] 1 All ER 972, in the Court of Appeal, Lord Denning said: 'To my mind it is a mistake to think that all contracts can be analysed into the form of offer and acceptance' and went on to say, 'You should look at the correspondence as a whole and at the conduct of the parties ...'. In *Gibson* the council had sent a letter to the plaintiff stating that it 'may be prepared to sell the house to you at ... £2,180', and asking the plaintiff to make an application. The plaintiff sent in his form, but in the meantime the political make-up of the council changed and the new council refused to sell. Lord Denning, in applying his approach to the facts of the case, concluded that there was a contract for the sale of the house, as clearly the council intended to sell and the plaintiff intended to buy. The House of Lords overruled this and said that in the circumstances, with detailed correspondence between the parties, there was no need to depart from the traditional approach. On the facts the council's letter indicating that it 'may be prepared to sell' was not an offer and the plaintiff's application could not be an acceptance, so no binding contract was made. Lord Diplock did accept that in 'exceptional' cases which did not fall into the normal offer and acceptance analysis, it would be possible to depart from the traditional approach.

In *Gibson* Lord Denning relied on the much earlier case of *Brogden* v *Metropolitan Railway Co.* (1877) 2 App Cas 666. Brogden supplied coal to the railway company. The company sent him a draft contract, which Brogden altered and returned. The contract was then put in a desk. Brogden continued to supply coal, but two years later a dispute arose and Brogden argued that there was no binding contract. It was held that Brogden had made a counter-offer by changing the draft contract and that this had been accepted. But the question was when was the counter-offer accepted — when the railway company ordered coal, or when they took delivery of coal? The House of Lords decided that it could have been at either point.

Another early example of a case not fitting the traditional pattern was *Clarke* v *Dunraven* [1897] AC 59, where the owners of two yachts entered a race organised by the yacht club. They were deemed to have made a contract with each other, accepting the rules as binding. Various suggestions have been made to explain this case in terms of offer and acceptance between the competitors for example, that the first competitor makes an offer which is accepted by the second who in turn makes an offer which is accepted by the third and so on. This has been criticised by Treitel, who points out that it would not work unless each competitor knew of the previous existence of competitors. A second suggestion is that when the race starts the competitors make offers and acceptances to each other, but again this has been criticised as unworkable as the competitors would be making cross-offers which do not make a contract.

The courts have also had to deal with unilateral contracts, which do not fit into the normal mould of offer and acceptance. The normal type of contract is bilateral, where each party agrees to do something for the other, which lends itself to offer and acceptance analysis. In a unilateral contract the promisor promises to do something for the other if that other carries out a particular task; but the other party does not have to do that task. In *Carlill* v *Carbolic Smokeball Co.* [1892] 2 QB 484, the company promised to pay £100 reward to anyone who used their smokeballs correctly and still caught influenza. It was argued on behalf of the company that Mrs Carlill had not accepted their offer as no formal acceptance had been received. But the court said that in such contracts, the acceptance consisted of carrying out the required task. Mrs Carlill had done this by purchasing the smokeball and using it according to the instructions, so a binding contract had been made.

The problem of a case which did not fit into the offer and acceptance analysis re-emerged in *Trentham* v *Luxfer* [1993] 1 Lloyd's Rep 25. Trentham were the main contractors to build a factory, and they subcontracted the windows to Luxfer. Luxfer installed the windows and Trentham paid them. Trentham then claimed that there were defects in the windows, but Luxfer argued that there had been no offer and acceptance and therefore no contract. At first instance the judge said that there was a contract and explained it on the basis of offer and acceptance. In the Court of Appeal Steyn LJ did not follow this approach, but said that a contract had been made by performance 'even if it cannot be precisely analysed in terms of offer and acceptance'. In the course of his judgment he said that offer and acceptance would be the mechanism for forming a contract in the majority of cases, but not necessarily in contracts arising from performance. It was significant that the contract had been fully carried out, and it would have been difficult for the argument that there was no contract to succeed even though no precise offer and acceptance could be identified.

The traditional approach has been criticised by some judges. Lord Denning described it as 'out of date' in *Butler Machine Tool Co. Ltd v Ex-cell-O Corporation Ltd* [1979] 1 All ER 965. Lord Wilberforce described it as artificial and restrictive in *New Zealand Shipping Co. v Satterthwaite* [1975] AC 154, where he said:

> English law, having committed itself to a rather technical and schematic doctrine of contract, in application takes a practical approach, often at the cost of forcing the facts to fit uneasily into the marked slots of offer, acceptance and consideration.

In some circumstances it is unrealistic to argue that because there is no offer and acceptance there is no contract, although this conclusion was reached in *British Steel Corporation v Cleveland Bridge & Engineering Co.* [1984] 1 All ER 504, where most of the work had been carried out. The result is that there is no remedy available in contract and the parties would have to look to restitution. The case also illustrates the practice of some businesses to start performance of the contract before a formal agreement has been reached. If the contract is then carried out, should the courts allow one party to say there is no contract based on the 'technicality' that there is no offer and acceptance? In fact, the courts have allowed acceptance to date back to when the work started. In *Trollope and Colls v Atomic Power Construction Ltd* [1962] 3 All ER 1035 the court held that an agreement concluded in 1960 dated back to cover work done in 1959, thus giving the contract retrospective effect. This point was reiterated by Steyn LJ in *Trentham v Luxfer* (above), that for contracts made by performance it is possible to say that the contract retrospectively covers pre-contract performance.

These difficulties illustrate that departing from the traditional approach makes the law uncertain. If the decision of whether a contract is made is based on the intention or conduct of the parties, what must be proved to establish these? The concepts of offer and acceptance at least give the courts some way of establishing agreement. Departing from the traditional approach also creates uncertainty as to the exact time at which the contract was made. For example, in *Trentham v Luxfer*, if the contract was made by performance, when was it deemed to be made — when the work was started or finished, or at some other point?

The practice of the courts shows that they accept that not all contracts can be based on the 'offer and acceptance' model and that some flexibility is needed in determining whether a contract exists. In the majority of cases the courts do need to look for an offer and acceptance, a point which has been emphasised by the House of Lords. Whether *Trentham* v *Luxfer* has a significant effect in moving the courts away from the 'offer and acceptance' model has yet to be seen. In maintaining a balance between certainty and flexibility the courts must be careful not to take the rules of contract formation out of the commercial world they operate in, as to do so would result in their being ignored by business. If the courts become slaves to the doctrine of offer and acceptance this could happen. Atiyah has warned that the law on offers in self-service shops 'is out of touch with modern social conditions', as people would be surprised to learn that goods displayed on a shelf do not constitute an offer.

QUESTION 2

Adam is an accountant, who owns a large accountancy firm. He lives with his French girlfriend, Babs, who came to England a couple of years ago to work as an office cleaner at the firm; but when she went to live with Adam, she gave up work.

Last year Adam, acting on behalf of the firm, made a contract with Chris, under which Chris would supply the firm with personalised stationery for £10,000. Although Chris works from home, he has built up a good business. When Chris contacted Adam to arrange delivery, Adam said 'I'm only paying £8,000 and if you won't sell at that price, we don't want the stationery'. Chris later delivered the stationery.

Adam told Babs that the firm was in debt and that he needed £100,000 or it would have to close down. Adam said that they could raise the money by taking out a mortgage on their jointly owned home. The bank sent Babs to Donna, a solicitor, for independent advice. Babs went with Adam. Donna said to her 'Do you realise what this is?'. Babs glanced at the mortgage document, said that she understood it and signed it without reading it. Adam spent the money on gambling.

Chris now wishes to claim the £2,000 difference from Adam, and the bank wish to take possession of the house.

Advise Adam and Babs.

Commentary

This problem question is the sort found in the Oxford and NEAB examinations, or as part of a larger AEB question. It requires an understanding of the law on economic duress and undue influence, and the ability to apply it in a problem setting. The key points to deal with are.

● explanation of economic duress

● need for an illegitimate threat and no other choice

● effect of time lapse between duress and the claim

● explanation of undue influence,including actual and presumed

● boyfriend/girlfriend — need to prove trust

● effect of third party's undue influence on the bank

● what bank must do to stop undue influence affecting the mortgage.

Suggested Answer

Adam's contract with Chris may be affected by economic duress, but even if this is established there could be a problem over the lapse of time between the duress and Chris taking action. The mortgage between the bank and Adam and Babs may have been made as a result of undue influence by Adam, but this will affect the bank only if they have notice of it and have not taken reasonable steps to see that Babs made the agreement freely. Each of these matters will be discussed in further detail below.

The contract between Adam and Chris raises the possibility of economic duress. Economic duress is economic pressure put on the other party to the contract, which causes that party financial loss. Although the courts recognise that this sort of pressure can make a contract voidable, they have sought to distinguish it from normal commercial pressure. In *The Atlantic Baron* [1979] QB 705, the defendants were building a tanker for the plaintiffs and they refused to finish it unless they were paid 10% more. The plaintiffs paid, as they needed the tanker for a charter which they had already entered. In the circumstances this was economic duress, as the defendants had no right to make this threat and the plaintiffs had no real alternative but to pay. Later cases said there had to be coercion of the will, but in *The Universe Sentinel* [1983] 1 AC 366, Lord Scarman rejected the idea of the will being coerced. There are now two requirements for duress: an illegitimate threat, and no other practical choice open to the victim. Here, Adam has threatened not to accept the stationery, which is a breach of contract and sufficient to be an illegitimate threat, as in *The Universe Sentinel*, where the threatened industrial action was illegitimate. Did Chris have any choice but to agree to Adam's demands? Chris did not protest, which could be seen as acceptance but would not necessarily be so, as Chris might see the situation as hopeless. Chris could sue Adam, who is in breach of contract by not paying the contract price, but this might not be seen as practical, involving waiting months for the money. It may also be worth arguing that Adam's is a large business dealing with a small one, which puts Chris at a disadvantage. Although the common law does not recognise inequality of bargaining power between two trading companies, it may be that Chris is a sole trader and so the case can be distinguished from *CTN Cash and Carry Ltd v Gallaher Ltd* [1989] 1 Lloyd's Rep 229 (CA) where the claim for duress arose from a contract made between two limited companies. In *Atlas Express v Kafco* [1989] 1 All ER 641, the defendants were a small company, who had made a contract with the plaintiffs, a national carrier. The defendants relied heavily on their contract with Woolworths and could not get anyone else to deliver their baskets at short notice. Consequently the defendants' agreement to pay increased delivery charges to the plaintiffs was made under economic duress. In Chris's case the situation is similar, and his position is made worse by the fact that he cannot resell the goods elsewhere, because they are personalised and would be of limited use to anyone else. It would seem that Chris has a strong claim that he acted under economic duress.

The effect of economic duress on the contract is that the contract is voidable and the innocent party can rescind it. But rescission of the contract must be claimed as soon as practical after the pressure has stopped. We are told that this contract was made last year. In *The Atlantic Baron* (above), by waiting for eight months after the contract was completed until claiming, the plaintiff was regarded as affirming the contract and lost his right to rescind. Applying this here may mean that Chris will lose his right to rescission.

For Babs to avoid the mortgage with the bank, the first thing she will have to establish is undue influence by Adam. Undue influence means that one person puts improper pressure on another to make that person enter a contract. Babs may be able to show actual or presumed undue influence. The relationship of

Adam and Babs as boyfriend/girlfriend is not recognised by the law as leading to an automatic presumption of undue influence, as for example with a solicitor and client. It is therefore up to Babs to show that she put her trust in Adam. This may be quite easy to show, as they bought a house together; and as Babs was a cleaner and Adam an accountant, it may be argued that she trusted him in financial decisions. If Babs can establish a relationship of trust, then the presumption of undue influence applies and there is no need to prove actual undue influence. In fact Adam threatening Babs that the firm would be closed if she did not agree to the mortgage, may be sufficient to amount to actual undue influence if this firm is their only source of income, as Babs would be worried they might well lose their income. It must also be shown that the mortgage is to the 'manifest disadvantage' of Babs, as illustrated by *National Westminster Bank* v *Morgan* [1985] All ER 821. It would seem that this agreement is to the disadvantage of Babs as it may lead to her losing her home.

The next question is whether Adam's undue influence over Babs can affect the mortgage given to the bank. In *Barclays Bank* v *O'Brien* [1993] 3 WLR 786 the husband and wife signed a mortgage over their home to cover the husband's business debts, without reading it. The husband told his wife that the mortgage was for a much smaller amount than was the case. The House of Lords said that if the creditor knew that the parties were cohabitants, the mortgage was valid unless there was undue influence or misrepresentation by the husband. The creditor had to take reasonable steps to see that the wife made the agreement freely, otherwise the creditor would be deemed to have constructive notice of the wife's right to avoid the mortgage. These steps required the creditor to tell the wife of the risks, without the husband being present, and to tell her to take independent legal advice. Lord Browne-Wilkinson stated that the same principles apply in all cases where there is an emotional relationship, so they can be applied to Babs and Adam.

Have the bank got actual or constructive notice that Babs signed the mortgage under the undue influence of Adam? The bank do not actually know that Adam has exerted undue influence over Babs, but here the bank may know that they are cohabiting from the deeds to the house, which should put the bank on enquiry. The bank may also be put on enquiry as the transaction is not an obvious advantage to Babs, by putting her home at risk. (Although the bank could argue that it is to her advantage, as it keeps the business going.) Have the bank taken reasonable steps to see that Babs signed the mortgage freely? They sent her to an independent solicitor, but was that sufficient? In *Banco Exterior* v *Thomas* [1997] 1 All ER 46 Mrs D signed a mortgage over her house with the plaintiff bank to guarantee the business debts of M, a friend. The bank sent

Mrs D to a solicitor for advice. It was argued that Mrs D was under the influence of M. It was held by the Court of Appeal that the independent advice rebutted any presumption of undue influence. The bank did not have constructive notice of the undue influence as they were not under a duty to enquire about the relationship of those they did business with. Although the bank have sent Babs to a solicitor, it is not clear whether this has met the requirements outlined above. Adam and Babs went to the solicitor together, and Adam may have been present when the solicitor spoke to Babs, so the advice may not be seen as free from Adam's influence. It does not appear that the solicitor explained the nature and effect of Babs signing the mortgage, and it is not enough to ask her if she understands what it is. But should the bank be responsible for ensuring that the solicitor acts properly? In *Bank of Baroda* v *Rayarel* (1995) 27 HLR 387 the court said that if a bank knew that a customer had been advised by a solicitor, they were entitled to assume that they had been properly advised. Consequently the bank would not have constructive notice of Adam's undue influence. Perhaps it could be argued that as Babs is French, there is a greater duty to see that she understands what she is signing.

One other possible route for Babs to take is to argue that the mortgage is an 'unconscionable bargain'. Equity will set aside an agreement made by a 'poor and ignorant man', and Babs may say that in the circumstances she is in this position. But again the fact she has been given independent advice will defeat this claim. Similarly with Adam's misrepresentation about using the loan for the business when he spent the money gambling; Babs will not be able to claim that knowledge can be imputed to the bank.

To conclude, Chris could establish economic duress, but his claim is likely to fail because he did not act quickly enough after the duress ended. Babs would also have difficulty in sustaining her claim for undue influence because she has been given independent advice.

QUESTION 3

Few untrue statements made before a contract will amount to a misrepresentation because of the strict legal requirements imposed by the law. Discuss.

Commentary

Essay questions of this type are found on the Oxford, NEAB and Welsh board examination papers, or as part of a larger question in AEB examinations. This essay involves examination of what is needed to prove that a statement amounts to a misrepresentation, and also requires explanation of the exceptions to these legal requirements. It also needs some consideration of related areas. Lastly, it calls for an overview of the law and comment on the above statement.

The key points to make are:

- the definition of misrepresentation

- explanation of what is excluded from the definition

- exceptions to the legal requirements

- statement must induce the contract

- overall comment.

Suggested Answer

If an untrue statement made before a contract is a term of the contract, the innocent party will be able to claim for breach of contract. If an untrue statement is not a term, the innocent party will have a legal remedy in certain cases. The main one is if the innocent party can show that the statement is a misrepresentation, and this essay will examine the circumstances in which that may occur. But the law may also provide help if a statement is shown to be a collateral warranty or a negligent misstatement within *Hedley Byrne* v *Heller* [1964] AC 465.

A misrepresentation is a false statement of fact made by one party to a contract to the other, which induces the other party to make the contract. Although this definition seems fairly straightforward, on detailed examination it will be seen that it is quite complex. The statement must be a statement of fact, which must be distinguished from mere 'puffs', statements of law, statements of opinion, statements about the future or silence, none of which can generally be misrepresentations.

A mere puff is a statement about something which is simply 'sales talk', for example, 'this car drives like a dream'. Clearly such statements cannot be said to be true or false. A statement about what the law is cannot be a misrepresentation, as anyone can find out about the law. A statement of opinion is simply based on someone's beliefs and cannot be a misrepresentation because it is not a fact. This may be illustrated by *Bisset* v *Wilkinson* [1927]

AC 177, where the defendant was selling his farm, which had never been used for sheep, and told the plaintiff that it would support 2,000 sheep. Both parties knew that the farm had never been used for sheep. The plaintiff later found that the farm would not support a flock of that size and claimed misrepresentation. It was held that the defendant's statement was merely his opinion, and the plaintiff must have realised this. A promise to do something in the future cannot amount to a misrepresentation if the promise is not kept, as such a statement cannot be a statement of fact. A person making a contract is not under a duty to tell the other party all relevant facts. This is so even if he realises that the other party is mistaken, so the rule is that 'silence is not a misrepresentation'.

It would seem that defining misrepresentation as a statement of fact and as none of the above confines it within narrow limits. However, the law does recognise exceptions to the above rules in certain circumstances. A salesperson must be careful not to make statements which can be proved to be false, for example, 'This car goes at 100 mph'. If a person giving an opinion has special knowledge, the statement can be treated as one of fact, as seen in *Smith* v *Land & House Property Corporation* (1884) 28 ChD 7 (CA). In that case the seller of property described it as let to 'a most desirable tenant', knowing that the tenant was in arrears. It was held that the seller was in a position to know about the tenant and it could be implied he knew facts to justify this statement, so it could be treated as a misrepresentation. Similarly in *Esso* v *Mardon* [1976] QB 801, the plaintiffs made an estimate for sales at a petrol station which was wildly wrong. They argued that this was merely an opinion because there had never been a petrol station on that site, but this was rejected by the court because the plaintiffs had experience and skill in estimating petrol sales. The estimate was a statement of fact and the plaintiff's were in breach of a collateral contract which stood alongside the lease. A promise to do something in the future may amount to a misrepresentation if the person making it had no intention of doing it, because this misrepresents his present intention which is a statement of fact. In *Edgington* v *Fitzmaurice* (1885) 24 ChD 459, the directors of a company obtained loans by saying that they would use the money to expand the business. In fact they always intended to use the loans to pay off existing debts. It was held that the statement was a misrepresentation. There are also a number of exceptions to the rule that silence is not a misrepresentation. A duty to disclose may arise if a statement later becomes false. In *With* v *O'Flanaghan* [1936] Ch 575, the defendant doctor was selling his practice, and in January told the plaintiff that it was worth £2,000 per annum. The sale was not completed until May, when due to the defendant's ill health the value of the practice had dropped to £250 per annum. It was held that keeping quiet about the earlier statement of valuation amounted to a misrepresentation. If a statement is only a half truth there may be a duty to disclose, as in *Nottinghamshire Patent Brick and Tile Company* v *Butler* (1885) 15 QBD 261, where the statement that the vendor's solicitor did not know of any restrictive covenants on the land being sold was true only because he had not read the relevant documents. When the restrictive covenants were discovered the statement was treated as a misrepresentation. If a contract is one of *uberrimmae fidei* (which means of the utmost good faith) there is a duty to disclose. For example, in insurance contracts, each party is under a duty to disclose all material facts to the other party, so that keeping quiet in such circumstances may be a misrepresentation.

The next requirement to establish a misrepresentation is that the statement is made by a party to the contract. If the statement is made by a third party, there is generally no remedy in misrepresentation. However, if the requirements of *Barclays Bank* v *O'Brien* are met and one of the parties has notice or constructive notice of the misrepresentation, the contract may be avoided. In that case the husband misrepresented to his wife that the guarantee she signed with the bank for his business debts was for £60,000, when in fact it was for £135,000. It was held that the guarantee could be set aside. If the false statement is not made by the other party to the contract but by a third party, it may also be possible to establish liability for negligent misstatement under *Hedley Byrne* v *Heller*. This requires proving a 'special relationship' between the person who made the statement and the person who relied on it, which if established provides remedies of damages and rescision.

The misrepresentation must have induced the other party to make the contract. The means that the other party must have placed reliance on the statement in making the contract. The courts apply a subjective test: 'Was this plaintiff induced to make the contract?' (*Museprime Properties* v *Adhill* [1990] 36 EG 114). This is obviously in the plaintiff's favour and extends the circumstances in which a claim may be made for misrepresentation. The rules also provide that the misrepresentation does not have to be the only reason the party entered the contract. It may be one of many, as long as it had some influence on the party making the contract. In *Edgington* v *Fitzmaurice* (above), the plaintiff lent money to the company, but was influenced by the false statement in the prospectus and his own misunderstanding that he would have a charge over the company's assets. He was still able to claim misrepresentation. Another rule which favours the innocent party is that if the innocent party does not bother to check a statement, even if given the opportunity, he may still rely on misrepresentation. In *Redgrave* v *Hurd* (1881) 20 ChD 1, the defendant solicitor was buying a practice from the plaintiff and did not check papers which would have shown that a statement by the vendor was false.

Nevertheless, he could still claim rescission for misrepresentation. One rule works against the innocent party, though, who will not be able to show reliance on the statement made by the misrepresentor if the innocent party relied on his own judgement. In *Attwood* v *Small* (1838) 6 Cl & Fin 232, the buyer of a mine relied solely on his own agent's statement of earning capacity rather than on the seller's statement, and could not therefore claim misrepresentation when the seller's statement turned out to be false. Again, there can be no reliance if the innocent party did not know about the misrepresentation or knew that the statement was false.

The law of misrepresentation allows relief only for statements of fact. But in determining what amounts to a statement of fact the law has drawn the boundaries flexibly and widened the scope of misrepresentation. The requirement of inducement is also less restrictive than it seems. The statement only has to be one reason for making the contract, and there is no need to check it. A party who cannot establish a misrepresentation may be able to show that the statement should be treated as a term or collateral warranty, as was the case in *Esso* v *Mardon*. A party who makes statements before a contract should proceed with a degree of caution or he may be caught by the above rules. The law then provides the remedies of rescission of the contract, which puts both parties back in their original position, and damages.

QUESTION 4

Alex, the secretary of the Northampton University Students Union (NUSU), booked a coach with Carryme Coaches plc, with whom he regularly dealt, to take a party of students to the Grand National in Liverpool. It was agreed that the coach would leave the university at 8.00 am and return at midnight. Alex also bought 50 tickets for the enclosure at Aintree from Aintree Racecourse Ltd and paid £100 deposit. On Friday, the day before the Grand National, heavy rain caused a river alongside the racecourse to overflow, and the racecourse was flooded because the ditches blocked up. Aintree Racecourse Ltd cancelled all racing on Saturday to be on the safe side.

When Alex heard about this later on Friday, he immediately telephoned Carryme Coaches plc claiming that the contract for the hire of the coach was frustrated and saying that the NUSU no longer wanted the coach.

On the tickets from Aintree Racecourse Ltd it stated, 'No liability can be accepted for events cancelled due to industrial action, demonstrations or any other matters beyond our control'. Aintree Racecourse Ltd are now claiming the balance of £400 for the tickets.

Advise Alex.

Commentary

This type of question is found on the examination papers of all the boards apart from the AEB, where it could be part of a larger question. The question requires an understanding of the rules of frustration, including both the common law and statute. If frustration cannot be proved it should be noted that a party which does not carry out its contract will be in breach of contract.

The key points which should be dealt with are:

- outline the doctrine of frustration

- examine whether the contract with Carryme Coaches is radically different — is there more than one purpose?

- examine the contract with Aintree Racecourse — does self-induced frustration apply; what is the effect of the *force majeure* clause?

- apply the Law Reform (Frustrated Contracts) Act 1943.

Suggested Answer

This problem relates to the doctrine of frustration and whether it applies to the contracts for the coach and the tickets to the Grand National. It requires application of the Law Reform (Frustrated Contracts) Act 1943 to the £100 deposit paid for the tickets and consideration of whether Alex has to pay the balance. Other matters to take into account are whether the flood is self-induced and the effect of the *force majeure* clause.

Originally obligations under a contract were absolute and there was no excuse for not carrying them out. In *Paradine* v *Jane* (1647) Aleyn 26, a tenant thrown out of his house by an invading army was still held liable to pay the rent. The courts retreated from this position in *Taylor* v *Caldwell* (1863) 2 B & S 826, which involved the hire of a hall to hold a concert. The hall was burned down before the concert and the courts recognised that performance of the contract had become impossible. It was held that the contract could be regarded as frustrated, and neither party was liable under it. This doctrine was further developed to include situations where performance of a contract became impossible, illegal or radically different after the contract was made.

The contract between the NUSU and Carryme Coaches for the coach has not become physically impossible, as the coach is still available to travel to Liverpool, nor has it become illegal. But has the contract become radically different? It may be argued that the whole 'foundation' of the contract has been frustrated. In *Krell* v *Henry* [1903] 2 KB 740, the defendant hired a room from the plaintiff intending to watch the coronation procession. The procession was cancelled because of the King's illness. Although the defendant could still have sat in the room, the foundation of the contract had been taken away and the contract was frustrated. Even though watching the coronation was not stated as the purpose of the contract, it was understood by both parties that this was the whole basis of the contract. The fact that the cost of the room was £75 also supported this conclusion (see below). Did Carryme Coaches know the purpose of the contract for the hire of the coach? They may have done as the NUSU had used them for similar events. But even if the coach company knew that the students were going to Liverpool to see the Grand National, would this frustrate the contract? Even if the Grand National is cancelled, it may be argued that Alex could still demand that Carryme Coaches take the party to Liverpool, as the students are away for the whole day and the race meeting lasts only a few hours, so visiting Liverpool may be one of their purposes. In *Krell* v *Henry*, Vaughan Williams LJ gave the example of hiring a cab to go to Epsom on Derby Day, saying that if the Derby was cancelled, the hirer could still ask to be taken to Epsom. (In any event, *Krell* v *Henry* may be distinguished from the present case as the price of the room was grossly inflated, and this showed that it was not simply the hire of a room in the normal course of events.)

A similar situation arose in *Herne Bay Steamboat Co.* v *Hutton* [1903] 2 KB 683, where the defendant hired a boat from the plaintiff, 'for the purpose of watching the Naval Review and a day's cruise round the fleet'. The Review was cancelled because of the King's illness and the defendant claimed that the contract was frustrated. The Court of Appeal held that it was still possible to cruise round the fleet and the contract was therefore not frustrated. Thus it would seem that the contract for the hire of the coach is not frustrated here. In these circumstances Alex will be in breach of contract and Carryme Coaches will be entitled to damages, to cover their loss of profit. It is unlikely that they would be able to hire the coach to anyone else at such short notice.

As regards the contract between Alex and Aintree Racecourse, the race cannot be run on a waterlogged course, but does this mean that the contract is frustrated? It may be possible to run the race somewhere else. Simply because a contract becomes more difficult or more expensive to carry out does not mean that it is frustrated. In *Tsakiroglou & Co. Ltd* v *Noblee Thorl GmbH* [1962] AC 93, a contract was made to ship nuts from Port Sudan to Hamburg. The Suez Canal was blocked by the outbreak of war, but the court said that the contract was not frustrated as the ship could have gone round the Cape of Good Hope. But here both parties would understand that the race had to be run on this particular course due to its unique nature, and changing to another race course would not be running the 'Grand National'.

The doctrine of frustration applies only if neither party is at fault. The rule is that self-induced frustration does not amount to frustration. Is the fact the race is not taking place due to the flooding, or because Aintree Racecourse have cancelled it? In *The Super Servant Two* [1990] 1 Lloyd's Rep 1 a contract was made to move a drilling rig, which could be done only by one of two tugs, *Super Servant One* and *Super Servant Two*. The defendants intended to use *Super Servant Two*, and used the other tug for another contract. But *Super Servant Two* sank before the contract was performed and the defendants claimed that the contract was frustrated. It was held that the contract had not been frustrated because it was the defendants' own act which meant that the contract could not be carried out. By cancelling the race 'to be on the safe side', it seems that it is the act of Aintree Racecourse which brings about the event and they would not then be able to claim frustration.

Another possibility is that Aintree Racecourse may have been negligent in not checking or clearing the ditches in the first place, and it was this which led to the flooding of the racecourse. Although the point has not been decided it is unlikely they would be able to claim frustration if they have been negligent. Treitel has argued that negligence by one of the parties should exclude the doctrine of frustration.

The effect of the *force majeure* clause also has to be considered. Such clauses are used by the parties to allocate risks, and in such a case the court follows the clause and the doctrine of frustration does not apply. But does this clause cover the event? It may be argued that it is within 'other matters beyond our control'. If the flooding was not beyond the control of the racecourse, they cannot rely on this clause. Even if the flooding was not the fault of the racecourse and it is considered to be within the wording of the clause, it could be argued that the actual circumstances are more far-reaching than the parties had in mind, so frustration could still apply. In *Jackson* v *Union Marine Insurance Co.* (1874) LR 10 CP 125, even though there was a clause which provided 'dangers and accidents of navigation excepted', when the ship ran aground and was in dock for eight months the contract was treated by the court as frustrated because the clause was not intended to cover such an extensive accident. The strongest argument against the clause is that it could be interpreted according to the *eiusdem generis* rule, that where general words follow particular words, the general words are limited to 'things of the same kind'. Consequently the general words 'other matters beyond our control' would be limited to things caused by the actions of people, like industrial action and demonstrations, and would not cover a natural event like a river flooding. This is assuming for the moment that the flooding is not due to the negligence of the racecourse. Consequently the clause would not apply. It is also likely to be classed as an unfair term under the Unfair Terms in Consumer Contracts Regulations 1994, as it is in a consumer contract which has not been individually negotiated and which tries to exclude the consumer's rights for non-performance in a vague way.

If the contract to go to the Grand National is treated as frustrated, the effect is that the contract automatically comes to an end. The original common law rule was that 'loss lies where it falls' at the time of the frustrating event. The Law Reform (Frustrated Contracts) Act 1943 now provides that in certain circumstances, where it applies, money paid before the frustrating event is recoverable and money owed ceases to be payable (s. 1(2)). The proviso to this is that even where there is a total failure of consideration, the other party may have incurred expenses and the court, if it considers it just and reasonable, may allow recovery of those expenses up to the amount paid or payable. If the parties provide for the effects of frustration the 1943 Act does not apply (s. 2(3)), but here the clause does not cover the event. Alex could reclaim his £100 deposit less an amount for any expenses incurred in printing tickets etc. He would not have to pay the £400 balance, whether it was payable before or after the time of the frustrating event.

In conclusion, Alex's contract with Carryme Coaches is unlikely to be treated as frustrated as the students may still go to Liverpool; and if Alex refuses to carry on with the agreement it will be a breach of contract. The contract with Aintree Racecourse on the other hand can be regarded as frustrated. The burden of proving that the flooding was self-induced is on Alex, and this would be difficult to prove; but the *force majeure* clause is invalid. Alex would be able to reclaim most of his deposit.

QUESTION 5

Ali, Bill and Celia are all 19-year-old students. They go to Nero's Nightclub, which is owned and run by the Students Union. Ali and Bill pay on the door, but Celia is allowed in free as she has a complimentary ticket. A notice near the entrance states: 'The management cannot accept liability for injury or loss to persons using these premises.' The nightclub is dimly lit, and as Celia is going down a flight of stairs she trips on a loose carpet, sprains her ankle and as a result is confined to bed for a week, thus missing her weekend job. Bill, who regularly goes to the club, hands his expensive leather jacket to the cloakroom attendant. He pays £1 and is given a ticket, on the back of which it states: 'Nero's nightclub hereby limit their liability to £25 per item deposited.' When Bill returns to collect his jacket, he discovers that it has been stolen. Ali is sitting at a table when Ellie, a waitress, spills a drink over his new suit, ruining it. Ali did not see the notice at the entrance.

Advise Ali, Bill and Celia of any rights they may have in civil law.

Commentary

Questions on exemption clauses are found on the examination papers of all the boards and as part of the larger questions in the AEB examinations. The topic of exemption clauses lends itself to problem questions. Any such questions now require a knowledge of three sets of rules — common law rules, statutory rules, and the 1994 Regulations. The key points which should be made are:

- Ali's claim — has he been given reasonable notice? does the *contra proferentem* rule apply? what is Ellie's legal position? is the Students Union a charity rather than a business?

- Bill's claim — is the cloakroom ticket a contractual document; is there a regular course of dealing; explain the effect of the Unfair Contract Terms Act 1977, s. 2(2) and s. 11(4), and of the Unfair Terms in Consumer Contracts Regulations 1994

- Celia's claim — is she owed a duty of care in negligence, and the effect of s. 2(1) of the 1977 Act.

Suggested Answer

It is proposed to advise the three parties separately. Ali's claim will depend on whether he has been given reasonable notice and whether the clause covers what has happened. The success of Bill's claim depends on whether the clause is valid or whether he has been given notice before. Celia's claim revolves round the provisions about negligence in the Unfair Contract Terms Act 1977.

Can Ali claim for the damage to his suit, or is he bound by the exemption clause on the notice at the entrance to the club? If Nero's Nightclub wish to rely on the notice they must show that it has been incorporated in the contract made with Ali. They can do this by showing that Ali knows about the notice or that they have given him 'reasonable notice' of it. In *Parker* v *South Eastern Railway* (1877) 2 CPD 416, the plaintiff was given a ticket containing a limitation clause when he handed in his luggage. Although he did not read the ticket, it was held that he had been given reasonable notice of it. Even though Ali did not see the notice at the entrance, he may have been given reasonable notice of it. This depends on a number of factors like when the notice was given, how big the notice was, whether it was in a prominent place, if the notice was illuminated at night etc. If it is an easily read notice, in a prominent place and it is positioned *before* the place where Ali pays, then Ali has been given reasonable notice and it is binding on him, even though he did not actually see it. In *Olley* v *Marlborough Court Hotel* [1949] 1 KB 532, an exclusion notice on the back of the bedroom door of an hotel was held to be ineffective, as the contract was made at the reception desk.

If the exemption clause is regarded as part of the contract, it is still subject to interpretation by the court. The exemption clause could be seen as ambiguous, as the reference to 'injury' could be argued to be referring to bodily injury only rather than to Ali's clothes or possessions. The *contra proferentem* rule provides that an ambiguous exemption clause is interpreted against the party who relies on it. If this is applied the clause is interpreted against Nero's Nightclub and liability will not be limited to injury to persons, so the notice will cover the damage to Ali's suit.

If the exclusion notice is treated as part of the contract and as covering damage to property, it must still satisfy the requirements of s. 2(2) of the Unfair Contract Terms Act 1977. This provides that a person cannot exclude his business liability for damage to property resulting from negligence unless the term is reasonable. Ellie may be regarded as negligent in spilling the drink. In determining whether the exclusion notice is reasonable the relevant matters from sch. 2 of the 1977 Act are likely to be taken into account. If Nero's Nightclub are seen as doing enough to bring the notice to Ali's attention, this would be evidence that it was reasonable. However, the fact it is an individual dealing with a business, and that it would be unlikely Ali could go to another nightclub without such a notice, would show that on balance the notice was unreasonable. Consequently the exclusion notice would be invalid. Nero's Nightclub might be able to argue that the 1977 Act applies only to 'business liability' and as a Students Union body they may qualify as a charity. This point has not been decided and the fact that the club is run like a business could mean that the Act applies.

If Ali's claim against Nero's Nightclub was unsuccessful, Ali could take a personal action against Ellie in negligence. Ellie was not a party to the contract between Ali and Nero's Nightclub and cannot rely on the clause (*Adler* v *Dickson* [1955] 1 QB 158). However, this is not a practical proposition as it may be difficult to establish negligence and Ellie may not be able to pay compensation.

Bill was given the ticket at the time he made the contract for use of the cloakroom, and Nero's Nightclub complies with the rule in *Olley* v *Marlborough Court Hotel* (above) by giving notice before or at the time of making the contract. But in order to give 'reasonable notice' of the limitation clause the ticket must be a 'contractual document', which is something you expect to contain the terms of a contract. In *Chapelton* v *Barry UDC* [1940] 1 KB 532, the plaintiff hired a deckchair and was given a ticket containing an exemption clause. It was held that the ticket was simply a receipt and the clause was not binding. Even if the cloakroom ticket was treated as a contractual document, the fact that the limitation clause is on the back of the ticket might mean that it is not sufficient to bring it to the attention of Bill. However, an alternative way of giving notice of the clause is through a regular and consistent course of dealing. In *Hollier* v *Rambler Motors* [1972] 2 QB 71 it was held that using a garage four times in five years was not sufficient. Bill 'regularly' goes to the club, and depending how often this is — for example, if it was every couple of weeks over a period of months — it may well be sufficient to establish notice through a regular course of dealing. In order for Bill's dealings to be consistent, he would need to have used the cloakroom on these visits and to have been given the same sort of ticket. If this is established, it does not matter that Bill was not given reasonable notice on this occasion, the clause is binding on him.

Once it is established that the clause is part of the contract, the effect of the Unfair Contract Terms Act 1977 needs to be considered. The clause limits liability for damage to property, and under s. 2(2) the clause is subject to a test of reasonableness. The test is that the clause was fair and reasonable at the time the contract was made. As this is strictly a limitation clause, in determining reasonableness, under s. 11(4) the court must take into account the resources available to Nero's Nightclub and whether insurance against this loss was available to them. In assessing reasonableness the court is likely to take into account the factors mentioned in sch. 2 to the 1977 Act, although strictly these apply only to sales of goods. In applying these factors, Bill is in a relatively weak position compared to Nero's Nightclub — he ought to have known of the clause from previous dealings and it is likely that similar clauses are used in other clubs — but the Union have the resources and could insure, so it would seem on balance that the limitation clause is unreasonable. In *St Albans City and District Council* v *ICL* [1996] 4 All ER 487 the defendants limited their liability to the plaintiffs to £100,000. The facts that the defendants were a multi-national company and were insured for £50m against such losses, showed that such a clause was unreasonable and they could not rely on it. The Unfair Terms in Consumer Contracts Regulations 1994 may also apply. This is a consumer contract, but can it be regarded as being made on standard terms? If the cloakroom ticket is regarded as such, is the effect of the clause to cause a significant imbalance in the parties' rights to the detriment of Bill? Limiting liability to £25 for any item of clothing would seem to cause such an imbalance and therefore the clause will be invalid. Bill would then be able to claim the cost of another jacket.

Celia does not have a contract with Nero's Nightclub but she is owed a duty of care in negligence, as covered by s. 1(1) of the 1977 Act. Under s. 2(1) of the Act, a person cannot exclude or restrict business liability for death or injury resulting from negligence. Here Nero's Nightclub are negligent in having a loose carpet and/or dim lighting which has caused the injury to Celia. The exemption clause has no effect and the nightclub are liable in the tort of negligence under the principle laid down in *Donoghue* v *Stevenson* [1932] AC 562. Celia is entitled to compensation for her injury.

It may be, though, that Nero's Nightclub are not acting in the course of a business, because as a Students Union body they may be regarded as a registered charity. In such a case it can be argued that the 1977 Act would not apply and that only the common law rules are applicable. If this is the case Celia may have been given reasonable notice, subject to what has been said above about the position of the notice. The clause would then be binding. In *White* v *Blackmore* [1972] 2 QB 651 the defendants successfully relied on an exclusion notice to protect them from liability for negligence.

Ali, Bill and Celia would all seem to have strong claims against the nightclub, whose only chance of avoiding liability would be to establish that they were a charity.

QUESTION 6

'A promise to perform an existing duty is not valid consideration for a contract.'

To what extent do you agree with this proposition?

Commentary

This requires an explanation of consideration. It should be followed by an examination of the situation where someone agrees to carry out an existing duty as their consideration for a contract. It does not require all the rules on consideration to be discussed, just those about existing duties. It also needs some analysis of these rules and cases to show an appreciation of underlying policies behind some of the decisions of the courts. The key points which should be considered are:

- definition of consideration

- explanation of the rule that consideration must be sufficient

- statutory duties, existing contractual duties and duties owed to third parties

- exceptions to these rules

- the influence of public policy on decisions.

Suggested Answer

Consideration is one of the requirements for a legally binding contract unless the contract is made by deed. Consideration is what each party does or promises to do as their part of the contract. At one time consideration was seen in terms of a benefit given or a detriment suffered. Sir Frederick Pollock defined consideration as follows: 'An act or forbearance of the one party or the promise thereof, is the price for which the promise of the other is bought, and the promise thus given for value is enforceable'. The modern view is based on this, that each party provides something in return for what the other provides. As the doctrine of consideration grew, it developed a number of 'rules', one of which is that 'consideration must be sufficient', which means something the law regards as valid. If someone promises to do something which they are already legally bound to do, that promise is not regarded as 'sufficient' consideration, i.e., as legally valid. Under this rule there are three situations to be considered: an existing duty imposed by the law, an existing duty imposed by a contract, and an existing duty under a contract with a third party. But in applying the rules to cases the courts sometimes seem to 'concoct' consideration, which shows that factors like public policy are at work and that the courts are not simply applying the formal rules.

If someone is under a public duty imposed by the law to do something, carrying out that duty cannot be used as valid consideration for a contract. An example of this can be seen in *Collins v Godefroy* (1831) 9 LJ KB 1158, in which the plaintiff promised to attend court and give evidence, and the defendant promised to pay him six guineas. The plaintiff had been sent a subpoena and was legally bound to attend, so his promise to attend was not valid consideration. The law has recognised that if someone under a public duty does something more than their duty, though, then it will be regarded as valid consideration. In *Glasbrook Bros v Glamorgan CC* [1925] AC 270, where the police provided men stationed on mine premises to protect property during a miners strike, this was regarded as more than their public duty and was valid consideration. Therefore the police were entitled to payment. Another example of someone providing valid consideration in carrying out a public duty can be seen in the case of *Ward v Byham* [1956] 2 All ER 318. The father of an illegitimate child, who had left the mother, promised to pay her £1 per week if she looked after the child and made it happy. The mother of an illegitimate child was under a statutory duty to look after the child and the father later argued that she had not provided consideration for his promise. But it was held that by looking after the child well and ensuring that the child was happy, the mother had provided consideration.

If someone is bound by an existing contract to do something, a promise to carry out that duty cannot be valid consideration for a new contract. In *Stilk v Myrick* (1809) 2 Camp 317, two sailors deserted from a crew of nine and the captain promised the remaining crew extra money to sail back from the Baltic. The crew were already bound to do this under their contract, so sailing back was not valid consideration and they could not enforce the promise. Carrying out the duty cannot be a benefit to the promisor, who is already owed that duty. If someone does something more than their contractual duty, however, the courts have accepted that this may be treated as valid consideration. In *Hartley v Ponsonby* (1857) 7 E & B 872, where a majority of the sailors deserted, the captain promised the remaining crew extra money to sail home. This was held to be valid consideration, as crewing an under-manned ship was doing more than they were contractually bound to do.

The principle in *Stilk v Myrick* has been challenged by *Williams v Roffey Bros* [1990] 1 All ER 512. The defendants were the main contractors to refurbish a block of flats, and they contracted with the plaintiffs to refit the kitchens. The plaintiffs were behind schedule with the work and the defendants promised to pay them extra money to finish by the agreed date. The plaintiffs finished by this date, but the defendants argued that the plaintiffs were only carrying out their contractual duty and had not provided any new consideration. The Court of Appeal held that because the plaintiffs finished on time, the defendants had avoided payment under a liquidated damages clause in their contract with the owners of the building and they had avoided the trouble of getting someone else to finish the work. The plaintiffs had therefore provided consideration. The court did not overrule *Stilk* v *Myrick*, although it will not always be easy to apply *Williams* v *Roffey Bros* in future situations. The court seems to be taking notice of business practice which treats such renegotiated contracts as valid.

In the case of an existing duty owed to a third party, the law regards carrying out this duty as valid consideration. Two examples from the cases illustrate this rule. In *Scotson* v *Pegg* (1861) 6 H & N 295, S contracted to deliver coal to 'X or his order'. X sold the coal to P and told S to deliver to P. P promised S that P would unload at a fixed rate, but P did not keep this agreement. P argued that S had not provided consideration in delivering the coal, as S was already bound to deliver the coal under his contract with X. It was held that S had provided consideration because delivering the coal was a benefit to P, as P could sue S to enforce the agreement. This was approved by the Privy Council in *The Eurymedon* [1974] 1 All ER 1015. The owner of a machine made a contract with a carrier to take the machine to New Zealand. A clause in this contract exempted the carriers from all liability for loss or damage. The carriers made a contract with the stevedores to unload and (whilst unloading) the stevedores damaged the machine. It was held that the owner had made an implied promise to the stevedores that they could have the benefit of the exemption clause. The stevedores had provided consideration by unloading, even though they were already bound to do so under their contract with the carriers.

The statement that a promise to perform an existing duty is not valid consideration thus needs qualification. A promise to perform an existing public duty is not valid consideration unless it can be shown that a person is doing more than his or her public duty. The courts have sometimes been willing to 'find' the necessary consideration, as in *Ward* v *Byham* (above), where the majority said that keeping a child 'happy' was valid consideration. Denning LJ, while agreeing with the majority that there was consideration, gave a different reason, i.e., that the mother carrying out her statutory duty was a benefit to the father and that a promise to perform an existing duty should be valid consideration. In *Williams* v *Williams* [1957] 1 All ER 305, Denning LJ again said that a promise to perform an existing duty is sufficient consideration if there is nothing in the contract which is contrary to the public interest. But a promise to perform a duty under an existing contract is not generally valid consideration. Only if circumstances show extra consideration or that the requirements of *Williams* v *Roffey Bros* can be met, will carrying out an existing duty be valid consideration. A promise to perform a duty owed to a third party is valid consideration and contradicts the statement. But in some cases the courts have been influenced by public policy in making their decisions and the rules of consideration take second place. This was not apparent in *Stilk* v *Myrick*, but the court was concerned not to enforce the promise because, if it did, this might open the door to crews demanding extra money to sail home. In *Ward* v *Byham* the underlying policy was that the father of an illegitimate child paid maintenance for that child, and the court stretched the concept of consideration to achieve this. More recently in *Williams* v *Roffey Bros* the courts have accepted the business practice that agreeing to finish a job is acceptable as consideration. Although the rule that carrying out an existing duty is not valid consideration is still in place, the cases show that the courts sometimes apply it in a flexible manner.

QUESTION 7

In January, Wisdom College, Oxford, made a contract with their regular builders, Ace Builders Ltd, to construct a new sports hall complex. This was to include a swimming pool, which it was agreed would be 8' 0" at the deep end. The contract also provided that the sports hall would be finished by 1 October. A clause in the contract provided that 'Ace Builders Ltd will pay a penalty of £1,000 per week or part thereof that completion is late'. In fact the sports hall was not ready until 1 November. Meanwhile the college had to hire other sports facilities at a local hotel at a cost of £8,000. The college also had to cancel a booking for the hall by a touring Welsh choir, taken for mid-October, and had to return their booking fee of £2,000. When the work was completed it was discovered that the swimming pool measured only 6' 0" at the deep end. The only way to remedy this was to rebuild the pool to a depth of 8' 0", at a cost of £50,000.

Advise Wisdom College in respect of the above matters.

Commentary

This type of problem question can be found on the examination papers of all the boards, and it would be part of an extended question on the AEB papers. It involves consideration of the breaches of contract by Ace Builders Ltd and an examination of the effect of the penalty/liquidated damages clause. It is important to examine both sides of the argument. The key points which should be covered are:

- identify the claim for late completion — principle of remoteness of damage; duty to mitigate

- consider whether the clause is a penalty or liquidated damages

- apply the principle of remoteness to the loss of the fee for the choir

- examine the damages payable for the swimming pool — the difference in value or cost of cure.

Suggested Answer

There are two possible breaches of contract by the builders, in not finishing on time and in not complying with the agreed specifications. It must also be determined whether the clause in the contract is a penalty or a liquidated damages clause and the consequent legal effects. Other matters to consider are (i) can the college make the builders rebuild the swimming pool or are they entitled only to damages; and (ii) do the college need to mitigate their loss?

By not finishing on the agreed date Ace Builders are in breach of contract. As the contract makes provision for what should happen in the event of late performance, the parties do not intend to make time 'of the essence', and the college have allowed Ace Builders Ltd to continue with the contract, so the college do not have the right to repudiate the contract. They may, however, be entitled to claim damages. The aim of damages is to put the innocent party in the same financial position as if the contract had been carried out according to its terms. Damages are normally based on what the innocent party expected to obtain from the contract, i.e., expectation damages. But a party suffering a breach of contract cannot simply claim for all the losses arising, as the law restricts the damages which may be claimed as a result of a breach. It does this through the principle of remoteness of damage. This principle was first set out in *Hadley* v *Baxendale* (1854) 9 Exch 341. The defendants were in breach of contract by bringing the plaintiff's millshaft back a week late. The plaintiff had to close his mill during this time and claimed for the loss of a week's profits. The court said that in order to claim damages for a breach of contract the plaintiff had to show that the loss arose in the natural course of things, or that it was in the contemplation of the parties at the time of the contract. In applying this principle to the facts the court said that it was not in the natural course of things that the mill should have to close, and neither was it in the contemplation of the parties as the defendant did not know the special circumstances. Here the college would wish to recoup the cost of hiring alternative facilities. This loss can be seen as in the natural course of things, as the facilities were obviously going to be used by students, and if they were not available alternative facilities would have to be provided. It could also be argued that the loss was in the minds of the parties at the time of the contract, as the builders are the regular builders for the college and must know or be taken to know that the beginning of October was the start of term.

One difficulty with any claim for damages by Wisdom College over the late completion, is that the contract makes provision for compensation to be paid if completion is late. The law makes a distinction between penalty clauses and liquidated damages clauses, the former being an attempt to enforce the contract and the latter a genuine estimate of damages. The importance of the distinction is that a penalty clause is not binding, whereas a liquidated damages clause is. The legal effect of this distinction means that if a clause is deemed to be for liquidated damages, the innocent party is limited to claiming the amount provided under the contract, not its actual loss. In *Cellulose Acetate Silk Company Ltd* v *Widnes Foundry (1925) Ltd* [1933] AC 20, the plaintiff contractors agreed to instal machinery for the defendants and to pay a penalty of £20 per week for each week they were late. The plaintiffs were 30 weeks late. When the contractors sued for the contract price the defendants wanted to deduct their actual loss caused by the delay which was £5,850. It was held that the clause was a liquidated damages clause and the contractors were liable for £600 only. Applying this to Ace Builders, if the clause is classed as a liquidated damages clause, it will be binding and Wisdom College will be limited to £5,000 damages. The guidelines for distinguishing between penalty and liquidated damages clauses were laid down in *Dunlop* v *New Garage* [1915] AC 79:

(1)   using the words 'penalty' or 'liquidated damages' is not conclusive;

(2)   if a large sum is payable compared to the possible loss, it will be a penalty;

(3)   if the breach is a failure to pay a sum of money and the clause provides for payment of a larger sum, it is a penalty;

(4)   if a single amount is payable for both major and minor losses, it is a penalty;

(5)   if estimating the loss is difficult, a sum stated may still be liquidated damages.

These guidelines are only presumptions and may be changed. Here, simply by calling it a 'penalty' clause does not make it a penalty, so this does not stop this clause providing for liquidated damages. The amount payable under the clause (£1,000 per week) does not seem a punitive amount compared to the possible losses which could arise from the breach. It is therefore unlikely that this was intended to be a penalty. Although it is difficult to estimate the losses which might arise here, this would seem to be a genuine attempt to do so. Consequently the college will be limited to £5,000 damages as provided by the clause.

A further limit on the damages which the college may claim is possible under the principle of mitigation of damage, which provides that plaintiffs must take 'reasonable steps' to minimise their losses. As a corollary of this, plaintiffs must not take unreasonable steps which would increase the loss. Here, it is reasonable to hire other facilities, but could hiring hotel facilities be seen as unreasonable? This may depend on whether there are other, cheaper facilities available locally. If there are no cheaper facilities which are suitable, it will probably be reasonable to hire facilities at an hotel. If it was regarded as unreasonable, the college could not claim the amount by which the actual cost exceeded the cost of the cheaper facilities.

The loss of £2,000 from the cancellation of the booking for the choir is unlikely to be seen as in the natural course of things, as the facilities were to be used for sports by the students during term time. Unless the builders knew about the booking at the time the contract was made, neither was it likely to be within the contemplation of the parties. It may be compared to the claim for the loss of a special Government dyeing contract in *Victoria Laundry* v *Newman* [1949] 2 KB 528, for which the plaintiffs were not entitled to succeed as the defendant engineers did not know about it and it was not a loss that was 'at the time of the contract reasonably foreseeable as liable to result from the breach'. It was therefore too remote.

The claim in respect of the swimming pool raises some difficult problems. Financial loss for breach of contract can be measured as either:

(a)   the difference in the value of the work done and what should have been done; or

(b)   the cost of reinstatement.

What is the effect of the pool being 6′ 0″ deep instead of 8′ 0″ deep? If the pool was fitted with diving boards and it cannot be used for diving, the college have not obtained what they contracted for. In such circumstances, the difference in value may be similar to the cost of reinstatement. If the cost of reinstatement is less than the difference in value, the damages awarded will be the cost of reinstatement, because the plaintiff who then claims the difference in value would be failing to take reasonable steps to mitigate his loss. It is likely that with a large pool in a sports complex diving boards are provided, so this situation may be distinguished from the small family pool in *Ruxley Electronics* v *Forsyth* [1995] 3 WLR 118. As the pool is now 2′ 0″ shallower, diving may be restricted or even prevented altogether. The loss to the college is likely to exceed the £50,000 needed to make the pool deeper, and they would therefore be entitled to reinstatement. They would not be able to obtain specific performance of a building contract as it is possible to engage another builder to carry out the work.

If the pool could still be used for all the usual purposes and there was little or no difference in value to a pool built 8′ 0″ deep, the cost of reinstatement would be out of all proportion to the loss. In *Ruxley Electronics* v *Forsyth* the defendant had specified a pool 7′ 6″ deep, but when completed it was only 6′ 9″ deep. It was still safe for diving and the court said that the defendant was not entitled to the cost of reinstatement (£22,000) but only to damages for loss of amenity (£2,500). Here, if diving facilities were not provided and the swimming pool could be used in the normal way, the college would not be entitled to the £50,000 but would be limited to a small amount of damages to reflect the inconvenience.

In conclusion, the college will be limited to the amount in the liquidated damages clause and may be unable to claim the cost of hiring other facilities. The lost fee for the choir booking is too remote. However, they have a strong claim to have the swimming pool rebuilt.

QUESTION 8

John, a farmer, saw a 'Magicut' brand petrol-driven lawnmower on display for £500 in Fixitall Ltd. A label on the mower stated 'Made by craftsmen in Germany'. John had always believed that Germans were the best engineers and was impressed by this statement. The sales assistant demonstrated a mower, and John then tried it himself and decided to buy it. A few weeks later, Kate, John's wife, decided to mow the lawn. As she was putting the grassbox on the mower, she noticed that there was some rust on the underside of the grassbox.

While Kate was using the mower it suddenly burst into flames, injuring Kate and setting fire to her prize rose bushes (worth £250). John then examined the mower and noticed that the following was stamped on it: 'All parts made in Germany by Karl GmbH but assembled in England by Magicut Ltd.' John took the mower back to Fixitall Ltd for repair, and they returned it to Magicut Ltd who discovered a fault in the motor and replaced it. Soon after getting the mower back the same problem occurred. It is not clear whether the problem was caused by incorrect assembly, or because the component parts are faulty.

(a) Explain what action John can take under the Sale of Goods Act 1979, if any.

(b) Explain what action Kate may take, if any, at common law.

(c) If John had bought the mower with his credit card, explain what rights he would have against the credit card company.

(d) Explain any action which Kate may take under the Consumer Protection Act 1987

(e) What problems do litigants face in using the courts to settle disputes of this nature, and what alternatives are open to them?

Commentary

This question straddles the consumer law area of the syllabuses. It is typical of the questions on AEB paper 2, but parts of the question may be found on papers by the other boards. The question requires knowledge of a wide area of contract and consumer law, including privity, the implied terms of the Sale of Goods Act 1979, the Consumer Protection Act 1987, and negligence.

The key points which should be covered are:

Question 8(a)

- outline John's claims for breach of the implied conditions under the 1979 Act for description, satisfactory quality and fitness for purpose

- consider the effect of John's examination of the lawn mower on the condition of satisfactory quality

- examine whether John has accepted the lawn mower under s. 35 of the SGA 1979.

Question 8(b)

- explain that under the principle of privity Kate has no claim in contract

- identify the requirements of duty, breach and damage for a claim in negligence

- consider the significance of intermediate examination.

Question 8(c)

- explain the claim against the credit card company under s. 75 of the 1974 Consumer Credit Act for misrepresentation and breach

- explain the claim under s. 56 of the 1974 Act.

Question 8(d)

- outline the three requirements for Kate to claim under the 1987 CP Act

- examine who the producer is — component manufacturer and/or assembler

- explain the restriction on claims for property damage.

Question 8(e)

- identify that claims may be brought under the arbitration procedure in the county court or in the High Court

- outline the problems of cost, delay and uncertainty

- consider the alternatives of trade associations, arbitration and mediation.

Suggested Answer

(a) The Sale of Goods Act 1979, as amended by the Sale and Supply of Goods Act 1994, implies a number of terms into contracts for the sale of goods.

Goods must match their description (s. 13), be of satisfactory quality (s. 14(2)) and be fit for their purpose (s. 14(3)). Under s. 13, where there is a sale by description, there is an implied condition that goods must correspond with their description. This condition applies to both business and private sales, and here there is a sale in the course of a business so the condition would apply. Was this a sale by description? Even though John has seen the lawnmower, it is described on the label as 'Made ... in Germany' and John has read the label, so it is a sale by description. Similarly in *Beale* v *Taylor* [1967] 1 WLR 1193 the plaintiff read an advert in a newspaper which described a car as a '1961' model. He went and looked at the car and bought it, and then found that only half the car was made in 1961. It was held that even though he saw the car, a breach of condition had occurred as he had still relied on the description. Applying this to John's situation, there is a breach of s. 13 and John has the right to end the contract.

As this is a sale in the course of a business, s. 14(2) provides that there is an implied condition that the goods are of satisfactory quality. Section 14(2A) provides that goods are satisfactory if they meet the standard a reasonable person would regard as satisfactory, and in determining this s. 14(2B) provides that appearance and finish and freedom from minor defects are relevant. In deciding if the grassbox is of satisfactory quality, therefore, the rust may be seen as a minor defect, and (unless it was a very small area) a 'reasonable person' would not expect a new lawn mower to be rusty. Nevertheless, 'some rust' may be just a spot of rust which would constitute only a slight blemish on the goods and would not necessarily amount to a breach of s. 14(2). If the area was quite large then the lawn mower would not seem to be of satisfactory quality. However, under s. 14(2C) the condition of satisfactory quality does not apply where the buyer examines the goods and that examination ought to have revealed the defect. Here it would depend how thoroughly John examined the mower, whether he ought to have noticed the rust. He did try out the mower and perhaps should have noticed, although the rust is underneath the grassbox. It would also again depend on how large the area of rust was. If the rust covered a substantial portion of the grassbox, the fact it was on the outside of the machine points to the fact that John should have noticed it. In these circumstances the rust would not be treated as a breach of condition. Another potential problem with the rust is that it must be proved that it existed at the time of sale, rather than developing since. It seems that this claim is weak.

As regards the fault in the motor, this means that the mower is not fit for use. A reasonable buyer would expect a new mower costing £500 to work properly, so it would also not seem to be of satisfactory quality. The examination and use of the mower by John would be unlikely to reveal such a fault, so this defect would be a breach of that condition. Section 14(3) also applies to sales in the course of a business, as here, unless the buyer does not rely on the seller's skill. One possible argument is that as John is a farmer, he is relying on his own judgement. If John does rely on the skill of the seller then the mower is not fit for its purpose because it has burst into flames during normal use.

A breach of condition generally gives the buyer a choice of rejecting the goods or claiming damages. But will John have the right to reject the mower? Under s. 35(4), the buyer is deemed to have accepted goods if he does not tell the seller that he rejects them within a reasonable time. Under s. 35(6), the buyer is not deemed to have accepted simply because he asks for or agrees to repair of the goods. Prior to this amendment by the Sale and Supply of Goods Act 1994, if a buyer handed back goods for repair, this could mean losing the right to reject. The fact that John has asked for the mower to be repaired does not of itself mean that he has accepted it. Whether John has the right to reject the mower will depend on how long has passed since he first bought it. In *Bernstein* v *Pamson Motors Ltd* [1987] 2 All ER 220, the buyer of a new car, who had the car for three weeks, was held to have lost his right to reject it for breach of a condition. This case was decided before the change in the law, and it appears that since John has had the mower for a matter of only weeks he should still be able to reject it.

(b)   The principle of privity of contract means that only the parties to the contract have rights and duties under the contract. In *Dunlop* v *Selfridge* [1915] AC 847, Dunlop sold tyres to Dew, Dew sold them to Selfridge, and Selfridge agreed not to sell the tyres below list price and to pay £5 to Dunlop for each breach. Selfridge sold below list price and Dunlop sued them. It was held that Dunlop were not a party to the contract between Dew and Selfridge, and Dunlop's claim failed even though the contract was for their benefit. The contract for the lawn mower was made between John and Fixitall and, applying the principle of privity, Kate has no claim in contract against Fixitall. She could argue that John was acting as her agent, but this is unlikely to succeed.

Kate may be able to claim in the tort of negligence if she can establish that she is owed a duty of care, that the duty has been broken and that she has suffered damage as a consequence. In *Donoghue* v *Stevenson* [1932] AC 562, it was held that the manufacturer owes a duty of care to the ultimate consumer, as he can foresee that if he is negligent in making the product, the consumer will suffer damage. The difficulty will be in establishing who is negligent here — the seller (Fixitall Ltd), the assembler (Magicut Ltd) or the manufacturer of the parts (Karl GbmH). It is unlikely that Fixitall Ltd will owe a duty of care to Kate, unless the fault in the motor could be identified by intermediate examination and it was expected that the retailer would carry out such an examination, or there had been similar faults before so that Fixitall could have foreseen injury and loss. In *Grant* v *Australian Knitting Mills* [1936] AC 85, the court said that as regards the chemicals in the underpants produced by the manufacturing process there was no obligation on the buyer to wash the underpants before wearing them. By analogy, it was not up to the retailer, Fixitall Ltd, to carry out an intermediate examination of the lawnmower. The difficulty Kate faces is proving whether it is the manufacturer of the parts or the assembler who is in breach of duty. In *Evans* v *Triplex* [1936] 1 All ER 283, the windscreen of the plaintiff's car shattered and injured the passengers. The windscreen had been made by the defendants, but the plaintiff was unable to prove whether it was faulty manufacture or faulty fitting which caused it to break. Kate faces a similar problem. She may be able to surmount it by taking a third party action and suing both Magicut Ltd and Karl GmbH together. She would be able to claim for her injuries and for the damage to the roses, but not for the cost of a new mower.

(c)   If John had bought the mower using his credit card, the credit card company are not a party to the contract of sale and at common law (under the principle of privity) they cannot be made liable on the contract. The Consumer Credit Act 1974, s. 75 provides, however, that if the debtor has any claim against the supplier for misrepresentation or breach of contract, 'he shall have a like claim against the creditor'. To have a claim under s. 75 the goods must have a sale price of between £100 and £30,000, and there must be a 'business arrangement' between Fixitall and the credit card company. Here the price of the goods is within those bands and clearly there must be an arrangement for the store to accept the credit card. The three possible breaches are in respect of the description 'Made ... in Germany', the rust and the defective motor. The stronger claims would be as regards the description and the defective motor. John could sue the credit card company in these circumstances, but it would be an unusual course of action to take because he has a contract with Fixitall Ltd. If John did claim from the credit card company, they have a right to be indemnified by Fixitall Ltd.

The creditor may also be made liable for any misrepresentations made by the seller before the contract of sale was made. Under s. 56 of the Consumer Credit Act 1974, any negotiator in antecedent negotiations is treated as the agent of the creditor. The notice on the mower 'Made ... in Germany' may be regarded as a misrepresentation as it is on the lawn mower and is seen by John before he makes the contract. The credit card company will be liable under s. 56 and John can rescind the credit agreement for the mower and claim damages. Here the arrangement is a three-party debtor-creditor-supplier agreement and the debtor has a contract with the supplier so is less likely to use s. 56.

(d) A lawn mower is clearly a 'product' under the Consumer Protection Act 1987; and anyone who suffers damage from a defective product may sue, so Kate would be able to claim. Kate must prove that the lawn mower was defective, that she suffered damage, and that the damage was caused by the defect. A product is defective when the safety is not such as 'persons generally are entitled to expect'. This is an objective standard and all the circumstances are taken into account. It would not be expected that a new lawn mower would burst into flames, and it is clearly defective because the motor had to be replaced within a few weeks. Safety covers both injury and damage to property, and Kate will claim for both her physical injuries and the damage to her roses (but see below).

Kate has to decide who to sue. Under the 1987 Act liability is placed on the 'producer', which covers both the assembler and the manufacturer of the components, as under s. 1(2) the definition of 'product' includes components incorporated in the finished product. Here it all depends on whether the lawn mower is faulty because of a defectively made part, or because it was wrongly assembled. If there is a defect in a component, both Karl GmbH and Magicut Ltd are liable. If the defect is in the assembling then only Magicut Ltd are liable. The supplier, Fixitall Ltd, may also be liable, but only if they fail to identify the producer of the finished product.

Kate would be able to claim for her injuries, but no claim can be made for damage to property unless it is for more than £275, so the claim for the roses would fail. Neither could any claim be made for damage to the mower, as liability for damage to the product itself is excluded by s. 5(2) of the Act. The claim must be made within three years of when the damage was caused, under the Limitation Act 1980. One possible defence is that the state of scientific knowledge at the time of manufacture was not such that the producer might be expected to have discovered the defect, but there is little evidence that this applies here, as the mower is not described as a new development.

(e) The claims arising from the above cases would be by John, to reclaim his £500 for the lawn mower, and by Kate, for her injuries, in negligence and under the 1987 Act, and for the damage to the roses in negligence. It is likely that these claims would be brought in the county court. If the only claim was for a refund for the mower, this would be brought under the county court arbitration scheme for small claims (limit £3,000). But as regards Kate's injuries, it would depend on their severity whether the claim would go above the personal injuries limit of £1,000 and be tried in the county courts. If she was claiming over £50,000 the case would go to the High Court.

Bringing claims through the civil court system causes many problems for litigants. Probably the most significant one is the cost of legal representation, as over the small claims limit the general rule is that the losing party pays the costs of both sides. If a plaintiff is not entitled to legal aid, taking legal action means taking a financial risk. With claims of small value it is often not worth that risk. Legal aid in civil cases is not available to those with a disposable income of approximately £7,500 per annum and capital over a similar figure. Below these limits contributions are made on a sliding scale. The Government is continuing the policy of restricting legal aid. There is also the problem of delay and claims in county courts often take six to nine months after issuing the summons to come to court, with longer delays in the High Court. Taking legal action is very often a lottery because of the uncertain outcome and the possibility of appeals. Since 1995 a conditional fee system has operated, under which if litigants lose they do not have to pay their solicitors, but if they win their solicitors can charge them up to double the fee. This is available in personal injury claims. The Woolf Report, *Access to Justice* (1996), has made many suggestions for reforming the civil process, including a fast track procedure and fixed fees per day.

Parties to small value claims may find that retailers are members of trade associations who provide arbitration schemes. But these are limited to that particular business, for example, the motor trade. The parties may consider appointing an arbitrator themselves to settle the dispute between them. Each side pays its own fees and they share the cost of the arbitrator. This is both quicker and cheaper than going to court. A system of appointing mediators also operates for commercial cases, but unlike arbitrators the mediator deals with the parties separately. The system remains piecemeal and individuals still have difficulty in enforcing their rights in claims of small value.

7 Miscellaneous topics

INTRODUCTION

This chapter consists of four questions on four different areas of law, namely: public order; consumer; family and employment law. These subjects are not included in the syllabuses of the major boards, but are covered in other 'A' level syllabuses (such as the Welsh and EDEXCEL Foundation boards) to a greater or lesser extent. This chapter will therefore give students of boards other than AEB, NEAB and Oxford some additional coverage of the syllabus which they are studying. Each question is in the style of a situation-based or problem question, so that various topics in each area of law are covered.

As each question is on a different area of law, the commentaries are a little more detailed. You will note that they give some guidance as to the wider issues involved, so that you can consider the extra information which would be required for an essay style question on the same topics. The different approach which should be taken for an essay question is covered in chapter 1 'How to use this book', and can also be seen by comparing questions and answers on other areas of law elsewhere in the book. The criminal law on intoxication as a defence, for example, is covered in chapter 4 in situation-based questions such as numbers 1(**d**) and 2; but question 2 shows how the same law would need to be discussed in the context of an essay style question.

QUESTION 1

Adam, Rebecca, Thomas and Nawaz are followers of a pagan religion which holds that trees contain a source of spiritual power. On the day before Midsummer's Day they set out to travel to Billingham, a small village in the centre of England, where there is a famous ancient oak tree. The local police are aware that several people will be doing the same thing, and therefore obtain an order under the Public Order Act 1986, s. 14A(2), prohibiting assemblies within a two mile radius of the tree. Adam is approached by PC Surinder when he stops in a pub in Catchford (a village about two miles away from Billingham) for a drink. PC Surinder instructs Adam not to visit the ancient oak tree, and arrests him when Adam puts down his drink and walks away from the pub in the direction of Billingham. Rebecca and Nawaz are arrested by PC Miles while they are standing on a footpath (a public right of way) which runs through the wood where the ancient oak tree is situated. They are surrounded by several other people, but claim that they are merely chatting to acquaintances who they have just recognised. Adam, Rebecca and Nawaz are all charged with offences under the Public Order Act 1986, s. 14.

Meanwhile, Thomas has entered the wood because he has heard that Robert, the owner of the wood, is engaged in felling trees. He sees Robert carrying a chain saw, and notices that he is approaching a large oak tree. Thomas immediately goes up to the tree and starts to inspect it closely, despite protests from Robert that this is preventing him from cutting it down. PC Campbell sees what is going on and arrests Thomas. Thomas claims that he was merely studying the bark for his research into tree structures, and had no desire to obstruct Robert. He is later charged with the offence of aggravated trespass under the Criminal Justice and Public Order Act 1994, s. 68.

Advise Adam, Rebecca, Thomas and Nawaz.

Commentary

This question concerns a range of offences introduced into the law by the Criminal Justice and Public Order Act 1994. Note how there are three distinct sections to the problem, but that one issue is more complex than the other two. The offences concerned with trespassory assemblies were promulgated by way of amendments to the Public Order Act 1986, hence the references to that Act in the question; whereas the offence of aggravated trespass is a completely new crime. Either way, these are still relatively new crimes, and therefore there is little case law which can be applied. They are controversial offences, however, as there are already laws prohibiting violent or threatening behaviour generally, and offences such as criminal damage to cover vandalism. These new laws will criminalise peaceful protest, therefore, and as such there has been much speculation about how the courts will develop them, as well as critical comment on the extent to which they encroach on civil liberties.

In the context of a situation based, problem style question, you are not expected to make critical comment and should concentrate merely on stating the relevant law as clearly and concisely as possible and applying it to the facts of the problem. It is necessary sometimes to discuss how the courts might interpret certain provisions, and this gives you an opportunity to refer to civil liberties issues if you feel that such considerations could affect the way in which the courts would apply the law. You must be careful to strike the right balance, however, as even the European Convention on Human Rights is only of limited weight in the eyes of English judges, and the constraints of the time limits of an examination do not allow you much scope for digression from the main issues. Bear in mind also that these are criminal offences, and that therefore the basic principles of criminal law (e.g., the necessity for the *actus reus* and *mens rea* of the offence to be proved) apply. You should therefore concentrate on the following points:

- police powers to prohibit trespassory assemblies — definition of 'assembly'

- the offence of taking part in a prohibited assembly — what exactly is prohibited?

- Rebecca and Nawaz — have they exceeded the limits of their rights of access?

- Police powers to stop persons proceeding — requirements for a lawful order

- Adam — was he entitled to ignore PC Campbell's instructions?

- definition of the offence of aggravated trespass

- *mens rea* — did Thomas 'intend' to disrupt?

Suggested Answer

Under the Public Order Act 1986, s. 14A, (introduced by the Criminal Justice and Public Order Act 1994) the chief officer of police for an area has the power to apply to the district council for an order prohibiting 'trespassory assemblies'. An assembly is defined as 'an assembly of 20 or more persons'. There must be a reasonable belief that people are intending to hold an assembly on land where there is no public or only limited, right of access, and that the assembly would take place without the consent of the occupier of the land, or would exceed the limits on public access. There must also be a possibility that the assembly would result in 'serious disruption to the life of the community', or 'significant damage' to important land, a building or monument. In this case, we must assume that the district council properly made such an order, presumably on the grounds that a gathering of the followers of the pagan religion would disrupt the Billingham community, although it is possible that the land on which the oak tree stands could be regarded as of historical importance. The order can last for a maximum of four days, and cover an area with a maximum radius of five miles. The facts state that the restricted area has a radius of two miles from the Billingham oak tree, which is within the limits of the Act. It must also be assumed, therefore, that all the events take place within the time limits of the order, i.e., within a maximum of two days either side of Midsummer's Day.

Once such an order is in force, it operates to prohibit any assembly on land where there is no right of public access, or with limited public access where the assembly exceeds those limits. Under the Public Order Act 1986, s. 14B(2), a person who takes part in an assembly knowing it to be prohibited is guilty of an offence, and under s. 14B(4) a constable in uniform may arrest without warrant anyone she reasonably suspects to be committing the offence. With reference to the charges against Rebecca and Nawaz therefore, the key questions to be considered in this problem are:

(a)   were they taking part in an assembly as defined by the Act?;

(b)   did they know that an order under s. 14A had been issued?;

(c)   if there was an 'assembly', as they were standing on a public right of way, was the assembly outside the limits of the public rights of access?

We are not told if the police had informed the crowd of people that a s. 14A order had been made, and we must therefore assume that the police had adopted this procedure — their usual means of ensuring that such gatherings are about to be dispersed lawfully. That being the case, there would then be a question as to whether Rebecca and Nawaz were in a gathering of people which amounted to an 'assembly'. It must have comprised 20 or more people, but otherwise the term is not defined by the Act. The facts state that they were 'surrounded by several other people' and that they were 'chatting to acquaintances'. There seems to be clear evidence, therefore, that they were part of the gathering, and could not claim that they were separate from it. The only remaining question, therefore, is whether they were exceeding the limits of public access applying to a right of way. This issue was raised in the case of *DPP v Jones and another* (1997) 147 NLJ 162. A s. 14A order had been made prohibiting assemblies within a four mile radius of Stonehenge. The defendants had been arrested while taking part in a demonstration on a grass verge on a road running alongside the perimeter fence at Stonehenge itself, and were convicted by the local magistrates of an offence under s. 14B(2). The Crown Court allowed an appeal on the grounds that the defendants had not exceeded the public's limited rights of access to the road in question, in that the gathering was peaceful and did not cause an obstruction. The Divisional Court quashed the decision and ordered a rehearing. They ruled that the assembly in question was outside the purpose of passing and repassing, which are the rights of the public in respect of a highway (*Harrison v Duke of Rutland* [1893] 1 QB 142). One judge suggested that the actual use of the right of way need only be in breach of the order, as that in itself operated to limit the public's rights of access. Both judges also pointed out that holding a meeting or demonstration have nothing to do with passing or repassing, although 'passing the time of day with an acquaintance ... might well qualify.'

This decision can be questioned, as there is no law against holding a meeting on a highway, and the English constitution allows any activity which is not specifically prohibited. On that basis, a gathering would not be unlawful, and thereby outside the terms of public rights of access, unless something took place which was specifically prohibited. The existence of an order under s. 14A of the 1986 Act could not do this in itself, as it only operates to prohibit assemblies which are already trespassory. One judge in *DPP v Jones* drew a distinction between activities which are tolerated and therefore will not be stopped in practice; and those which are exercised because they cannot be stopped. By this reasoning, only the latter are 'rights'. This point of view is certainly supported by old cases such as *Ex parte Lewis* (1888) 21 QBD 191, where it was ruled that there was no 'right' to hold a public meeting in Trafalgar Square. But the modern view is that, if something is not positively unlawful, it must therefore be lawful and thus 'cannot' be stopped. Rebecca and Nawaz can therefore adopt two arguments. First, that their behaviour was lawful even within the terms of *DPP v Jones*, in that they were merely doing something which was incidental to the public right to pass and repass along the footpath. 'Chatting to acquaintances' could fall within this category, but in this case it would depend upon factors such as the amount of time that they had spent standing in one place, and how many different people they had been talking to. At some point, 'chatting' must become 'meeting and assembling'! The difficulty they would have to face, however, is that in *DPP* v *Jones* the court also ruled that all participants in an assembly are in breach of s. 14B(2) as long as some people in the gathering are exceeding their rights of access. Rebecca and Nawaz would only be successful on this point, therefore, if everyone else was doing the same — which seems unlikely. Secondly, they could argue that *DPP* v *Jones* was wrongly decided, and that there is a right to assemble on a public right of way as long as nothing unlawful is done. This approach would necessitate taking the case at least to the Divisional Court on appeal, as the decision in *DPP* v *Jones* is binding on a Crown Court or magistrates' court. The implications that the case has for civil liberties are such that it seems a suitable case for a higher court.

Adam has been charged with an offence as a result of his apparent refusal to comply with PC Surinder's instructions. Under the Public Order Act 1986, s. 14C, a constable in uniform has certain powers if he reasonably believes that a person is on his way to a prohibited assembly. These powers allow the constable to stop the person and direct him not to proceed 'in the direction of the assembly'. This power can only be exercised within the area covered by the prohibition order, however. If the person refuses to comply, he is committing an offence and can be arrested without a warrant. There is no provision in the section stipulating that the person must know of the prohibition order, or even that the constable must inform him of that fact, but it is clearly not sufficient that the person is merely going towards the prohibited area — there must be reasonable belief that he is going to the assembly. There is no doubt in this case that Adam was on his way to the Billingham oak, but there may be scope for him to argue that he was not going to the assembly itself. During a debate on the Bill in the House of Lords, the government spokesman stated that: 'Directions can be given only where a police officer believes a person to be going to the gathering, not just to the place where it is for some unconnected purpose'. But the section stipulates that the constable must believe that the person is on his way to an assembly, not merely 'to the place where it is'. It is therefore possible for Adam to argue that his purpose was merely to visit the tree, not to join a gathering there. The fact that his purpose is identical to that of the other people going to the site does not necessarily mean that he wants to join with them — he might be a very private person who hates crowds! If the courts were to allow this argument, however, it would reduce the effectiveness of the Act considerably; there is also the practical point that the key element is the constable's reasonable belief that the person is intending to join the assembly, and it might be difficult for a person in this situation to convince a constable that he hates crowds! Adam is therefore guilty of the offence as charged, as he has proceeded in the direction of the Billingham oak after being directed not to do so. This is only an offence, however, if the pub in Catchford is within the area covered by the order, i.e., within a two mile radius of the Billingham oak tree. The facts of the question leave some room for doubt on that issue. The wording of the section seems to be absolute, in that the constable's reasonable belief only applies to the fact that the person is £on his way to an assembly . . .'. If the Catchford pub is, in fact, outside the area, the powers to stop and direct are not exercisable, and Adam would not have committed the offence of failing to comply with PC Surinder's direction.

Finally, Thomas has been charged with aggravated trespass. This offence is committed when a person trespasses on land in open air and does anything which is intended to intimidate, obstruct or disrupt a person engaging in a lawful activity. Thomas seems to have committed the *actus reus* of the offence, in that his detailed inspection of the tree has prevented Robert from cutting it down. In *Winder* v *DPP* (1996), the Divisional Court held that the offence was committed by a man running after a hunt in order to get close enough to disrupt it, even though the act of running in itself had no effect (nor was it intended to). With such a wide interpretation of the statute being taken, there does not seem to be any room for Thomas to argue with the basics of the offence. The mens rea of the offence requires the prosecution to prove that he 'intended' to obstruct the activity, however. Thomas claims that he was merely studying the bark for his research into tree structures, and had no desire to obstruct Robert. In *R* v *Hancock and Shankland* [1986] 2 WLR 357 the House of Lords ruled that 'desire' is irrelevant to the issue of intention, and in *R* v *Nedrick* [1986] 1 WLR 1025 the Court of Appeal stated that the jury are entitled to infer intention if the defendant knew that his actions were 'virtually certain' to have the relevant effect, and furthermore that such an inference 'may be irresistible'. As Robert told Thomas that his inspection was preventing him from cutting down the tree, a jury would almost certainly believe that Thomas knew that his behaviour was having that effect, and therefore the jury would be entitled to infer that he 'intended' to obstruct Robert.

QUESTION 2

Andy runs his own business from home. He visited Bob's Motors Ltd, where he was attracted by a sticker on the windscreen of a Ford Mondeo, which stated, 'Only 10,000 miles'. The sticker had been put on the windscreen by Bob's Motors Ltd, based on the mileometer reading. Andy examined the car, went for a test drive and then decided to buy it, intending to use it for both business and private purposes. Shortly after this he discovered that at the time of the sale, the car had done 20,000 miles. Bob's Motors Ltd had bought it from another dealer, who unknown to Bob's Motors Ltd had turned back the mileage. Last week, Eric, a salesman, called at Andy's home and demonstrated a new vacuum cleaner to Andy's wife, Carol, which Eric said was the most effective on the market. When Carol hesitated, Eric said that he could arrange finance through Dodgy Finance Ltd. Carol then signed a hire purchase agreement made with Dodgy Finance Ltd, under which she agreed to pay £360, in equal instalments, over 12 months. She was then given a copy of the agreement. Carol no longer wants the vacuum cleaner.

Advise Andy of what action may be taken in civil and criminal law in respect of the car; and Carol of her legal position as regards the vacuum cleaner. How would your advice to Carol differ, if she had paid five monthly instalments?

Commentary

This type of question is found on the examination papers of the London Board (now EDEXCEL Foundation) and the Welsh Board, in sections entitled 'The Market' or similar. It could also be found as part of a larger question on NEAB examination papers. This area of law could be examined in an essay question involving both an explanation of the law and comment on its effectiveness from the consumer's point of view. For example, the use of exclusion clauses in consumer sales can often prevent the purchaser of goods from enforcing their rights under consumer protection legislation.

This question should take approximately 45 minutes. It requires a knowledge of the Sale of Goods Act 1979, the Trade Descriptions Act 1968, the Consumer Credit Act 1974 and some common law principles. The following points should be considered:

- sale by description SGA 1979, s. 13 implied term

- false trade descriptions TDA 1968, s. 1 — an offence

- defences under TDA, s. 24

- formalities needed for a regulated consumer credit agreement

- cancellation and termination under the CCA 1974

Suggested Answer

Andy will need to consider whether the sale of the car is a sale by description and whether there is a breach of the Sale of Goods Act 1979. In criminal law the possibility of action against Bob's Motors Ltd and the other dealer, under the Trade Descriptions Act 1968 should be considered. With regard to Carol's contract, it needs to be considered whether the formalities for a valid consumer credit agreement have been complied with and even if they have does Carol have a right of cancellation or termination?

In civil law Andy has made a contract with Bob's Motors Ltd. The first question to determine is whether this is a sale 'by description'. The Sale of Goods Act 1979, s. 13 provides that where there is a sale of goods by description, there is an implied term that the goods will correspond with that description. This section applies here, as it applies to all sales, whether business or private. Every statement about goods does not automatically become part of the description. Descriptive words which are not within s. 13 could be representations and, if so, Andy could have a claim for innocent or negligent misrepresentation as regards the mileage covered by the car. In *Harlingdon & Leinster Enterprises Ltd* v *Christopher Hull Fine Art Ltd* [1990] 3 WLR 13 the Court of Appeal said that for a sale to be 'by description', the buyer had to rely on the description so that it became an essential part of the contract. In that case the defendant seller of two paintings described them as 'by Munter'. The defendant was not an expert on such paintings and said this to the plaintiff buyer. The paintings were fakes. It was found that the buyer had not relied on this description, but on his own judgment, therefore the sale was not by description. The mileage is often an important part of the description of a second hand car. It seems that Alan was attracted to the car because of the low mileage and it could be argued that even though he had examined and driven the car, he relied on the notice about the mileage and it is part of the description. But this description is wrong because the actual mileage is greater and there is, therefore, a breach of the implied term. It is likely to be treated as a condition because of the importance attached to it by Andy.

The seller's duty under s. 13 is strict and even slight variations from the description have been treated as breaches of condition. In *Re Moore* [1921] 2 KB 519 the seller of tinned fruit delivered the correct quantity but some of it was in cases of 30 and not 24 as requested. This was held to be a breach of s. 13 and the buyers could reject the goods. However, the Sale and Supply of Goods Act 1994 provides that if the breach is so slight it would be unreasonable to reject the goods, the breach should be treated as a breach of warranty. This provision does not apply to a buyer who 'deals as consumer'. The question here is whether Andy 'deals as consumer' as provided by the Unfair Contract Terms Act 1977? The requirements are that the buyer does not make the contract in the course of a business; the other party does make the contract in the course of a business; the goods are of a type ordinarily supplied for private use. Even though Andy is running a business, he may be within this definition, as the purchase will not be in the course of the business unless it is integral to the business. In *R & B Customs Brokers* v *UDT* [1988] 1 WLR 321 a company involved in ship broking bought a car for the use of directors, which was only the second or third time they had done so. This was held to be a consumer sale. In Andy's case it would depend how often he bought cars for the business. Even if this was a regular occurence he could argue that the car was also for private use and was not therefore bought in the course of a business. As Andy found out about the false mileage shortly after buying the car, it is unlikely he will be treated as keeping it more than a reasonable time, and thereby accepting it under s. 35, as such acceptance would mean that he could not reject it. If the above arguments are successful Andy will have the right to reject the car for breach of the condition about description.

The Trade Descriptions Act 1968 makes it an offence to falsely describe goods in the course of a business. Under s. 1(1) anyone who in the course of a trade or business (a) applies a false trade description to any goods; or (b) supplies any goods to which a false description is applied, commits an offence. What can be regarded as part of the description is set out in s. 2, which includes '(j) other history, including previous ownership or use'. The mileage is within the 'use' of the car and therefore is part of the description. Bob's Motors Ltd are acting in the course of a business and as the mileage on the sticker is false, they could be charged under s. 1(1)(b) for supplying goods to which a false description has been applied. The prosecution may also say that putting the notice on the windscreen is 'applying' a false trade description and the court may accept that they have committed an offence under s. 1(1)(a).

There are two possible defences which Bob's Motors Ltd could put forward. There is a general defence under s. 24 of the Act if Bob's Motors can prove that

(a) the commission of the offence was due to ... reliance on information supplied to him or to the act or default of another person ... and (b) that he took all reasonable precautions and exercised all due diligence to avoid the commission of such offence by himself or any person under his control.

If prosecuted under s. 1(1)(a) for *applying* a false trade description, Bob could say that he relied on information supplied i.e., the mileage reading on the car.

He would also have to show that he took all reasonable precautions to stop an offence being committed. He may be able to show that he had a system for checking the mileage or that he had bought the car from a reputable dealer, but it may be difficult to establish the defence in the light of the following case. In *Simmons* v *Potter* [1975] RTR 347 the defendant car dealer had sold a car with a false mileage which had been changed by a previous owner. The court said that the defendants did not have a defence under s. 24 because by not putting up a disclaimer notice, that they could not guarantee the correct mileage, they had not taken all reasonable precautions to avoid commission of an offence. It may be that the sticker on the car windscreen was put up by an employee and Bob could use the 'act or default of another person'. In *Tesco* v *Nattrass* [1971] AC 153, Tesco's were not guilty of an offence under the Act because an employee had changed a price without following Tesco's stringent system of checks to avoid such an offence. If Bob's Motors Ltd are charged under s. 1(1)(b) for *supplying* goods there is an alternative defence provided by s. 24(3) that the defendant did not know and could not with reasonable diligence have ascertained that the goods did not conform to the description. If Bob could show that he had checked the mileage was accurate with the dealer who sold to him and that it was difficult to tell the difference between a car which had done 20,000 miles and one which had done 10,000 miles, for example if this Ford Mondeo was only six months old, then he may be regarded as acting with reasonable diligence and have a good defence. But as a car dealer, Bob could be expected to know the difference between two such cars and the defence is not likely to be successful.

If there is a conviction under the TDA the court may make a compensation order in Andy's favour, but any amount awarded would be taken into account in assessing damages in any civil claim he makes.

Carol has made a 'regulated consumer credit agreement' under the Consumer Credit Act 1974, which is an agreement under which the creditor provides credit not exceeding £15,000. This is a hire-purchase agreement, which involves three parties, the owner, the creditor and the debtor. The owner (Eric) sells the goods to the creditor (Dodgy Finance Ltd), who in turn lets the goods on credit to the debtor (Carol). There is no obligation on the debtor to buy the goods, although the debtor may do so when they have paid all the instalments, usually by paying a nominal sum. The first matter to check is that both Dodgy Finance Ltd and Eric (as a credit broker, who introduces customers) hold a licence from the Director General of Fair Trading. It is a criminal offence to act without a licence and any agreement made whilst doing so cannot be enforced against the debtor. In this case, Eric's licence must cover canvassing off trade premises. Assuming they both hold appropriate licences, the Act lays down certain formalities in ss. 60–65 which must be followed and the Consumer Credit (Agreement) Regulations 1983 set out the details. The agreement must be in writing and must contain information about the cash price, the amount of credit, the annual percentage rate etc. It must also give the debtor information about certain statutory rights, for example, the right to cancel and the right to settle early. This agreement was in writing but it must be ascertained that it contains all the required details. If these requirements are not met, then the agreement is treated as improperly executed. The effect is that the creditor cannot enforce the agreement without a court order and the court would only enforce it, if this was just in the circumstances.

Under ss. 62 and 63 the debtor must be given a copy or copies of the agreement. Carol has been given a copy but this does not necessarily mean the requirements of the Act have been met, as it depends on who signed first. If the form given to Carol had already been signed by Dodgy Finance Ltd, when Carol signs, the agreement becomes executed. Carol must then be given one copy and no further copy need be given. But if Carol is the first to sign, the agreement is unexecuted and she must be given one copy when she signs and a second copy later. When she is entitled to the second copy will be explained below.

The other important right which Carol may be entitled to is the right to cancel the agreement. Under s. 67 two conditions must be fulfilled to have a right to cancel:

(i)   before the agreement, oral statements are made in the debtor's presence by a negotiator; and

(ii)   the debtor signed the agreement away from trade premises of the creditor. Here Eric is a negotiator and has made statements about the effectiveness of the vacuum cleaner before Carol signed the agreement. The agreement has also been signed away from trade premises. This gives Carol the right to cancel the agreement. This right of cancellation must be related back to the requirement for copies of the agreement. If Carol executed the agreement by signing she must be given one copy. As the agreement is cancellable, it must contain her right to cancel. She must also be sent a notice of her right to cancel, by post, within seven days of her signing the agreement. If Carol signed first, she must be given one copy when she signed and must be sent a second copy by post within seven days of the agreement being made, which will be when it is signed by the creditor (Dodgy Finance Ltd). It would seem that in making a hire-purchase agreement in these circumstances, the debtor (i.e. Carol) is usually the first to sign. Carol has a right of cancellation and can exercise it by sending a notice of cancellation to the creditor (Dodgy Finance Ltd) or the owner (Eric) or his agent. This must be done within five days after the debtor receives their second copy of the agreement or their notice of cancellation. We are not told that Carol has received a second copy or a notice of cancellation, so she has five days from receiving such a document. It is more likely that she is entitled to a second copy as by signing the proposal form she is making the offer, which is accepted when the credit company sign.

If Carol exercises her right to cancel the agreement, the effect is that Carol does not have to make any further payments and any payments made must be returned. Carol must return the vacuum cleaner, which in effect means that she must make it available for collection.

If Carol had paid five monthly instalments then she loses her right to cancel as she has continued with the agreement. Under s. 99 of the CCA a debtor has a right to end or terminate a regulated agreement any time before paying the last instalment. The debtor must:

(a)   give notice in writing of termination to the creditor (Dodgy Finance Ltd);

(b)   pay any instalments owing;

(c)   pay an amount to bring the amount paid up to one half the total price payable;

(d)   allow the creditor to take the goods;

(e)   pay compensation for any damage to the goods.

Carol would have to pay any sums owing after five months and pay another £30 to bring the total paid up to £180. She would also have to give back the vacuum cleaner to Dodgy Finance Ltd. Carol would be advised not to follow this course of action as she would lose financially. It would be better for her to sell the cleaner with the creditor's permission and use the money obtained to pay off the hire-purchase agreement.

QUESTION 3

Roberta and her parents, Warren and Meryl, emigrated to England from the USA some years ago when Roberta was two years old. Warren and Meryl are adherents to a little-known religion which forbids marriages outside their faith, and discourages contact with anybody who is not part of their religious community. Roberta is now 17 years old and has been brought up very strictly within her parents' religion and has very little contact outside a small community of like-minded people.

Last month Warren and Meryl informed Roberta that they wished her to marry Clinton, a distant cousin from another town. Roberta objected, but her parents told her that their religion forbade her from disagreeing with their wishes, and that if she did not go through with the wedding she would have to leave their house and never speak to them, or anybody else in their community, again. Roberta therefore agreed, and a date was fixed for the Register Office ceremony and a subsequent religious ceremony. Two weeks ago the Register Office ceremony took place. Roberta was horrified to find that Clinton was an extremely ugly man with chronic halitosis and rampant body odour, but she allowed the ceremony to proceed. Subsequently, she has put off the religious ceremony by various subterfuges and has now come to you for advice. Roberta is adamant that she does not wish to divorce Clinton because of her religion, but wishes to be free to marry someone else in due course.

Advise Roberta as to the validity of her marriage to Clinton.

Commentary

This question focuses on the law of nullity, which originates in the Nullity of Marriage Act 1971 but is now set out in the Matrimonial Causes Act 1973. Nullity is one way of terminating a marriage, along with divorce and the little used procedure for decree of presumption of death. When judicial separation is included, these are the 'final decrees' which enable the courts to exercise wide powers to award (*inter alia*) lump sums and transfer of property orders. The decree of nullity is something of an anachronism. It derives from canon law theory that a marriage is invalid if there is something wrong with it at the very beginning, and the grounds are supposed to reflect the range of possible problems. Legally the marriage will be valid until a decree is obtained, however, unlike a wedding which falls foul of the rules concerning void marriages. The rules concerning void marriages are regarded as covering fundamental defects, such as a wedding where the parties are not respectively male and female, and technically therefore no 'marriage' has taken place in a legal sense. Divorce law, on the other hand, enables a marriage to be terminated because of problems which have arisen after the date of the wedding. The availablity of these alternative grounds for invalidating a marriage is seen as useful for those people who disagree with divorce, on religious or moral grounds, and for whom a divorce might be seen as a disgrace by their community. Whether they are still appropriate for a modern, secular legal system is a matter of dispute.

The problem requires a knowledge of several aspects of the law of nullity, and the way in which different grounds can interrelate. The case law shows that these issues are still very much relevant to those sections of contemporary society which have an aversion to the concept of divorce. The restrictions which Roberta places on your advice also means that you must have a sound knowledge of all the different processes which can be used to bring about an end to married life. For example, her comments have the effect of ruling out not only divorce, but also judicial separation, as she wishes to be able to re-marry. The following points should be covered in your answer:

- legal background for termination of a marriage — divorce, nullity, presumption of death, judicial separation, void marriages.

- outline of the law on voidable marriages

- wilful refusal and incapacity to consummate a marriage

- lack of consent — duress

Suggested Answer

There are several ways of terminating a marriage, and one process which effects a permanent separation without allowing remarriage. Under different provisions in the Matrimonial Causes Act 1973 (MCA), one party to a marriage can petition for a divorce (s. 1); nullity (s. 12); or for a declaration that the other party is dead (s. 19). A permanent separation can be obtained by petitioning for a decree of judicial separation under s. 17, but although this will bring to an end the usual rights and obligations arising out of the status of being married, and enable the court to make full and final orders for financial relief, neither party will be able to remarry. If there is a fundamental flaw in the marriage (the requirements for a valid marriage are set out in s. 11), it will simply not have taken place in the eyes of the law and a declaration to that effect can be obtained under the Family Law Act 1986. Roberta's situation is such that only the law relating to nullity is relevant. She does not wish for a divorce, but judicial separation is useless as she wants to be able to remarry. All the requirements of s. 11 appear to have been met, and so the marriage is valid until declared otherwise by a court order.

The grounds for annulling a marriage are set out in the MCA, s. 12. Briefly, they allow one party to apply to annul the marriage where:

(a)   the other party has wilfully refused to consummate the marriage;

(b)   either party is incapable of consummation;

(c)   either party did not give a valid consent;

(d)   either party was suffering from a mental disorder at the time of the ceremony;

(e)   the other party was suffering from a venereal disease at the time of the ceremony; and

(f)   if the other party was pregnant by another man at the time of the ceremony.

The last two grounds can only apply if the applicant was unaware of the venereal disease or pregnancy at the time. The facts of the problem give no indication that either party was suffering from a mental disorder, nor do the last two grounds appear relevant. Roberta is therefore left with the issues of non-consummation and lack of proper consent.

Non-consummation means that sexual intercourse has not taken place since the time of the wedding. All that is required is an erection on the part of the man, and penetration of the vagina for a reasonable length of time (*W* v *W* [1967] 2 WLR 218). The ability of the man to reach orgasm is not required, let alone the capacity of either party to have children (*SY* v *SY* [1963] P 37). Sexual intercourse before the marriage is irrelevant, but that does not appear to be an issue in Roberta's case. The grounds are more specific than just non-consummation, however, in that they require either wilful refusal or inability to consummate. Furthermore, the applicant can only petition on the grounds of the other party's wilful refusal. This means that Roberta cannot use this ground, assuming that Clinton would be willing to have sexual intercourse with her. Clinton, however, could petition on this ground if he could be persuaded to accept the realities of the situation. A petition can be founded on the inability of either party, however, so Roberta should consider this as a possibility. The first point is that the inability need not be physical. Psychological impotence is just as valid a ground as physical impotence, and furthermore it need only be with the other party. In *G* v *M* (1885) 10 App Cas 171, for example, a petition was granted despite the fact that the medical evidence suggested that the man 'might succeed with other women' (given time, encouragement and 'a little champagne'!). The problem must amount to 'invincible repugnance', however. Thus, in *Singh* v *Singh* [1971] P 226, the petition of a 17 year old girl was rejected on those grounds, as the only evidence was that she refused to have sexual intercourse with the man because she did not want to marry him. Clinton's appearance and personal problems are clearly insuperable difficulties for Roberta, and she may therefore be able to convince a court that it would be impossible for her to have sexual intercourse with him. She may have to produce medical evidence, however, suggesting that it is a true psychological inability to have sexual intercourse with Clinton, not just extreme distaste.

Roberta's other possible ground for annulling the marriage would be that she gave no valid consent during the actual ceremony. Under the MCA s.12(c), a marriage is voidable on the grounds that either party did not validly consent to it, 'whether in consequence of duress, mistake, unsoundness of mind or otherwise'. Roberta could claim that her consent was invalidated because of the pressure put on her by Warren and Meryl, her parents, in that they threatened that she would have to leave their house and never speak to them, or anybody else in their community if she refused to go through with the marriage. The cases on this area have shown the courts struggling to reconcile conflicting principles. On the one hand, society's interest in maintaining the institution of marriage demands that an apparently valid marriage should not be set aside without firm and objective evidence. On the other, there is a modern emphasis on freedom of choice and action, and it is unjust to subject a person to the rights and obligations of marriage against his or her will. This conflict is particularly pronounced where there has been pressure on a particular individual which has fallen short of direct compulsion such as threats of violence; but in practice has amounted to irresistible pressure which that individual has been unable to stand up to. In *Singh* v *Kaur* (1981) 11 Fam Law 152, the Court of Appeal refused a decree of nullity to a 21 year old man who had been told by his parents to enter an arranged marriage, or disgrace his whole family and give up his job in the family business. The court pointed out that there was no evidence of threats to the petitioner's 'life, limb or liberty', and that they were bound by previous English authorities, such as *Singh* v *Singh* (*above*). In that case, a 17 year old girl went through an arranged marriage in the register office, but then refused to go through the necessary religious ceremony (she had been told that her husband would be 'educated and handsome', and he was neither!). Her evidence was limited to an explanation that she felt constrained by a 'proper respect' for her parents and her religion, and the court refused her petition as there was no evidence of fear. In other cases, however, the courts have been readier to accept the realities of the petitioner's situation. In *Szechter* v *Szechter* [1971] 2 WLR 170, for example, the marriage was necessary to enable the applicant to get out of a Poland when that country was being ruled by a totalitarian regime, and when it was apparent that she would not be able to survive a period of imprisonment which had been unjustly imposed upon her. What was clear from these cases was that only threats of personal violence ('life, limb and liberty') would be taken into consideration, with some uncertainty as to the degree to which the courts would take a subjective approach by concentrating on a particular applicant's ability to withstand the threats she or he was under. In *Hirani* v *Hirani* [1982] FLR 232, the Court of Appeal took a flexible line on both issues. The petitioner was a 19 year old girl who had been instructed by her parents to renounce her friendship with a boy from another religion, and to marry a man chosen by them. She had been told that if she disobeyed them, she would simply have to leave their house. As she had been completely dependent upon her parents up until then, and now faced being ostracised by them and her community, the pressure upon her was extreme, and she went through with the marriage. It did not last long, however, and after three weeks she moved in with her original boyfriend and applied to annul the arranged marriage. The Court of Appeal allowed her petition, stating that the key test was 'whether the pressure is such as to destroy the reality of consent and overbears the will of the individual'. Roberta could argue that she was unable to resist the pressure from her parents, because she was afraid of the consequences of being cast out from her home and community. The fact that she had been brought up inside that community for the whole of her adult life would mean that she would be less able to cope with such a situation than a person who had lived a 'normal' life, with wide social contacts.

If this case of *Hirani* is followed, Roberta's petition on that basis would be allowed. Although *Hirani* seems contrary to the previous case law, it does have the support of more recent decisions in the Scottish courts. In both *Mahmood* v *Mahmood* 1993 SLT 589 and *Mahmud* v *Mahmud* 1994 SLT 599, the applicants for a decree of nullity had suffered social and psychological pressure from their families which resulted in them marrying partners chosen for them against their wishes. The woman in *Mahmood* was threatened with ostracism and the loss of her job in the family shop. The man in *Mahmud* suffered blame from his family for causing the death of his father by his 'obstinacy', and pressure to comply with his father's dying wish. The Scottish courts accepted that duress need not be purely physical as long as it had the effect of vitiating true consent, and granted a decree in each case. Although these decisions are only persuasive precedents for English courts, they lend such powerful support to the decision in *Hirani* that it seems likely that it will be followed. On that basis, Roberta's petition for nullity would be granted.

QUESTION 4

Steelers plc produce steel and employ a large number of people in their foundry. Keith has worked in the foundry for a number of years, pouring the molten metal into moulds. The company provide steel capped boots but they know that some employees wear their own boots, rather than those provided. Keith frequently wears his own boots and on one of these occasions he suffered severe injuries to his feet, when molten metal splashed on to his boots. Lyn is a personal assistant to one of the managers and her work involves using a wordprocessor. After one busy period producing the annual report she developed repetitive strain injury (RSI). Mick, an independent contractor, is engaged to clean out the furnaces and he provides all his own equipment. While he was working, one of his light bulbs broke, ignited gases which had built up in the furnace and caused an explosion, which badly burned him.

Advise Keith, Lyn and Mick of any legal action which may be taken in civil and criminal law in the above situations.

Commentary

Questions on employment law are found on the EDEXCEL Foundation (London) and Welsh boards in sections such as 'The Workplace'. This question should take approximately 45 minutes. Essay questions may also be asked on this topic and they would require an explanation of the relevant law and some comments or criticism of it. For example, how effective the HASAW Act 1974 is in preventing accidents in the workplace, and in particular whether the punishments for breaches of the Act are adequate when a death has resulted. Other questions could look at such related topics as discrimination legislation and its effectiveness in practice, as women still only earn 75 per cent of men's pay.

This question requires a broad knowledge of both the civil and criminal aspects of employers liability. The key points should include the following:

- distinguish between civil (common law) and criminal (statutory) duties

- duty to provide a safe system of work at common law and corresponding duty under HASAWA 1974

- duty owed to independent contractors under s. 3 HASAWA and application to Mick.

Suggested answer

Keith, as an employee, is owed duties both at common law and by statute. At common law an employer owes a number of civil law duties to employees. These duties can be seen as based on implied terms in the contract of employment or a concurrent duty based on negligence in the law of tort. One of the common law duties is that the employer must ensure that there is a safe system of work. Steelers plc owe a duty to Keith to provide a safe system of work in this foundry. This is a very wide duty and includes providing training, instituting safe procedures and providing supervision. The important factor is whether the employer has acted 'reasonably'. In deciding if a duty of care has been breached a number of factors are taken into account, in a similar way to establishing liability in negligence under *Donoghue* v *Stephenson* [1932] AC 562. In the present case the nature of the risk, the likelihood of injury, the characteristics of Keith and the cost of prevention are all relevant. The nature of the risk is suffering severe injury. We are not told of how often injuries occur but it is certain they are not unknown in this type of work and may be likely to happen. The company also know that employees do not always wear the boots provided. But do they know that Keith is one of these employees? The cost of prevention also needs to be considered if the company had to provide a team of boot inspectors. The fact that Keith has been there for a number of years does not mean that the company can avoid their duty by saying he is experienced. Given the fact that there is grave danger to the employees if proper boots are not worn and that the company know there is slackness in wearing the boots provided, there is a strong argument that the company are under a duty to supervise the wearing of the boots provided. In *Bux* v *Slough Metals Ltd* [1973] 1 WLR 1358 the company provided goggles but an employee was injured in the eye when not wearing them. The company knew about employees not wearing goggles and put up some posters advising employees to wear the goggles provided. The court said they were in breach of their duty for not providing a system of supervision.

However, the company may be able to raise certain defences to a claim by Keith. Firstly, they could say that Keith had consented to the risk by wearing his own boots. The courts are reluctant to accept that employees can give a valid consent to the risks of their jobs and this defence is not likely to succeed here (*Smith* v *Baker* [1891] AC 325). Secondly, the company could say that Keith had been contributorily negligent and if this were to succeed his damages would be reduced to the extent the court thought just under the Law Reform (Contributory Negligence) Act 1945. The courts are also reluctant to say that employees have been contributorily negligent, but it does seem that Mick has been partly to blame here.

In criminal law the Health and Safety at Work Act 1974, s. 2(1) provides that the employer must ensure, so far as is reasonably practicable, the health, safety and welfare of all his employees. This includes a safe system of work and is thus a parallel duty to that owed at common law. The employer in consultation with employees must have a safety committee and safety representatives to assist in producing policies and suggestions to make the work place safe. As the company employ more than five people they must have a written health and safety policy. The Act is enforced by the Health and Safety Executive through an inspectorate. Health and Safety inspectors can issue an 'improvement notice' if they believe an employer is in breach of the Act, and such a notice requires the employer to remedy the situation. Inspectors can also issue a 'prohibition notice' if they believe that an activity is likely to cause serious personal injury. The employer is not strictly liable for breach of the Act but only has to do what is 'reasonably practicable'. In *Associated Dairies* v *Hartley* [1979] IRLR 171 ASDA allowed employees at a warehouse to buy boots at cost price. An employee fractured a toe when a roller truck went over his foot. The inspector issued an improvement notice requiring ASDA to provide free footwear. The court held that as the cost would be £20,000 in the first year and there had only been one injury in five years, this did not justify the expenditure and the improvement notice was cancelled. The present case may be distinguished, as it is far more dangerous working in a steel foundry than a warehouse. It may be that an improvement notice or prohibition notice could be issued against the company subject to a condition that the company make their boots compulsory and put a system of supervision in place. It should be noted that breach of the HASAWA 1974 does not give any rights to sue for damages in civil law.

Under the HASAWA 1974, s. 7 there is also a duty on employees to take reasonable care for their own safety and a duty to co-operate with their employer to help the employer meet their obligations under the Act. It would seem here that Keith was in breach of both duties and could also be prosecuted.

Lyn is owed both common law and statutory duties. The company owe a duty of care at common law to provide a safe system of work. This includes both safe practices and sufficient staff to carry out the job properly. In Lyn's case the employer knows she spends much of her time working on wordprocessors and is under a duty to provide varied tasks to prevent injury. In *Pickford* v *ICI plc* [1996] IRLR 622 the plaintiff secretary spent most of her time typing. The HSE had issued information about the dangers and the company had warned typists to take breaks but not secretaries. It was held that this failure to warn was negligent. In Lyn's case it seems that the injury has developed just at a busy time of year, when she is producing the annual report. This would suggest that there should be more staff to deal with the typing of the report and the company could easily take on temporary staff. It would seem that the company are negligent and in breach of this duty.

There is also a breach of the corresponding duty under the Health and Safety at Work Act 1974, s. 2(1) to ensure the health, safety and welfare of employees. Under the Health and Safety (Display Screen Equipment) Regulations 1992 the employer must provide for breaks and changes of activity. The company would also seem to be in breach of the regulations. Breach of these regulations is both a criminal wrong and gives the right to sue for damages for breach of statutory duty.

Mick is an independent contractor and at common law an independent contractor is responsible for their own safety. However, under the HASAWA 1974, s. 3 an employer is under a duty to conduct his undertaking in such a way that, as far as is reasonably practicable, anyone not in his employment is not exposed to risks from his undertaking. The situation is similar to *R* v *Associated Octel* [1996] 1 WLR 1543. The defendants owned a chemical works and engaged an independent contractor to repair tanks. An employee of the contractor was cleaning a tank using acetone, which is inflammable, when a naked light bulb he was using broke and caused an explosion. The House of Lords held that the activity of cleaning the tanks could be treated as part of the employers undertaking and the company were guilty of an offence under HASAWA, s. 3. In applying this case here, even though Mick is working for himself, the cleaning of the furnaces could be seen as part of the undertaking of Steelers plc and Mick is injured as a result of the company's breach of duty. They should have warned him of the gases and suggested or provided a sealed light unit. However, breach of the Act does not in itself give Mick any rights to sue for compensation, unless it involves a breach of regulations.

Index